SELECTED DIALOGUES

LUCIAN (born about AD 120, died sometime after 180) was the most enduringly enjoy   fluential of ancient comic writers, though Greek was   He was born at Samosata on the Euph   years as a pleader and tr sequently in Athens and G and turned to literature, wh satiric writer. Towards the end   HE U   had a ment post in Egypt, but the p   and year of his death a unknown. His main originality and his lasting importance in the world of literature were in the development of the comic dialogue as a technique of satire. He achieved this by adapting the long estab-lished philosophical dialogue and using it primarily as a vehicle for humour, thus offering inspiring models to numerous subsequent writers in many languages. His favourite targets were false philo-sophers, sham prophets, and pseudo-historians (*How to Write History*); but he respects and praises decent, honest men; he enjoys telling stories (*The Lovers of Lies*); and his most famous piece (*A True History*) is an extended piece of narrative fantasy – an import-ant departure from his favourite dialogue form.

C. D. N. COSTA is Emeritus Professor of Classics at the University of Birmingham. He is the author of *Greek Fictional Letters* (Oxford, 2002).

LUCIAN

Selected Dialogues

Translated with an Introduction and Notes by
C. D. N. COSTA

OXFORD
UNIVERSITY PRESS

OXFORD
UNIVERSITY PRESS

Great Clarendon Street, Oxford OX2 6DP

Oxford University Press is a department of the University of Oxford.
It furthers the University's objective of excellence in research, scholarship,
and education by publishing worldwide in

Oxford New York

Auckland Cape Town Dar es Salaam Hong Kong Karachi
Kuala Lumpur Madrid Melbourne Mexico City Nairobi
New Delhi Shanghai Taipei Toronto

With offices in

Argentina Austria Brazil Chile Czech Republic France Greece
Guatemala Hungary Italy Japan Poland Portugal Singapore
South Korea Switzerland Thailand Turkey Ukraine Vietnam

Oxford is a registered trade mark of Oxford University Press
in the UK and in certain other countries

Published in the United States
by Oxford University Press Inc., New York

First published 2005
First published as an Oxford World's Classics paperback 2006

British Library Cataloguing in Publication Data

Data available

Library of Congress Cataloging in Publication Data

Lucian, of Samosata.
[Dialogi. English. Selections]
Lucian, selected dialogues / translated with an introduction and notes
by Desmond Costa.
p. cm. — (Oxford world's classics)
Includes bibliographical references and index.
1. Lucian, of Samosata—Translations into English. 2. Dialogues, Greek
—Translations into English. 3. Satire, Greek—Translations into English.
I. Costa, Charles Desmond Nuttall. II. Title. III. Title: Selected dialogues.
IV. Series: Oxford world's classics (Oxford University Press)
PA4231.A5C67 2005 887′.01—dc22 2005023165

Typeset in Ehrhardt
by RefineCatch Limited, Bungay, Suffolk
Printed in Great Britain by
Clays Ltd, St Ives plc

ISBN 0-19-280593-2 978-0-19-280593-5

CONTENTS

INTRODUCTION

LUCIAN was one of the most gifted and entertaining of comic satirists, and he was notably influential on a very diverse range of subsequent writers. Yet few details of his life can be regarded as certain; with the exception of a disputed passage in the Greek doctor Galen, no contemporary writer mentions him, and we have to piece together what we can of his life and activities mainly from a scattering of allusions in his own works. He was born probably around AD 120 and died sometime after 180. His birthplace was Samosata, a town on the Euphrates, in the old kingdom of Commagene, which had been incorporated by the conquering Romans into the province of Syria. That much seems clear.

Both the period of his lifetime and the area in which he busied himself are important in assessing the nature of Lucian's work. The area which we now call Asia Minor and the Middle East had been, since the conquests of Alexander the Great and under his successors, a Greek-speaking society, at least in its upper classes, and dominated by Greek cultural ideals and traditions. When the imperial Roman sway spread eastwards and absorbed the Greek world of Asia Minor and beyond, there seems to have developed on the whole a mutually tolerant coexistence of Roman political domination and the existing Greek cultural traditions, with respect shown by each side to the qualities and achievements of the other. The local Greek and Greek-influenced elements could not and did not usually question the imperial superiority of their rulers; and the Romans tolerated and respected, as they had always done, the cultural achievements of their Greek subjects. There are innumerable friendly references in Lucian to the emperors of the time, and to local Roman-appointed governors.

Falling within the second century AD, Lucian's lifetime coincided with a period of crucial importance in the story of later Greek literature. This was a phase, which is usually called the Second Sophistic, in which writers thought it highly desirable to recall and imitate the language and the style of what they regarded as the golden age of Greek literature, the Attic prose which was written in the fifth and fourth centuries BC, taking as models, for instance, Plato in philosophy, Thucydides in history, and Demosthenes in forensic oratory. We have a great deal of surviving works from this later period, and many of the writers were remarkably successful in recapturing the earlier vocabulary and style. Among them Lucian is unsurpassed as an Atticizer, even though Greek was probably an adopted language for him and he originally spoke Aramaic. (A good parallel to this achievement might be the Pole Joseph Conrad, who spoke hardly any English until he was over 20 and became one of the greatest of English novelists.) This harking back to earlier literary ideals was a very basic element in both Greek and Latin literature, and it was part of the almost universal practice of *mimesis*, or creative imitation of chosen models. This was not slavish plagiaristic copying, but an imaginative reworking of a theme on which the writer set his own individual stamp. It might of course take the form of comic parody, as in Lucian's own *The Syrian Goddess*, which is a pastiche of the Herodotean style. But *mimesis* was commonly more allusively linked with its model, as with his *Dialogues of the Courtesans*, in which the themes and situations are recognizably derived from those of Greek New Comedy and the mime.

Thus *mimesis* formed a core element in the educational system at the period of the Second Sophistic and Lucian's lifetime, and among the most important and influential men who had gone through this educational mill were the sophists. These were professional speakers or 'rhetors', who not only worked in the courts as pleaders, but also travelled around giving declamations, or show-piece speeches, on a wide range of historical or fictitious topics. Many of them were also distinguished teachers, they found employment as secretaries to great men, and the more illustrious were asked to serve as ambassadors. It would be hard to exaggerate the prestige and influence of the sophists in the intellectual and literary world of the second century, and it was perhaps inevitable that a man of Lucian's talents would be attracted to try his hand at professional rhetoric.

What we know of his life and his travels has to be derived mainly from his own works, and this information is often delivered in an oblique and allegorical way; as when in *The Dream* he tells us that when he was a youth the personified figures of Craft and Culture competed for his allegiance, and he chose Culture; or when in *The Double Indictment* he faces dual accusations from personified Rhetoric and Dialogue: Rhetoric reproaches him for deserting her, and Dialogue complains that Lucian has devalued him from his serious philosophical role to become a vehicle for comedy. Putting together those bits of evidence it seems reasonable to trust, we have something like the following picture of his career. He would have had the standard education of that time, with its strong rhetorical basis. It is not clear whether he formally took up the career of a professional sophist (he does not actually say this), but he seems to have spent his early years as a pleader and travelling lecturer in Asia Minor, and subsequently in Athens and Gaul. Then at about 40 he abandoned his oratorical career, if not his interest in the techniques of rhetoric, and after experiencing a passing interest in philosophy, turned to literature. Later in his life (the date is disputed) he took a minor government post in Egypt, working in the retinue of the prefect there. He died sometime after 180: Marcus Aurelius, who died in that year, is referred to as dead in *Alexander* 48.

As we have seen, Greek prose at this period was deeply infused with the techniques and the rhetorical productions of the professional speakers and teachers, the sophists, and Lucian's works show many examples of the traditional exercises of the orators. One of the most important of these exercises was the 'practice speech' (*melete*), either forensic or deliberative, a declamation on a set historical or fictitious theme: Lucian's *Phalaris* is a clear example of this type. Then there was the 'display speech' (*logos epideiktikos*), a term which applied to a wide range of occasional oratory, and in particular speeches of praise and blame: in our selection *The Fly* is a whimsical specimen of this class. A third form was the 'introductory speech' (*prolalia*), a more informal, usually short, preliminary talk before a public performance. Lucian enjoyed writing these pieces: we have eleven of them, including *The Dream* in this selection.

These were all traditional categories which Lucian inherited, and his virtuosity made expert use of them, whether as straight exercises or with humorous adaptation. His real originality, and his lasting importance in the history of satiric literature, lies in his development of the comic dialogue. The dialogue had of course long been used by writers of philosophical treatises: Plato was the most famous exponent; and Cicero also favoured this form of dramatic presentation in some of his treatises. But these were serious works, though of course they had plenty of room for humour and light relief. What Lucian did was to transform the function of the philosophical dialogue and make it a vehicle primarily for humour. It clearly had the potential for this, offering scope for vivid characterization, cut-and-thrust comic back-chat, and so on; and Lucian made full use of all this, as well as adapting from Plato the Socratic method of insidious questioning and demolition of an opponent (see *Hermotimus* and introductory note to it). Lucian is very clear about his achievement here—and his debts. In *The Double Indictment* he portrays himself as being accused by Dialogue for having wronged and debased him, dragging him down from the serious and elevated philosophical position he used to occupy, taking away his tragic mask and replacing it with the mask of comedy or farce. To make matters worse, says Dialogue, Lucian even imposed on him the old Cynic Menippus, and made a complete buffoon of him. Lucian's defence is in effect that he has actually done Dialogue a favour by making him more popular, attractive, and approachable; and that by associating him with comedy he has given him a new lease of life (*The Double Indictment* 33–4). The Menippus mentioned here was a Cynic writer from Gadara (third century BC), who is thought to have originated a serio-comic style of satire in a mixture of prose and verse. There is no doubt about Lucian's obvious debts to him, but the exact extent of them is not easy to assess because of the loss of Menippus' works. Lucian's affinity with Menippus seems to be noted also by implication by the later Greek sophist Eunapius (flourished *c.* AD 400), when he characterized Lucian as 'serious in his mockery' (*Lives of the Sophists* 454).

So it is generally agreed that Lucian invented a new literary genre, the comic dialogue, and much of his best and funniest work is written in this form. Yet, though many of his pieces are in dialogue form throughout, some include a dialogue element only as part of a more complex layout; and it is a feature of Lucian's virtuosity that he combines different literary forms within the same work. For example, the *Nigrinus* has a letter and dialogue as a frame for the central section of Nigrinus' long harangue; and *The Lovers of Lies* has a dialogue framework for the main narrative with its long series of stories. And when he chooses Lucian abandons the dialogue form altogether, and gives us straight narrative, as in his most famous work, *A True History*, or a narrative delivered in the form of a letter (*Peregrinus*, *Alexander*). Apart from the four sets of minor dialogues (*The Dead*, *Gods*, *Sea-Gods*, *Courtesans*), where the characters are clearly mythical, literary, or invented, a large number of Lucian's speakers are real people, and many others can be assumed to be, even if we cannot identify them.

The link with the Cynic Menippus brings us to the question of Lucian's own philosophical sympathies. These are not easy to decide, and no dogmatic statement is possible, as there seems to be a good deal of ambivalence in his attitude to the different schools and their representatives. The Platonists and the Pythagoreans are usually treated somewhat dismissively and with good-natured banter. There is little doubt of his antipathy to the Stoics, who are consistently given rough treatment throughout many of the works. The Aristotelians or Peripatetics are referred to less than the other schools, but the attitude to them seems to be cynical and unenthusiastic. His ambivalence is most noticeable regarding Cynicism: he is enthusiastically friendly to the Cynic Demonax, but he makes a stinging attack on another Cynic, Peregrinus. Perhaps the explanation is that Cynicism was a more loose-textured and elastic creed, and that differences between prominent individual Cynics could be critical. He seems most sympathetic to the Epicureans (see particularly the *Alexander*), though this favour is qualified in places by minor attacks on certain practices of the school. What is clear is that he was committed to no single creed, and that for his satiric purposes it was the pompous or the ridiculous that appeared in any philosophical stance and whatever school, which he seized on and castigated. Philosophical virtue and good deeds are praiseworthy, but make for dull satire.

Just as we cannot safely line Lucian up with any one philosophical creed, so we cannot label him with any distinct social or moral viewpoint. But we can say that along with the aim of showing us his paces as an expert literary artist is the aim, in the dialogues at least, of sharing with his readers a laugh at the expense of silly and pretentious people. He is not trying to mend the world but to extract humour from it. Even when the humour appears to be literary, as in *A True History*, with its extended parody of the popular vogue for incredible travellers' tales, his targets are the stupid liars who make them up and do not even have the honesty to admit to their deceptions. There are of course straight portraits of decent men saying wise things, like Nigrinus and Demonax; but they also serve to contrast with other behaviour which is stupid or base. It might be urged that in some works at least, like *How to Write History*, Lucian offers genuine and sensible advice, and in the case of this treatise that is certainly true; but here too the advice highlights by contrast the howlers and the lunacies perpetrated by the would-be historians he is attacking.

It must be clear by now that Lucian ranged very widely in his writings. Almost eighty works have come down to us under his name which are generally regarded as genuine, as well as a handful usually agreed to be spurious. Some idea has already been given of the spread of his interests, which largely reflect the educational ideals and the rhetorical practices of his time. But he must not be thought to be slavishly following received models, and even when we can point to a traditional structure in which he has cast one of his pieces, we also observe that he allows himself plenty of room for his free-wheeling humour, and his iconoclastic jabs at revered and august figures like, say, Plato or Pythagoras. Lucian was one of the wittiest writers in antiquity, but he was not a profound thinker, he did not have a particularly original mind, and he had no detectable moral or philo-sophical stance. He wrote for educated and literate readers, who he could assume were sufficiently intelligent and well read to appreciate the subtleties of his humour and to pick up his (sometimes allusive) quotations. As we have seen, earlier Greek literature provided him with a quarry of subject matter for his own exercises in *mimesis*; but the Graeco-Roman society he lived in also offered him a rich field of targets for his satire: silly or hidebound philosophers, charlatans of all kinds, pseudo-historians. His own presence as a stage-manager in his works varies, from lurking unobtrusively in the background to playing a full part in a dialogue under his usual pseudonym Lycinus (as in *Hermotimus*).

The selection of fourteen pieces offered here will, I hope, give a representative picture of his literary qualities and the range of his themes. Several of them show his preoccupation with philosophy and philosophers (*Nigrinus*, *Demonax*, *Peregrinus*, *Hermotimus*); the recurrent motif of a journey (either way) between heaven and earth can be seen in *Charon* and *Icaromenippus*, with a variation in *A True History*; *The Dream* illustrates the rhetorical *prolalia*, and is one of the works that give us interesting autobiographical details of the author; the *Alexander* shows us Lucian going for the jugular in one of his most intensely bitter personal attacks; by contrast, *The Lovers of Lies* illustrates his fondness for telling stories, and the *Dialogues of the Courtesans* are a light-hearted look at a familiar aspect of Greek society, and clearly derive from earlier Greek literature.

Something should be said of Lucian's influence on later literature, which was long-lasting and pervasive, though only a brief survey is possible here.* His extraordinary impact on subsequent writers as

---

* A useful and detailed account of this topic can be found in Christopher Robinson's *Lucian and his Influence in Europe* (London, 1979), to which I am much indebted.

distinguished as Erasmus and Sir Thomas More can be seen most obviously in three of his own favourite literary forms, the philosophical dialogue, the fantastic voyage, and the dialogue with the dead. But recognition of his influence and even allusion to his name were long in coming. No contemporary refers to him, though it seems clear that Alciphron (probably contemporary) was influenced by the *Dialogues of the Courtesans*. The same is true of the much later Aristaenetus (perhaps *c.* AD 500); otherwise there are only isolated references to him, and it is not until the Byzantine period that we can see evidence of his works being rediscovered, starting with the epigrams of Leon the Philosopher (early tenth century). After this there is plenty of evidence of Lucianic influence, and Byzantine interest in him can be typified by the *Philopatris*, an anonymous dialogue written around the mid-eleventh century in clear imitation of Lucian, which has survived attached to the corpus of his genuine works.

Moving on from Byzantium, it may be helpful to list the early translations of Lucian in the Renaissance and afterwards, as translations were often the trigger for imitations, especially when knowledge of Greek was limited. The landmarks were: the translation into Latin of selections by Erasmus and Thomas More (1506), and three important vernacular versions, Perrot d'Ablancourt's French translation (1654); the Dryden Lucian in English (1711)—a version by several hands, with a Life of Lucian by Dryden; and Wieland's German translation (1788/9). So, from the late seventeenth century reading Lucian became widespread and popular, and among his admirers he never looked back.

Prior to these translations, however, there were humanist scholars and writers who could read their Lucian and write Lucianic pieces of their own, and mention should be made of one of the most important, Alberti (1404–72), the most deeply dyed Lucianist of his age. Soon after Alberti, Lucian appeared in print in 1496, with the consequently greatly increased dissemination of his works, and a few years later appeared the ground-breaking translation of Erasmus and More. Erasmus was the most distinguished scholar of the Renaissance, and his admiration for Lucian must in itself have been a decisive influence on others. He commended Lucian for the clarity and elegance of his Greek, and many of his most important works are deeply imbued with the style and flavour of Lucian. This can be seen particularly in the *Colloquies* (1522–33), and in his most famous work, the *Praise of Folly* (published 1511). Thomas More in his *Utopia* (1516) combined two favourite Lucianic motifs, the satirical dialogue and the fanciful journey. Later on, Swift's *Gulliver's Travels* (1726) reflects the imaginary voyage, and his knowledge of Lucian is otherwise well attested. This has brought us into the eighteenth century, where Voltaire is a major witness to the Lucianic style. The greatest French satirist of his day openly acknowledges his debt to the greatest Greek one, which can be seen in his dialogues, particularly the one entitled *Conversation de Lucien, Erasme et Rabelais dans les Champs Elysées* (1765). Finally, we should note Fielding, in whose works many Lucianic motifs are obvious; and a curious, much later homage to Lucian in Walter Pater, who included an extensive translation of the *Hermotimus* in chapter 24 of *Marius the Epicurean* (1885).

These are simply a few highlights in the astonishing story of Lucian's popularity, and his influence on some very great and diverse writers. He would have liked to know that story, and he would have enjoyed the thought of successive Papal Indexes banning his works in 1559 and 1590—and of his surviving them unscathed. Individuals pass away, but the types that Lucian loathed, the charlatan, the conceited, the self-important, the plain stupid, are always with us; and perhaps we can still learn a little from him in dealing with these plagues in human society.

NOTE ON THE TEXT

THIS translation is based on the standard edition of Lucian by M. D. Macleod published in the Oxford Classical Texts series (1972–87).

The marginal numbers in the translation relate to section divisions in this edition. Asterisks in the text refer to the explanatory notes at the back of the book.

SELECT BIBLIOGRAPHY

Translations

Apart from the complete translation in the Loeb series two others are worth noting: the version (with omissions) by the brothers H. W. and F. G. Fowler (Oxford, 1905), which is lively and very readable, but sometimes strays rather far from the Greek; and the Penguin selection, *Lucian, Satirical Sketches*, by Paul Turner (Penguin, 1961).

General Background

Bowersock, G. W., *Greek Sophists in the Roman Empire* (Oxford, 1969).

Reardon, B. P., *Courants littéraires des IIe et IIIe siècles après J.-C.* (Paris, 1971).

Russell, D. A., *Greek Declamation* (Cambridge, 1983).

Swain, S., *Hellenism and Empire* (Oxford, 1996).

Taplin, O. (ed.), *Literature in the Greek and Roman Worlds* (Oxford, 2000).

Critical Studies

Anderson, G., *Lucian: Theme and Variation in the Second Sophistic*, Mnemosyne Suppl. 41 (Leiden, 1976).

—— *Studies in Lucian's Comic Fiction*, Mnemosyne Suppl. 43 (Leiden, 1976).

Bompaire, J., *Lucien écrivain: imitation et création* (Paris, 1958).

Hall, J., *Lucian's Satire* (New York, 1981).

Helm, R., *Lucian und Menipp* (Leipzig and Berlin, 1906).

Hirzel, R., *Der Dialog: Ein literarhistorischer Versuch* (Leipzig, 1895).

Homeyer, H. (ed.), *Lukian: Wie man Geschichte schreiben soll* (Munich, 1965).

Jones, C. P., *Culture and Society in Lucian* (Cambridge, Mass., and London, 1986).

Peretti, A., *Luciano: un intellettuale greco contro Roma* (Florence, 1946).

Robinson, C., *Lucian and his Influence in Europe* (London, 1979).

Reference Works

The following are referred to in the notes by authors' names or by initials.

Kock, T., *Comicorum Atticorum Fragmenta* (Leipzig, 1880–8).

Leutsch, E. L., and Schneidewin, F. G., *Corpus Paroemiographorum Graecorum* (Göttingen, 1839–51).

Nauck, A., *Tragicorum Graecorum Fragmenta* (2nd edn., Leipzig, 1889).

Otto, A., *Die Sprichwörter und sprichwörtlichen Redensarten der Römer* (Leipzig, 1890).

Oxford Classical Dictionary (3rd edn., Oxford, 1996). (*OCD*)

Further Reading in Oxford World's Classics

Apuleius, *The Golden Ass*, trans. P. G. Walsh.

Catullus, *The Complete Poems*, trans. Guy Lee.

Juvenal, *The Satires*, trans. Niall Rudd.

More, Sir Thomas, *Utopia*, in *Three Early Modern Utopias*, ed. Susan Bruce.

Shakespeare, William, *Timon of Athens*, ed. John Jowett.

Swift, Jonathan, *Gulliver's Travels*, ed. Claude Rawson and Ian Higgins.

THE DIALOGUES

PRAISE OF THE FLY

THIS little piece is a specimen of the paradoxical or humorous encomium, essentially a parody of serious speeches of praise, but practised as an exhibition of rhetorical skills. The structure of *The Fly* parodies the pattern of serious encomia, which discussed the subject's origins, virtues, and accomplishments, and we should note here the strong stress on the fly's virtues. The main point of the piece is thus the ingenuity shown in applying the techniques of a serious oratorical form to a ridiculously trivial subject, so that we find, for example, the august authority of Homer invoked where appropriate to support the writer's laudatory claims. Furthermore, where Lucian quotes the story that the fly is in origin a girl called Muia, he is using an aetiological fable of a kind familiar to us from the many transformations described in Ovid's *Metamorphoses*.

The fly is not the smallest of winged creatures if you compare it with 1 gnats and midges and even tinier things, but it is as much larger than those as it is smaller than the bee. It is not feathered like other creatures, with both plumage covering its body and wing-feathers to fly with; but like grasshoppers, cicadas, and bees it has membranous wings which are as much finer than theirs as Indian fabrics are softer and more delicate than Greek ones. What is more, it has all the colours of the peacock if you look closely at it when it spreads its wings in flight against the sun. Its flight is not like bats with a steady 2 wing-beat as of oars, or like the jumping of grasshoppers, or the buzzing of wasps, but it turns easily to any part of the air it wants. It has another characteristic too: its flight is not silent but tuneful—not harsh like midges and gnats, nor a deep humming like bees, nor fierce and threatening like wasps, but much more melodious, just as pipes are more sweet-toned than trumpet and cymbals. As for the rest of its 3 body, the head has a very slight attachment to the neck, and moves around easily, not being an integral part of it like the head of grass-hoppers. The eyes are prominent and have a very horny appearance. The chest is firm, and the feet grow right from the waist, which is not constricted like that of wasps. The abdomen too is fortified, and like a breastplate in having wide bands and scales. But it defends itself not with its tail-end like wasps and bees, but with its mouth and the proboscis, which it possesses as elephants do, and which it uses to forage, seizing and gripping things firmly with a sort of sucker at the end of it. There is also a tooth projecting from it with which the fly makes a puncture and drinks blood (for though it drinks milk too it likes blood), but its punctures do not hurt much. It has six feet but walks only on four, using the front two as hands. So you can see it standing on four legs and holding up a piece of food in its hands, just like us humans.

4   It is not born fully formed like this, but starts life as a maggot from the carcass of a man or other animal. Then gradually it develops legs, sprouts wings, and from a creeping creature becomes a flying one, which itself conceives and produces a little maggot, the future fly. Living in men's society and sharing their food and table, it eats everything except oil—to drink that is fatal to it. It is short-lived anyway, having been allotted a brief life-span, and delights most in daylight and pursues its activities there. It rests at night, neither

5   flying nor buzzing, but hiding quietly away. I can also report its considerable intelligence in avoiding the designs of its enemy the spider, watching carefully as he lays his traps against it and dodging his attack, so as not to be trapped and caught by falling into the creature's meshes. I need not speak of its courage and bravery, but leave it to that most mighty-voiced of poets, Homer. When he wants to praise the greatest hero,* he doesn't liken his spirit to a lion's or a leopard's or a boar's, but to the courage of the fly and its fearless and persistent attack—and it is courage he attributes to the fly, not recklessness. For even if driven away, he says, it does not give up but persists in trying to sting. He is so strong in his praise and affection for the fly that he mentions it not just once or twice but frequently: so much does the mention of it contribute to the beauty of his verses! Now he describes them flying in a mass looking for milk;* elsewhere, when Athena deflects an arrow from hitting Menelaus in a vital spot, he compares her to a woman caring for her sleeping child and uses the fly again in the simile.* What is more, he has dignified them with the impressive epithet 'thronging' and in calling their swarms 'nations'.

6   The fly is so strong that its bite wounds not only a man's skin but that of an ox and a horse, and it even causes an elephant distress by burrowing into his wrinkles and stinging him as far as the length of its own proboscis allows. They have a very relaxed approach to sex, love, and mating: the male does not mount the female and straightway jump off like roosters, but covers her for a long time. She carries her mate and they fly together, not endangered in this aerial copulation by

PRAISE OF THE FLY

the movement of their flight. If a fly's head is cut off its body goes on living and breathing for a long time.

I want now to tell you the most remarkable fact about the fly's 7 nature, and it is the only point I think Plato overlooks in his discussion of the soul and its immortality. If ash is sprinkled on a dead fly it recovers, and from this second birth it has a whole new life. Everyone accepts this as clear proof that flies too have an immortal soul, since it departs and then returns, recognizes and revives its body, and makes the fly take wing again. This also confirms the story about Hermotimus of Clazomenae,* that his soul often left him and went off on its own, subsequently returning to occupy his body again and bring him back to life.

The fly has a life of ease and idleness, enjoying the fruits of others' 8 labours and finding itself a full table everywhere. Goats produce milk for it; the bee toils specially for flies and men; cooks season their dishes for it; it tastes the food of kings before they do, walking all over their tables and sharing their enjoyment of all that they feast on. It doesn't build a nest or lair in one particular place, but like the 9 Scythians it adopts a roaming flight, and makes its home and its bed wherever night happens to overtake it. But, as I said, it is not active in the dark, not deigning to do anything by stealth, and not even considering any shameful action which would disgrace it if done in daylight.

There is a story that long ago there was a girl called Muia:* she 10 was extremely pretty, but over-talkative, gossipy and fond of singing, and she was a rival to Selene for the love of Endymion. She kept disturbing and waking the lad in his sleep with her chattering and singing, so that he got annoyed and Selene in anger turned her into her present form. This is why in memory of Endymion the fly still grudges all sleepers their rest, especially if they are young and tender, and even its bite and blood-thirstiness is not a sign of cruelty but of love and kindliness. It is getting what enjoyment it can and taking a sip of the flower of beauty.

There also lived among the ancients a woman of the same name, 11 a very pretty and skilful poetess;* and another who was a famous Athenian courtesan, of whom the comic poet wrote:

'Twas Muia bit him to the heart.*

So the spirit of Comedy did not disdain the name of Fly or ban it from the stage, and parents have not been ashamed to call their daughters by it. In fact, Tragedy too has high praise for the fly, as in these lines:

> Strange that the fly with mighty strength
> Should spring on men athirst for blood,
> While soldiers armed should dread the foeman's spear.*

I could say a lot too about Muia the Pythagorean* if her story were not familiar to all.

12   There are also some very large flies which many people call soldier-flies, and others dog-flies. They have a very strident buzz, fly very fast, and are extremely long-lived. They can last through the whole winter without food, mostly hiding under roofs. They are chiefly remarkable for being bisexual, mounting and mounted by their mates in turn, like the child of Hermes and Aphrodite who had a mixed nature and twofold beauty.*

But I must stop though I have still a lot to say, lest you think, as the proverb puts it, that I am making an elephant out of a fly.*

THE DREAM OR LUCIAN'S CAREER

THIS is an introductory speech or *prolalia* (see Introduction, ix), presumably delivered by Lucian to an audience in his native Samosata on his return there after achieving fame and fortune in Italy, Gaul, and Athens. The piece is interesting as it gives some of the few biographical details we have about Lucian, and there seems no good reason not to trust what he tells us about his family and his early choice of career. Yet he gives a literary cast to that choice in the form of a fable of a familiar type, of which the most famous example is Prodicus' myth of 'The Choice of Heracles' between Virtue and Vice, recounted by Xenophon (*Memorabilia* 2. 1. 21–34).

When I was beginning to be grown-up and had just left school, my 1 father discussed with his friends my further education. Most of them considered that an academic education involved a lot of effort, time, and expense, and required a well-endowed position in life; whereas ours was modest and actually needed some timely assistance. But if I were to learn one of your ordinary crafts, I would straightaway earn an adequate living from it and not be a drain on my family at such an age, and before long my father would be enjoying a share of my earnings.

So the next point to settle was which was the best craft and the 2 easiest to learn, while being suitable for a man of free birth, requiring easily accessible equipment, and bringing in an adequate income. Each recommended a different craft, as his own inclination and experience dictated, but my father looked at my uncle—my maternal uncle was present and highly regarded as a sculptor—and said, 'It would be quite wrong to give preference to any other craft with you here. Take this boy' (indicating me) 'and train him to be a good sculptor, mason and statuary: as you know, he has a natural gift for this.' This remark he based on the way I used to play with wax. For when school was over, I would scrape the wax off my tablets and mould it into cattle or horses or indeed people, and he thought they were lifelike. I got caned by my teachers for this, but now I was praised for having a natural talent, and that modelling gave them good hopes that I would quickly learn the craft.

So as soon as it seemed a suitable day to begin my training, I was 3 handed over to my uncle and the arrangement seemed pretty good to me: in fact, I thought it a delightful pastime and a way of impressing my comrades, if I were seen to be carving gods and creating little statues for myself and my special friends. Then I experienced what usually happens to beginners. My uncle handed me a chisel and told me to give a light tap to a stone tablet lying before us, quoting the proverb 'Well begun is half done.'* But being inexperienced I hit it too hard, the tablet broke, and in a rage he grabbed a nearby stick and gave me an initiation which was neither gentle nor encouraging: thus my apprenticeship began with tears.

4   So I ran away and went home, sobbing continuously and my eyes full of tears. I told them about the stick and showed them my bruises, and I accused my uncle of great brutality, adding that he had done it through envy that I might excel him in his own craft. My mother consoled me and strongly abused her brother, but that night I fell asleep still crying and thinking of the stick.

5   So far my story is funny and childish, but from now on, gentlemen, it must be taken seriously and it deserves a very attentive audience. To quote Homer:

> In my sleep came a dream from the gods
> Through the night divine*

so vivid that it seemed completely real. Even after all this time I can still see the figures in the vision and still hear their words: it was all so clear.

6   Two women held me by my hands and each was trying with violent force to drag me to herself: in fact, in their struggle against each other they nearly pulled me apart. Now one of them would prevail and almost have me entirely, now the other would have me. And they kept shouting at each other, one saying, 'He's mine and I'm going to keep him', and the other, 'It's no use your claiming what isn't yours.' One was masculine in appearance, like a workman, with dirty hair, calloused hands, and clothes tucked up, and covered with marble dust, just like my uncle when he was cutting stone. The other had a lovely face, a fine figure, and a neatly worn cloak. At length they let me decide which of them I wanted to live with, and the rough, masculine one spoke first.

7   'I am the craft of Sculpture, dear boy, which yesterday you began to learn, having close family ties with you on your mother's side. For your grandfather (naming my mother's father) was a sculptor, as are both your uncles, who enjoy much fame thanks to me. If you will

8

ignore this woman's foolish nonsense (pointing to the other), and come and live with me, you will be looked after generously and have broad shoulders; you won't suffer from any sort of envy; you'll never go abroad, leaving your country and your family; and everyone will praise you not just for your fine words.

'Don't look down on my shabby figure and dirty clothes. Pheidias 8 looked like this when he produced his Zeus, and Polyclitus when he created his Hera, and Myron when he was praised and Praxiteles* when he was marvelled at. These men indeed are worshipped like gods. If you join their ranks, how can you fail to achieve fame yourself among all men, while making your father the object of envy and your country of admiration?'

This and still more said Sculpture, with much stuttering and out-landish jargon, hastily stringing her words together in her efforts to persuade me. But I can't remember it all, for most of it has now escaped my memory.

Anyway, when she had finished the other one began like this: 9

'I am Culture, my child, already known and familiar to you, even though you are not yet fully acquainted with me. What benefits you shall gain if you become a sculptor you have heard from this woman. You will simply be a workman, with your only hope of livelihood in manual labour. Living in obscurity you will have meagre and sordid returns and an abject spirit; you will count for nothing in public, neither sought after by your friends nor feared by your enemies nor envied by your fellow-citizens—just a workman and one of the masses, cowering before your superiors and paying court to the eloquent, living a hare's life* and providing a godsend to any-one stronger than you. And even if you should turn out to be a Pheidias or a Polyclitus and produce many marvellous creations, everyone will praise your skill, but no one in his senses who saw you would long to be like you. Whatever your real qualities you will be regarded as a mere artisan, a labourer who lives by the work of his hands.

'But if you'll be persuaded by me, I will first of all show you many 10 works of men of old, and tell you of their marvellous words and deeds, and make you familiar with practically everything. I shall adorn your soul, the most essential part of you, with many noble ornaments—moderation, justice, piety, gentleness, fairness, understanding, endurance, love of beauty, and a yearning to achieve the sublime. For these are the purest adornments of the soul. You will miss nothing in the past and nothing which is now due to happen, and you will even foresee the future in my company. In short, I shall very soon impart to you all knowledge, human and divine.

11   'You are now poor and the son of a nobody, and you thought of taking up such a sordid craft. Soon everyone will admire and envy you; you will be praised and honoured, enjoying high esteem for the finest qualities, respected by the rich and the noble, wearing clothes like this,' (pointing to her own brilliant attire) 'and considered worthy of office and precedence. If you go abroad, not even on foreign ground will you be unknown or unnoticed. I shall put such identification marks on you that everyone seeing you will nudge his neighbour

12   and point to you, saying, "That's the man." If anything serious happens to your friends or even to the whole city, they will all turn to you. Whenever you make a speech the crowd will listen open-mouthed, marvelling and congratulating you on your eloquence and your father on his good fortune. Some men are said to become immortal: I shall make this true of you. For even after you yourself die, you will always have the company of men of culture and associate with the noblest people. Look at Demosthenes and what I made of him in spite of his birth. Look at Aeschines:* his mother played the tambourine, but through me he was courted by Philip. Socrates himself was nurtured by Sculpture here;* but as soon as he knew better he deserted her side for mine, and you know how everyone sings his praises.

13   'On the other hand, if you reject such distinguished men as these, along with glorious deeds and noble words, a decent appearance, honour, reputation, praise, precedence, power, office, popularity for your eloquence and esteem for your sagacity, you will then put on a dirty apron and look like a menial, handling crowbars, gravers, mallets, and chisels, bent down over your work, physically and mentally grovelling on the ground and utterly abject. You will never hold up your head, or have manly or liberated aspirations; and though careful to produce works that are well balanced and shapely, you will give little thought to making yourself well balanced and elegant, accounting yourself of less importance than the stone you work with.'

14   While she was still speaking and not waiting for her to finish, I stood up and gave my decision. Turning away from the ugly work-woman I went joyfully over to Culture, especially with the thought of that stick in my head, and the many blows it had dealt me as soon

as I started working the day before. At first when Sculpture was abandoned she was angry, beating her hands together and grinding her teeth, but at last, like Niobe* in the tale, she stiffened into stone. Don't be surprised at her strange fate—dreams can work wonders.

The other one looked at me and said, 'I shall accordingly repay you 15 for making this wise and just decision. Come now, get up on this chariot,' showing me one drawn by winged horses like Pegasus, 'so you can learn how much you would have missed if you had not joined me.' I got up and she took the reins and drove off, and I was carried high up, so that travelling from east to west I viewed cities, races, and peoples, sowing something over the earth like Triptolemus.* What I sowed I cannot now remember, except that the people looking up from below applauded me and everyone I passed over in my flight sent me on my way with blessings. Having shown all this to me and 16 me to my well-wishers, she brought me back no longer wearing the same clothes as when I started my flight: I seemed to have come back in fine purple dress. She found my father standing and waiting for me, and showed him these clothes and the figure I presented on my return; and she also reminded him of the plans they had come close to making for me.

That is the vision I remember having when I was a mere boy, and I suppose it arose from my agitation and terror at the beating I'd had.

While I've been talking somebody remarked, 'Gracious me! What a 17 tedious argumentative dream!' Then somebody else interrupted, 'Must have been a winter dream, when the nights are longest; or perhaps it took three nights to conceive, like Heracles.* What possessed him to tell us this rubbish, and to go on about a night in his childhood and ancient, antiquated dreams? Such stale and frigid waffle. Does he think we are dream-interpreters?'

No, my friend; and when Xenophon described his dream* in which his father's house seemed to be on fire, and the rest of it—I'm sure you know the passage—he did not offer the vision as an exercise in interpretation or aim just to talk nonsense. After all, there was a war on and things were desperate, with the enemy pressing round them: no, the story had a real point to it.

And so it is with me. I have told you about this dream in order that 18 the young may take the better course and embrace Culture, especially if Poverty should make any of them play the coward and ruin a noble nature by inclining towards the worse path. I am sure that any such will be strengthened by hearing my story and taking me as a fitting example for himself. He will realize both what I was when I eagerly went after all that is noblest and set my heart on culture, not flinching before the poverty I then suffered; and what I am now I have come back to you,—if nothing else, at least as highly esteemed as any sculptor around.

CHARON OR THE OBSERVERS

A DIALOGUE between Hermes and Charon, the ferryman of the dead. Hermes at Charon's request shows him a bird's-eye view of mankind and some of its varied activities, on which Charon gives a mordant and satirical commentary. We find the mechanism of the sightseeing and the theme of the futility of human achievements elsewhere in Lucian. In *Icaromenippus* Menippus also goes up to a great height (heaven) partly to have a good view of men's activities; and *Icaromenippus* and *Menippus* are like *Charon* in preaching the vanity of human aspiration and the mutability of fate—themes derived in part from the teaching of the Cynics. We should note also that the characters and events observed here belong to the sixth century BC, which is in line with many writers of the Second Sophistic, who harked back to an earlier society as well as an earlier Greek language.

HERMES. What's the joke, Charon? Why have you left your ferry and come up to our world here? You're not in the habit of visiting the upper world.

CHARON. I was eager to see what the life of man is like, Hermes, and what they do in it, and what they all grieve to lose when they come down to us: for none of them has crossed over without weeping. So, like that Thessalian youth,* I asked Hades for a day's shore leave to come up to the light of day, and I seem to be in luck meeting you: for I'm sure you will go round with me, guiding and showing me everything, seeing that you know it all.

H. No time, ferryman: I'm off on an errand concerned with human affairs for the upper Zeus.* He is short-tempered, and I'm afraid that if I linger over it he will consign me to the lower darkness and let me be yours completely; or, as he treated Hephaestus* recently, he will grab me by the foot and hurl me from the threshold of heaven, so that I too will cause them mirth as I limp around and pour their wine.

C. So you'll let me roam about aimlessly on the face of the earth, and you're supposed to be my friend and shipmate and fellow-conductor? Well, you ought at least to remember, O son of Maia, that I've never yet ordered you to bale water or help at the oar. Instead, even with those broad shoulders you stretch out on the deck snoring, or if you find some chatty corpse you talk to him all through the trip; while in spite of my age I take both oars alone. Come, dear old Hermes, in your father's name don't abandon me: show me around all there is in life, so I can go back having seen something. If you desert me I'll be no better than the blind; for they slip and fall about being in darkness, while you see on the contrary I'm dazzled by the light. Do me this favour, Cyllenian,* and I'll always remember it.

2 H. This business is going to cause me a thrashing—I can see already that my guided tour will certainly earn me some hard blows. Still, I must help you: what can one do when a friend is so urgent?

Now, it's impossible for you to see everything in close detail: that would take us many years. Moreover, Zeus would have to advertise for me like a runaway slave; you would be prevented from doing Death's work and would cause Pluto's realm a loss by not bringing over the dead for a long time, and then the toll-collector Aeacus would be irritated at not collecting even an obol.* So we must see to it that you view just the main things that are happening.

C. You decide what is best, Hermes. Being a stranger here I know nothing of things on earth.

H. The important thing, Charon, is that we must have a high spot from which you can look down on everything. If you could go up to heaven we shouldn't have a problem: you would have a clear bird's-eye view of everything. But since one who spends his time with ghosts is not allowed to set foot in Zeus' court, we must now find some high mountain.

3 C. You know what I usually tell you all on the boat, Hermes. When a sudden gust of wind hits our sail athwart and the waves rise high, then in your ignorance you urge me to take in sail or slacken the sheet a bit or run before the wind; but I tell you to keep quiet for I know best. In the same way you are now the skipper and you must do whatever you think best; and like a good passenger I'll sit quietly and do anything you say.

H. Quite right: I shall know what's to be done and I'll find a suitable look-out. Let's see: would Caucasus do us, or Parnassus, or Olympus over there, which is higher than either? No, but looking at Olympus gives me rather a good idea. But I'll need some help, and you'll have to give me a hand.

C. Tell me what to do and I'll give a hand in any way I can.

H. The poet Homer tells us that the sons of Aloeus,* two of them as we are, when they were still children decided to heave Ossa up from its base and place it on Olympus, and then to put Pelion on that, thinking that this would provide a suitable ladder to get into heaven. Well, those two lads were punished for being presumptuous; but as we two aren't planning this to hurt the gods, why shouldn't we also make a similar structure, rolling the mountains on top of each other, to give us a clearer view from higher up?

C. Can just the two of us, Hermes, lift up Pelion or Ossa and put it in place? 4

H. Why ever not, Charon? You don't think we are inferior to those two brats?—and we are gods.

C. No, but the task seems to me incredibly laborious.

H. Naturally, for you're an amateur with no poetic vision at all. But noble Homer in just two verses has given us the path to heaven, so easily does he assemble the mountains. I'm surprised you think this so marvellous, as of course you know Atlas, who on his own holds up the sky itself with the weight of all of us. And I expect you've also heard how my brother Heracles once relieved Atlas of his burden for a while by taking over the weight himself.

C. Yes, I've heard that—but only you and the poets, Hermes, know if it's true.

H. True as anything, Charon. Why should wise men lie? So let's first lever up Ossa, as the master-builder Homer instructs us in his poem:

Then upon Ossa Pelion with quivering leaves.*

See how easily and poetically we've done it? Now let me climb up and see if we need to build it up any more. Oh dear, we are still 5 down in the foothills of heaven. In the east I can barely see Ionia and Lydia; in the west no further than Italy and Sicily; in the north nothing beyond the Danube; and over there a dim view of Crete. It looks as if we'll have to raise up Oeta too, ferryman, and then Parnassus on top of them all.

C. Right you are. Just take care that by making the structure incredibly high we don't make it too frail: then we'll come crashing down with it, crack our heads open, and bitterly regret our shot at Homeric architecture.

H. Don't worry, it will all be quite safe. Get Oeta moving: roll Parnassus up on top of it.

C. There you are.

H. I'll go up again. Good: I can see everything. Up you come now.

C. Give me a hand, Hermes: this is a monstrous contrivance you are making me climb.

H. Yes, if you really want to see everything, Charon: a curious sightseer has to take risks. But here's my hand, and take care not to step where it's slippery. Good, you are up too. Since Parnassus has two peaks, let us each take one and sit on it. Now, take a good look around at the whole prospect.

6 C. I see a large tract of land with a big lake surrounding it, and mountains, and rivers bigger than Cocytus and Pyriphlegethon, and very tiny men and some sort of dens they have.

H. Those 'dens' are their cities.

C. In that case, Hermes, we've achieved nothing, and it's all to no purpose that we've shifted Parnassus, Castalia and all, and Oeta and the other mountains.

H. Why?

C. I can't see anything clearly from up here. I didn't want just to look at cities and mountains as in paintings, but at men themselves and what they are saying and doing. For example, when you first met me and saw me laughing and asked me what was the joke, I was hugely amused by something I'd heard.

H. What was that?

C. Somebody had been asked to dinner, I think, the following day by a friend. 'I'll be there without fail,' he said, and as he was speaking a tile fell on him from the roof, dislodged by something, and killed him. I couldn't help laughing at this promise that he couldn't keep; so I think I'll now go back down to see and hear better.

7 H. Steady on: I'll put that right too for you, and quickly make you as keen-sighted as any, borrowing a charm from Homer for this too. When I recite the lines remember you are no longer to be short-sighted but to see everything clearly.

C. Go on then.

H.   See, I have taken the mist which covered your eyes,
    So now you can clearly distinguish a man from a god.*

    Well? Can you see now?

C. Splendidly! Lynceus* would be blind compared with me. So carry on with your information and answer my questions. But do you want me to question you in Homeric style so you'll know I've studied Homer too?

16

H. How can you know anything of him when you spend all your time sitting at an oar on a boat?

C. Now look here, that's a slander on my profession. When he died and I was ferrying him over, I heard him reciting a lot of poetry, some of which I still remember even though a pretty bad storm caught us at the time. For he began to sing a song which was rather inauspicious for the passengers, all about Poseidon gathering the clouds and stirring up the sea by plunging in his trident like a ladle, and raising all the storm winds, and all that sort of thing.* The result was his verses churned up the sea, storm and darkness suddenly fell on us, and our boat all but capsized. Then he himself got seasick and vomited up most of his lays, including Scylla and Charybdis and the Cyclops. So it wasn't difficult for me to salvage some of all that vomit. So tell me: 8

> Who is that stout fellow, goodly and great,
> Topping his fellows by a head and broad shoulders?*

H. That's Milo,* the athlete from Croton. The Greeks are applauding him for lifting up a bull and carrying it through the middle of the stadium.

C. It would be much more fitting, Hermes, if they praised me. I shall soon be grabbing Milo himself and putting him on the boat, when he comes to us after being thrown by Death, the most invincible opponent of all—and he won't even know how he was tripped up. Then, no doubt, he will be moaning to us as he remembers these victory garlands and the applause he won; but now he is full of pride at the admiration he is getting for carrying the bull. So what? Can we suppose that he expects that he too will die one day?

H. How should he think of death when he is at his peak?

C. Never mind him: he'll soon give us a laugh when he is on the boat and with no strength left to lift a mosquito, let alone a bull. But tell 9 me,

> Who is that other, that majestic one?

He doesn't seem Greek, to judge from his clothes.

H. That's Cyrus,* son of Cambyses, Charon, who has now annexed to the Persians the old empire of the Medes. He has also recently conquered the Assyrians and imposed terms on Babylon, and now he seems to be planning a campaign against Lydia so as to crush Croesus* and rule the world.

c. And where is this Croesus?

H. Look over there at that great citadel, the one with the triple wall. That is Sardis, and you can see Croesus himself sitting on a golden couch, talking to Solon the Athenian. Shall we listen to what they are saying?

c. Certainly.

10 CROESUS. My Athenian guest, you have seen my wealth and treasures, all my gold bullion and the rest of my riches: tell me who you think is the most fortunate of mankind?

c. What is Solon going to answer?

H. Don't worry: nothing ignoble, Charon.

SOLON. Few men are fortunate, Croesus, but of those I know, the most fortunate I consider to be Cleobis and Biton, the priestess's sons.

H. He means the Argive priestess: they died together just recently, after yoking themselves to a wagon and drawing their mother on it all the way to the temple.

CROESUS. All right, let them be first in good fortune. Who is second?

SOLON. Tellos the Athenian, who lived a good life and died for his country.

CROESUS. But what about me, you wretch? Don't I seem fortunate to you?

SOLON. I don't know yet, Croesus, as you haven't come to the end of your life. Death is the real test in such things, and living in good fortune right to the end.

c. Well said, Solon, as you haven't forgotten us and insist that such a
11 decision is made at the ferry itself. But who are those men Croesus is sending out, and what have they got on their shoulders?

H. They are gold ingots he is offering to Apollo* as payment for oracles which will actually destroy him soon. But the man is a real fanatic for divination.

c. So that's what gold is, that bright, shining stuff with a tinge of red? I've always heard of it but never seen it till now.

H. That's it, Charon—men praise it in song and fight wars for it.

c. I don't really see what's so good about it, except just the fact that it is heavy to carry.

H. Well, you don't know what it has led to—all the wars, plots, robberies, perjuries, murders, imprisonments, trading trips, and enslavings.

c. All because of this, Hermes—something not much different from bronze? I do know bronze, since I collect an obol, as you know, from each of my passengers.

h. Yes, but there's plenty of bronze, so men don't value it very highly; whereas miners have to dig this up a little at a time from a great depth. Otherwise it is like lead and other metals in coming out of the earth.

c. How terribly stupid men are, from what you tell me, if they are so greedy just for a heavy yellow bit of property.

h. Well, at least Solon over there doesn't seem to love it. As you see, he is laughing at Croesus and his barbarian arrogance, and I think he wants to ask him a question. So let's listen.

SOLON. Tell me, Croesus, do you really believe that Apollo needs these ingots?   12

CROESUS. Of course: he has no offering at Delphi to compare with them.

SOLON. So you think you'll make the god happy if he has gold ingots on top of his other offerings?

CROESUS. Why not?

SOLON. You're saying that heaven is extremely hard up, Croesus, if they have to send to Lydia for gold when they want it.

CROESUS. Where else is there such a supply of gold as with us?

SOLON. Tell me, is iron found in Lydia?

CROESUS. Not much of it.

SOLON. So you are lacking the superior metal.

CROESUS. How can iron be better than gold?

SOLON. You'll find out if you answer some questions without getting annoyed.

CROESUS. Carry on, Solon.

SOLON. Who are the better men, those who rescue others or those who are rescued by them?

CROESUS. Obviously those who rescue others.

SOLON. Then if, as the rumours go, Cyrus attacks the Lydians, will you supply your army with golden swords or will you then need iron?

CROESUS. Iron, of course.

SOLON. And if you didn't provide it your gold would go off captive to the Persians.

CROESUS. Don't suggest it!

SOLON. Let's hope not. But, anyway, you obviously agree that iron is better than gold.

CROESUS. Are you then telling me to recall the gold and offer the god iron ingots?

SOLON. He won't need iron either, but whether you offer him bronze or gold your offering will become a lucky windfall for others, the Phocians or the Boeotians or the Delphians themselves, or some tyrant or brigand. The god himself has little interest in your goldsmiths.

CROESUS. You're always attacking my wealth—you're just envious.

13 H. The Lydian can't bear this honest outspokenness, Charon. He thinks it strange if a poor man doesn't toady to him, but says openly whatever comes into his head. Yet he'll remember Solon before long, when he is fated to be led a prisoner of Cyrus to the pyre. For I heard Clotho* the other day reading out everyone's allotted fate, including this programme, that Croesus is to be captured by Cyrus, and Cyrus in turn to be killed by that woman of the Massagetae.* Do you see her—the Scythian woman riding a white horse?

C. Oh yes.

H. She is Tomyris, and when she has cut off Cyrus' head she will put it into a wineskin full of blood. And do you see his young son too? That's Cambyses. He will succeed his father, and after countless misfortunes in Libya and Ethiopia he will eventually die raving mad after killing Apis.*

C. What a joke! But who would now dare to look them in the eye, so scornful are they of everyone else? Who would believe that shortly one will be a prisoner and the other have his head in a wineskin of

14 blood? But who is that, Hermes, with a purple cloak fastened about him and wearing a crown? A cook is giving him a ring he has just cut out of a fish—

In a sea-girt isle: he claims to be some king.*

H. A good parody, Charon. You're looking at Polycrates,* tyrant of Samos, who thinks himself entirely fortunate. But even he will be betrayed to the satrap Oroetes by Maeandrius, the servant standing beside him. He will be crucified, poor wretch, overturned from his good fortune in a moment of time. I heard this too from Clotho.

C. Good for Clotho—a spirited lady! Burn them, my dear, chop off their heads, crucify them, so they'll know they are only human. Meanwhile, let them exalt themselves: the higher they are the more painful their fall. I shall laugh when I recognize them on my skiff, each of them naked, carrying with them neither purple raiment nor tiara nor golden couch.

H. That's what is coming to them. But do you see that throng of 15 people, Charon, sailors, warriors, litigants, farmers, money-lenders, beggars?

C. I see varied occupations and lives full of turmoil. Their cities look like beehives, where everyone has his own sting and stings his neighbour, and a few like wasps ravage and plunder the weaker ones. But what is that crowd that flits in the darkness about them?

H. Hopes and Fears, Charon, Ignorance, Pleasures, Greed, Anger, Hatred, and such like. Of these Ignorance mixes with them lower down and shares their lives, and so indeed do Hatred, Anger, Jealousy, Stupidity, Doubt, and Greed. But Fear and Hope hover above them, Fear sometimes swooping down to shock them into a cowering panic, while Hope, dangling overhead, flies up and away just when a man most thinks he will grasp her, and leaves him gaping after her—just as down below you see Tantalus treated by the water. And if you look closely you will also see the Fates above, 16 working a spindle for each man, from which it happens that every-one is suspended by a slender thread. Do you see what look like cobwebs coming down to each man from the spindles?

C. I see that each has a very slender thread, and that most of them are entangled, one with another and that one with yet another.

H. Of course they are, ferryman; for that man is destined to be killed by this man, and this man by another; and this man to be heir to that man, whose thread is shorter, and that man in turn to this one. That is the meaning of the entangling. Anyway, you see that they all hang from slender threads, and here is one man who is drawn up higher in the air. Soon his thread will snap under his weight and he will fall with a great crash. But here is another one raised only a little from the ground, so if he falls it will be a noiseless fall, scarcely audible even to his neighbours.

C. This is all very ridiculous, Hermes.

H. Indeed, Charon, you couldn't find words adequately to express 17 how absurd it is, particularly their tremendous exertions and how in the middle of their hopes they are carried off, a prey to our fine friend Death. You can see that he has a great many messengers and servants—agues, fevers, consumptions, inflammations, swords, robberies, hemlock, juries, tyrants—and men have no thought at all for any of these while they are prospering, but when disaster strikes the air is full of 'Oh!' and 'Ah!' and 'Woe is me!' If only they realized from the start that they are mortal, and that after a short sojourn in this life they will go away as from a dream, leaving all they had on earth behind, they would live more reasonably and be less grieved at dying. As it is, they expect that what they have now they will have forever, so that when Death's servant appears in order to summon and drag them off in the bonds of fever or consumption, they complain at the summons, never having expected to be dragged from their possessions. For instance, that man who is eagerly building himself a house and urging on the workmen—what would he do if he knew that as soon as it is finished and has the roof on, he will be on his way, leaving his heir to enjoy it, and not even, poor wretch, having a meal in it? And what about that one rejoicing because his wife has borne him a son, and entertaining his friends on the occasion, and giving the boy his own father's name—if he knew that the boy would die at 7 years old, do you think he would rejoice at his birth? The trouble is he sees before him that man there who is fortunate in his son, the father of an Olympic victor; but he doesn't notice his own neighbour who is burying his son, and he doesn't know what sort of thread his own son hangs by. Again, you can see how many there are who quarrel about boundaries; and all those who build up masses of money, and then before they can enjoy it are summoned away by the messengers and servants I mentioned.

18 C. Yes, I see it all, and it makes me wonder what pleasure they have in life and what there can be that they are grieved to lose. If you take their kings, who are reckoned the most fortunate of all, apart from the insecurity and uncertainty, as you put it, of their position in life, you will find that their pleasures are outweighed by their distresses—fears, alarms, hostilities, plots, rage, flattery are all around them. I don't count the sorrows, diseases, and general calamities which obviously control their lives impartially: but if they have a rough time of it, one can reasonably guess at the sort of lives led by ordinary people.

19   Come, Hermes, I'd like to give you an analogy of men and the whole life of men. You must have noticed the bubbles caused by a spring of water splashing down—I mean the way they gather together to cause a foam? Some of them are small and quickly burst and are gone; some last longer, and as others join them they swell and grow enormously: yet inevitably they too burst in due course,

as they must. Such is the life of man.* They are all inflated with the breath of life, some bigger, others smaller. Some have a short-lived inflation, doomed to early death; others die at the moment of birth: but they must all burst in the end.

H. Your simile is just as good as Homer's, Charon: he compares the race of men to leaves.*

C. And though they are like that, Hermes, you see the sort of things   20
they do: how ambitious they are, contending against each other for office and honours and possessions, all of which they will have to leave behind except a single obol when they come down to us. Now we are on a height, would you like me to shout out in a loud voice, urging them to desist from their vain endeavours, and to live with the prospect of death always before their eyes? I can say: 'You fools, why are you so eager for these things? Cease your labours, for you won't live forever. Nothing highly honoured here is eternal, nor can a man take anything with him when he dies. On the contrary, he must go hence naked, and his house and his land and his gold will be forever changing their owners and belonging to others.' If I were to shout this or something like it so that they could hear, would it not help them vastly in their lives and make them much more reasonable?

H. My dear fellow, you don't realize what ignorance and deceit have   21
done to them, stopping their ears with so much wax (as Odysseus did to his companions for fear they might hear the Sirens), that no drill could bore through them. So how could they hear you even if you burst yourself with shouting? Ignorance performs the same function here as Lethe* does with you, though there are a few who don't allow their ears to be waxed, who respect truth, and who have a keen insight into the real nature of things.

C. Then let's shout to them at least.

H. There would be no point telling them what they already know. You notice that they stand aloof from the majority, laughing at what's going on and not at all pleased with it. They are obviously planning already to escape from life to you, and with good reason, being hated for their exposure of men's follies.

C. Well done, noble fellows! But there are very few of them, Hermes.

H. These are enough. But let us now go down.

C. There was one more thing I wanted to know about, Hermes, and   22
once you have shown it to me you'll have completed your guided tour. I'd like to see the storage places where they bury their dead.

H. They call them barrows or tombs or graves, Charon. Do you see those mounds and columns and pyramids in front of the cities? They are all sepulchres and mausolea for their corpses.

C. Then why are those people putting flowers on the stones and anointing them with myrrh, and why are others, who have built pyres in front of the mounds and dug a trench, burning those lavish meals and pouring wine and some honey mixture, it seems to be, into the trenches?

H. I don't know, ferryman, how these things can affect those in Hades. However, the belief is that the souls, coming up from below, take what food they can flitting about the smoke and steam, and drink the honey mixture from the trench.

C. Eat and drink, when their skulls are dry as anything? But silly me for trying to tell you that, since you bring them down every day. You should know whether they can ever return to earth once they are down below. I would be a laughing-stock, Hermes, and have an awful lot of trouble, if they had to be not only taken down but brought up again to have a drink. Oh fools and idiots! They don't realize how great is the barrier between the worlds of the living and the dead, and what things are like with us:

> They are equally dead, the buried and unburied;
> And Irus the beggar has just the same honour as lord
>   Agamemnon;
> Fair-tressed Thetis' son is not greater than Thersites.
> For all are alike, feeble frames of the dead,
> Naked and withered in the asphodel mead.*

23 H. Goodness me, what masses of Homer you are spouting! But now you've reminded me, I'd like to show you Achilles' tomb. Do you see it by the seashore? Trojan Sigeum is over on that side, and opposite to it is Rhoeteum, where Ajax is buried.

C. The tombs are a bit small, Hermes. But now show me the famous cities we hear about down below—Nineveh of Sardanapalus, Babylon, Mycenae, Cleonae, and Troy itself. I remember ferrying over a great many from there, so that for ten years running I couldn't dock and clean out my boat.

H. Well, Nineveh has long since disappeared, ferryman, and there's no trace of it left: you couldn't even tell where it was. But there is Babylon for you, with its fine towers and great wall—and it too will soon be as hard to find as Nineveh. As for Mycenae and Cleonae,

24

I'm ashamed to show them to you, and Troy in particular. You will certainly throttle Homer when you return for his exaggeration of them in his poems. Yet they had their days of glory long ago, though now they too have perished. Cities too die as men do, ferryman, and even more oddly, so do whole rivers. Why, there's not even a ditch left in Argos where the Inachus once flowed.

c. So much for your praises, Homer, and your epithets—your 'holy' and 'wide-streeted' Troy, and your 'well-built'* Cleonae. But, by 24
    the way, who are those people fighting over there, and why are they slaughtering one another?

h. You are watching Argives and Spartans, Charon, and the dying general there is Othryadas, inscribing the trophy with his own blood.*

c. But what is the war about, Hermes?

h. About the plain itself on which they are fighting.

c. Fools!—not to know that even if each of them acquired the whole Peloponnese he would get scarcely a foot's breadth of ground from Aeacus. As for that plain, other nations will be tilling it one after another, and many times will they turn up that trophy, base and all, with the plough.

h. Yes, indeed. But let's go down now and put the mountains back in place. Then we must be on our way, I to my errand and you to your ferry. I'll catch you up soon with another batch of the dead.

c. Thank you very much, Hermes: you will be recorded forever as a benefactor. Thanks to you I have much enjoyed my trip. What a troubled existence ill-starred humanity does have, with its kings and gold ingots and sacrifices and battles—and never giving a thought to Charon!

TIMON THE MISANTHROPE

TIMON, the archetypal misanthrope who retired to a solitary tower in disgust with his fellow men, reputedly lived at Athens during the time of Pericles. Apart from this dialogue our knowledge of him derives mainly from Plutarch's *Life of Antony* (70), though he is mentioned by Aristophanes (*Birds* 1549, *Lysistrata* 809); the comic poet Antiphanes (fourth century BC) wrote a play *Timon*; and the historian Neanthes of Cyzicus (third century BC) wrote his life. In later Greek literature his continuing popularity is evidenced in Alciphron (*Letters* 2. 32) and Libanius (*Declamation* 12), while the type of the morose misanthrope appears in New Comedy, notably in Menander's *Dyscolus*. We learn too from Pausanias (1. 30. 4) that 'Timon's tower' survived as a tourist attraction in his time (mid-second century AD). He has a secure place in English literature through Shakespeare's play of that name, in which the resemblances to Lucian are very obvious.

The dialogue has a sustained brilliance and vigour which mark it out as one of Lucian's best. Apart from the surface humour of the knockabout scenes, there is a seriously satiric look at wealth and the problems it brings. Lucian attacks both its misuse in Timon's hands, where his thoughtless over-generosity backfires terribly on himself, and also the elbowing and scrambling for it shown by the flatterers and the parasites. These are stock types in the literature and life of the time; another is the randy philosopher (Thrasycles), a stern moralist to his pupils, but when off duty he emphatically does not practise what he preaches. Once more too we have the favourite Lucianic motif of gods intervening in human life and physically appearing among men.

1 TIMON. O Zeus, protector of friends and guests and comrades and the hearth, wielder of lightning, guardian of oaths, gatherer of clouds, pealing thunderer, and whatever other names the crackbrained poets call you by—especially when they are in difficulties with their lines, as a string of your epithets can support their faltering metre and fill up the gaps in their scansion—where now is your pealing lightning, your loud-roaring thunder, the blazing flash of your terrifying bolt?* All that turns out to be nonsense and just poetic humbug, except for the resonance of the epithets. That much-vaunted, far-shooting weapon ready to your hand has somehow been utterly quenched and gone cold: it hasn't got even a tiny
2 spark left of anger against evildoers. In fact anybody planning to

26

commit perjury might as soon be afraid of a smouldering lamp-wick as of the flame of your all-subduing thunderbolt. You seem to threaten them with only a brand from which they need not fear fire or smoke, and the only damage they expect is to be covered in soot.

That is why Salmoneus* dared even to rival you in thundering, and he was by no means unconvincing, with his fiery deeds and his great boastings to set against a Zeus whose anger had gone cold. And why shouldn't he, when you lie asleep as if drugged with mandragora, neither hearing perjurers nor noticing wrongdoers? Your eyes are dim and you're half-blind to what's going on and you've become as deaf as an old man. At least when you were still 3 young and quick-tempered and your wrath had an edge to it, you were energetic against wrongdoers and bullies and you gave them no respite then. Your thunderbolt was in full operation, your aegis shook threateningly, your thunder pealed, the shafts of your light-ning were like a continuous bombardment. The earth was shaken by quakes like a sieve, snow fell in heaps, we were stoned by hail (to use a vulgar expression), rain poured down fast and furious, every drop like a river. So in Deucalion's* time such a disaster occurred in a moment, that when all else had sunk beneath the waters barely one little chest survived, which landed on Lycoreus preserving a spark of human seed to breed future generations of greater wickedness.

That's why you are reaping the fruits of your laziness from men, 4 with no one now sacrificing or garlanding your statues. Someone may do so as an act incidental to the Olympic games, but not in the belief that it is at all essential: he is just keeping up an ancient custom. They have deposed you from your place of honour, O noblest of gods, and are gradually turning you into a Cronus.* I won't mention how many times already your temple has been robbed; but some have even laid hands on your very person at Olympia, and you, High Thunderer, were too frightened to rouse the dogs or summon the neighbours to rush to your aid and catch the fellows while they were still preparing their escape. Instead, you noble Giant-Slayer and Titan-Conqueror, you just sat there letting them cut your hair off, a ten-cubit thunderbolt gripped in your right hand!

Well then, you strange being, when will this careless disregard for things cease? When will you punish all this wickedness? How many Phaethons* and Deucalions will it take to deal with such

5   overwhelming human arrogance? For example, if I may leave aside generalizations and speak personally, I have given so many Athenians a leg-up in their lives, made some rich who were desperately poor, helped all who needed it; indeed I have poured out my money in heaps to serve my friends. But now that I have become poor through all this, I am cut dead and don't even get a glance from those who previously bowed and cringed to me and hung on my nod. If I happen to meet any of them in the street, they pass me by as they would an ancient tombstone that has fallen over through age, without even stopping to read it. Others, seeing me in the distance, take the next turning off: not long before I was their saviour and benefactor, and now I am a disagreeable and ill-omened

6   sight to them. That is why I've been driven by my wrongs to put on a leather jacket and dig this field at the back of beyond for four obols a day, meditating on solitude and on my fork. Here at least I can enjoy the advantage that I don't have to see a lot of people prospering undeservedly—that would certainly be more painful.

    So come on now, son of Cronus and Rhea, shake off that nice deep slumber—you've already beaten Epimenides' record sleep*— rekindle your thunderbolt, or light another one from Etna, and make a great blaze to show the wrath of a vigorous young Zeus— unless what the Cretans say about you and your grave there is true after all!*

7 ZEUS. Who is that, Hermes, yelling from Attica by the foothills of Hymettus, the filthy, squalid fellow in a leather coat? He seems to be bending over and digging; loquacious too, and insolent. He must be a philosopher, or he wouldn't be carrying on with such blasphemy against us.

  HERMES. What, father? Don't you recognize Timon, son of Echecratides, of Collytus? He's the one who has often feasted us with perfect sacrifices; he was newly made rich, offered whole hecatombs, and used to entertain us lavishly at the Diasia.*

  ZEUS. Dear me, what a change! Is this the fine and wealthy gentleman, who had so many friends about him? So what happened to a man like that, who seems now a squalid wretch, digging for hire and heaving such a massive fork?

8 HERMES. Well, you could say it was his goodheartedness and kindness that ruined him, and his compassion to anyone in need; but in truth it was his folly and simplicity and lack of judgment regarding

his friends. He didn't understand that he was being generous to ravens and wolves, and while all those vultures were tearing at his liver* the poor devil thought they were his friends and comrades, enjoying their food because they liked him. But when they had carefully stripped his bones and gnawed them clean, and very thoroughly sucked out any marrow in them, they departed leaving him as dry as a tree with its roots cut off, no longer recognizing him or giving him a glance (why should they?), or offering him any help, or repaying his generosity. That's why you see him with fork and leather coat, having left the city through shame. He tills the land for hire, half-crazed with his wrongs, as those he has made rich pass by him in utter disdain, not even knowing that his name is Timon.

ZEUS. Well, we must not ignore or neglect this man: with his mis- 9 fortunes he had good reason to be so irritated. We too would be behaving like those abominable flatterers if we forgot someone who has burnt all those fat ox and goat thigh-bones on our altars: I can still savour them in my nostrils. But I've been so busy, what with this upsurge of perjurers and assaulters and plunderers; and then there's the fear of temple-robbers—so many of them and hard to guard against, and they don't let you close your eyes for a moment. So it's ages since I even looked towards Attica, especially since philosophy and disputation became so prevalent there; for what with their wrangling and shouting at each other, it's impossible to hear any prayers. The result is you have to sit with your ears stopped up, or else be ground down with deafening discourses on 'virtue' and 'incorporeals' and other rubbish. That's why I come to have neglected this man though he's no paltry figure.

However, go to him quickly, Hermes, and take Wealth with you; 10 and let Wealth take Treasure with him too, and let them both stay with Timon and not abandon him so readily, however much he wants to drive them from his house again through his good-heartedness. And as to those flatterers and the ingratitude they showed him, I'll be seeing to them in due course and they'll get their deserts, as soon as I've had my thunderbolt repaired. Its two biggest prongs got broken and blunted the other day, when I was a bit too energetic in firing a shot at the sophist Anaxagoras* for teaching his disciples that we gods don't exist. I missed him, as Pericles put up his hand to shield him, and the bolt glanced off onto the Anaceum,* set that on fire, and almost shattered itself on the rock. But meanwhile it will be punishment enough for them to see Timon exceedingly rich.

11 HERMES. It certainly pays to yell out and make yourself troublesome and impudent: it's useful not only if you are pleading in court, but praying to the gods too. Here's Timon moving from poverty to riches in a moment, just because he attracted Zeus' attention by his loud outspoken prayers. If he'd just bent over his digging in silence he'd still be digging unnoticed.

WEALTH. But I can't go to him, Zeus.

ZEUS. Why not, my dear Wealth, since I've told you to do just that?

12 WEALTH. Because, by Zeus, he insulted me, ruined me, cut me up into little pieces, even though I was a family friend. He virtually pitchforked me out of the house, like someone hurling a live coal from his hands. So am I to go back again just to be handed over to parasites and flatterers and courtesans? Send me, Zeus, to those who will appreciate the gift, who will treat me well, who will value and love me. Let these idiots stick to the poverty which they prefer to me: they can get a leather coat and a fork from her, poor fools, and be content with four-obol wages after heedlessly throwing away ten-talent presents.

13 ZEUS. Timon will not treat you like that now. Unless his loins are totally impervious to pain, his digging will have taught him a clear lesson that you are preferable to poverty. But you do seem to me to be too critical: you find fault with Timon now because he opened his doors to you and let you wander around freely, and didn't lock you up jealously. But at other times you took the opposite line, complaining that the rich kept you locked up so closely with bolts and keys and seals that you couldn't even peep out and see daylight. At any rate that was your complaint to me, that you were stifled in total darkness. That's why you appeared so pale and careworn, your fingers distorted with constant counting on them, and you threatened to run away if you got the chance. In a word, you thought it frightful to have to lead a virgin life like Danae in a bronze or iron chamber,* under the care of those strict and horrible
14 guardians, Interest and Accounts. Actually, you used to say that they behaved ridiculously in loving you extravagantly but not daring to enjoy you though they could; and though quite free to indulge their passion, instead they stayed awake to guard you, staring unblinkingly at their seals and bolts. They thought it was sufficient enjoyment not to enjoy you themselves but to prevent

others enjoying you, like the dog in the manger which didn't eat the barley herself nor allow the hungry horse to have it.* What is more, you laughed at them scraping and saving and even, absurdest of all, feeling jealous of themselves, but quite unaware that a cursed house-slave or jailbird of a steward would secretly slip in and cause mayhem, leaving his wretched, unloved master to sit up poring over his interest payments by the dim light of a narrow-necked lamp with a thirsty wick. So, isn't it inconsistent in you to criticize that sort of behaviour in the past and now to blame Timon for doing the opposite?

WEALTH. Actually, if you consider the thing realistically you'll 15 realize that I have good reason for both my attitudes. This utter carelessness of Timon can only be regarded as negligent and unfriendly towards me. On the other hand, those who kept me shut up in dark boxes, taking care to make me grow fat and overweight, not touching me themselves nor showing me to the light of day in case someone saw me—those I thought stupid and arrogant. What had I done wrong for them to let me rot away in such a prison, not realizing that in a short time they would pass away and leave me to some other lucky man? So I have no time for either that lot or the 16 others who are too free with me, but for those who follow the best course, which is moderation in this matter, and who neither abstain from spending altogether nor squander all they have.

In Zeus' name, Zeus, look at it like this. Suppose a man should legally marry a pretty young woman, and then put no restrictions on her and feel no jealousy about her whatsoever, but let her wander freely night and day and see anyone who wanted her company—or rather, himself encourage her to commit adultery, flinging open his doors and playing the pander by inviting all and sundry to come to her: would you think that such a man loved her? You wouldn't say so, Zeus, with all your experience of love. But suppose, on the other hand, a man takes a freeborn woman 17 in due form into his house to bear him legitimate children, but neither himself touches the girl in the bloom of her beauty, nor lets anyone else look at her, but keeps her locked up to live a life of barren virginity, claiming, however, that he loves her, and proving it by his pallor and wasted flesh and sunken eyes. Surely such a person would be thought to be out of his wits, when he could be having children and enjoying his marriage, but instead lets such a lovely and desirable girl wither away by keeping her all her life like a priestess of Demeter. That's the sort of thing I get angry about too, because some people kick me about shamefully and lap me up greedily and pour me away like water, while others keep me in irons like a branded runaway slave.

18 ZEUS. Why are you angry with them? Both sorts pay a fair penalty. The latter are hungry and thirsty and dry-mouthed, like Tantalus,* just gaping at their gold; while the others, like Phineus,* have their food snatched from their throats by the Harpies. Come on, off you go to Timon: you'll find him much more sensible now.

WEALTH. Why, will he ever stop eagerly pouring me out of a leaky sieve, as it were, even before I've finished streaming in, trying to beat the inflow and stop me overflowing and drowning him? I think I'll just be carrying water to the Danaids' jar* and filling it in vain, as the vessel leaks and empties almost before you've filled it—the outflow is so much wider and nothing stops me from running out.

19 ZEUS. Well, if he's not going to stop that hole and it's been opened up for good, you will quickly run out and he will find his leather coat and his fork again in the dregs of the jar. But off with both of you and make him rich. And remember, Hermes, on your way back bring the Cyclopes from Etna, so that they can sharpen and repair my thunderbolt: I'll soon need it with a good point.

20 HERMES. Let's go, Wealth. What's this? Are you limping? My dear fellow, I didn't know you were lame as well as blind.

WEALTH. Not always, Hermes; but whenever I go to somebody on an errand from Zeus I somehow get sluggish and lame in both legs, so that I barely make it to my destination, and sometimes the man who's expecting me has grown old before I get there. But when I am due to leave you'll see me growing wings and much swifter than dreams. The starting gate is hardly opened before I am announced winner of the race, having leapt round the course so fast that the spectators sometimes don't even see me.

HERMES. That's not true: I could name you many people who yesterday didn't have an obol to buy themselves a noose, but suddenly today they are teeming with riches, and driving a pair of white horses, though previously they couldn't even afford a donkey. And they go about wearing purple clothes and rings on their fingers, though I bet they still can't believe their wealth isn't just a dream.

21 WEALTH. That's quite different, Hermes. I don't go on my own feet then, and it's Pluto not Zeus who sends me to them—he too gives wealth and splendid gifts, as you can tell from his name.* When I

have to migrate from one man to another, they put me into a will, seal me carefully, bundle me up and carry me off. The corpse lies in some dark corner of the house, covered from the knees in an old sheet, to be fought over by weasels; while those who have hopes regarding me hang about in the public square with their mouths gaping, like chirping swallow chicks waiting for their mother to fly back to the nest. And when the seal is broken, the thread is cut, and 22 the will opened, my new master's name is revealed. He is either some relative or flatterer, or a lecherous slave who was once a favoured boyfriend, with his chin still scraped smooth—this fine fellow now reaps a rich reward for all the many and varied pleasures he gave his master even when past the age to give such service. Whoever it is, he grabs me, will and all, and rushes off with me, changing his name from Pyrrhias or Dromo or Tibius to Megacles or Megabyzus or Protarchus, and leaving the others staring at each other, their mouths open in vain, and in real mourning now that a tunny-fish like this has escaped from the folds of their net after swallowing such a lot of bait. But the man who has suddenly fallen 23 into riches, a vulgar, thick-skinned fellow, who still shudders at the thought of shackles, pricks up his ears if someone passing just cracks a whip, and pays reverence to a mill-house* as if it was a holy shrine—he is quite insufferable to those he meets, insulting free men and whipping his fellow-slaves, to see if he too is allowed to behave like that now. At length he becomes involved with a tart, or acquires a mania for breeding horses, or gets into the hands of flatterers who swear that he is more handsome than Nireus, nobler than Cecrops or Codrus, craftier than Odysseus, and richer than sixteen Croesuses* put together: and so the poor wretch squanders in a moment what he gradually amassed through all his perjuries, his swindles, and his villainies.

HERMES. That's pretty well what happens. But when you go on your 24 own feet how do you find the way, blind as you are? And how do you recognize the people Zeus sends you to, who he thinks deserve to be rich?

WEALTH. Do you imagine I discover who they are? Not on your life; otherwise I wouldn't have abandoned Aristides and gone over to Hipponicus and Callias* and many other Athenians who didn't deserve an obol.

HERMES. But what do you do when you are sent down to earth by him?

33

WEALTH. I wander up and down, pottering about until I come across somebody unawares. Then whoever first encounters me takes me off to keep me at home—and pays homage to you, Hermes, for his windfall.*

25 HERMES. So Zeus is deceived in thinking that you follow his wishes and enrich those he thinks deserve riches?

WEALTH. Yes indeed, my dear fellow, and deservedly. He knows I'm blind, but he kept sending me to look for an object exceedingly hard to find and long since extinct in the world: not even Lynceus* could easily find something so small and shadowy. So you see, the good being few and far between, and the wicked completely crowding the cities, it's easier for me to come across them as I wander around, and to get caught in their nets.

HERMES. Then how do you escape easily when you leave them, not knowing the way?

WEALTH. Somehow I get keen-sighted and swift-footed then, but only for the moment of escape.

26 HERMES. One more question. Though you are blind (that can't be denied), and what is more, pale and heavy-footed, how do you come to have so many lovers that everyone looks longingly at you, and if they find you they think themselves happy, but if they miss you life isn't worth living? Indeed, I know quite a few so madly in love with you that they went and hurled themselves 'into the deep-yawning sea' and 'down from the lofty crags',* thinking you disdained them, when in fact you just couldn't see them. But I'm sure even you will admit, if you know yourself, that they must be crazy to be infatuated with such a lover.

27 WEALTH. Do you think they see me as I really am, lame and blind and so on?

HERMES. Why not, Wealth, unless they are just as blind themselves?

WEALTH. They are not blind, my good fellow, but ignorance and deceit, which are everywhere now, cloud their vision. Moreover, to avoid being totally ugly, I put on a most alluring mask before I meet them, all gold and jewels, and dress myself in gay colours. So they think the beauty they see belongs to me as a person, fall in love with me, and are ready to die if they can't have me. If anyone stripped me naked and revealed me to them, no doubt they would be accusing themselves for being utterly short-sighted and falling in love with an object so hateful and hideous.

28 HERMES. Then why is it that even those who have become rich and

have themselves put on the mask are still deluded, and if anyone tries to take it off them they would sooner part with their head than their mask? They are surely not likely then to be unaware that your beauty is painted on, having seen all that's under it.

WEALTH. I have quite a lot of help with this too, Hermes.

HERMES. Like what?

WEALTH. When someone first meets me and opens his door to welcome me in, others come in secretly along with me—Pride, Folly, Arrogance, Effeminacy, Insolence, Deceit, and countless more. Once his soul has been possessed by all these, he admires what he should not admire, longs for what he should avoid, and stands in wonder at me, the parent of all these intruding vices who attend me, and he would suffer anything rather than have to part with me.

HERMES. What a smooth, slippery thing you are, Wealth, how elusive 29 and evasive: one can't get a firm grip on you, but somehow you escape through the fingers like an eel or a snake. On the other hand, Poverty sticks and holds on to people: she has countless hooks growing all over her body, so that anyone coming near gets caught at once and cannot easily get away. But while we've been chattering we have forgotten something fairly important.

WEALTH. What's that?

HERMES. We haven't brought Treasure with us, and we must have him.

WEALTH. Don't worry about that. I always leave him back on earth 30 when I come up to you, with instructions to stay at home with the door locked, and not to open to anyone unless he hears my voice.

HERMES. In that case let's now go to Attica. Hold on to my cloak and follow me until I come to the wilderness.

WEALTH. You're wise to hang on to me, Hermes. If you leave me behind I'll wander around and maybe run into Hyperbolus or Cleon.* But what is that noise like iron hitting stone?

HERMES. This is Timon, not far off digging a stony bit of mountain 31 ground. Aha, and here's Poverty with him, and Toil over there, and Endurance and Wisdom and Courage, and all that multitude of Hunger's troops—a much better lot than your own bodyguards.

WEALTH. Then shouldn't we take ourselves off as quickly as possible, Hermes? We can't do anything worthwhile with a man surrounded by such an army.

HERMES. Zeus thought differently: let us not be cowards.

32 POVERTY. Where are you off to, Slayer of Argus,* leading that fellow by the hand?

HERMES. We've been sent by Zeus to Timon here.

POVERTY. Wealth sent to Timon now, when I have taken him over in a terrible state because of Luxury, and made a noble and worthwhile man of him, giving him into the care of Wisdom and Toil? Do you really think that I Poverty am so contemptible and so easy to injure, that I can be robbed of my one and only possession, that I have carefully brought to perfection in virtue, only for Wealth to take him over once more, entrust him to Insolence and Pride, make him once more soft and degenerate and stupid, and then give him back to me worn to a rag?

HERMES. That's the will of Zeus, Poverty.

33 POVERTY. I'm off: come along with me, Toil and Wisdom and the rest of you. This fellow will soon realize what he is giving up in me—a good helping hand and teacher of all that's best. With me he kept going, healthy in body and strong in mind; he lived the life of a man, keeping his independence, and rightly regarding all these excesses and extravagances as alien to him.

HERMES. They're leaving: let's go to him.

34 TIMON. Who are you people, damn you? What do you want, coming here to annoy a working man trying to earn his wages? You'll go away regretting it, wretches all of you: I'll straightaway beat you up with these clods and stones.

HERMES. Stop, Timon: don't throw them at us—we're not men. I am Hermes, and this is Wealth. Zeus has heard your prayers and sent us; so cease your toils, welcome prosperity, and good luck to you.

TIMON. You'll still suffer, even if you are gods as you claim. I hate everyone, men and gods alike; and as for this blind fellow, whoever he is, I intend to crush him with my fork.

WEALTH. In Zeus' name, Hermes, let's go before I suffer harm: the man looks absolutely crazy to me.

35 HERMES. Don't be stupid, Timon: stop this terribly harsh and savage behaviour, and stretch out your hands to accept your good fortune. Be rich again, play a leading part in Athens, and despise the ungrateful while you keep your prosperity to yourself.

TIMON. I don't need anything from you: stop bothering me. My fork is wealth enough for me, and otherwise I'm happiest if nobody comes near me.

HERMES. Must you be so unsociable, my friend?

36

Must I take up to Zeus a speech so harsh and so stubborn?*

Indeed you may well hate men after they have treated you so badly, but there's no reason to hate the gods who are showing such concern for you.

TIMON. All right, Hermes, I'm most grateful to you and to Zeus for 36 your concern, but I'm not having any of this Wealth.

HERMES. Tell me, why?

TIMON. Because in the past he caused me countless troubles, handing me over to flatterers, bringing plotters against me, stirring up hatred, ruining me with good living, exposing me to envy, and in the end suddenly deserting me with such bad faith and treachery. But that good woman Poverty trained me in manly toils, talked to me with frankness and truth, rewarded my labours with life's necessities, and taught me to despise my former wealth. She made me depend upon myself for my hopes of a livelihood, showing me what my real riches were, which I could not lose to a fawning flatterer or threatening blackmailer or angry mob, or voter in the assembly or plotting tyrant. So, made hardy by my labours I toil 37 away with a will on this field, seeing nothing of the evils of the city, and earning my daily bread amply and sufficiently with my fork. So turn round and be off, Hermes, and take Wealth back to Zeus. As for me, I'd be satisfied if I could cause all men, young and old, to grieve aloud.

HERMES. That's no way to talk, my friend: they don't all deserve to grieve. Do drop this childish show of bad temper and accept Wealth. Gifts from Zeus shouldn't be rejected.

WEALTH. Are you willing for me to state my case, Timon? Or will you be angry if I say anything?

TIMON. Say on—but don't be long about it, and no preambles like those damned orators. I'll put up with a few words from you for Hermes' sake.

WEALTH. I really ought perhaps to be making a long speech in view 38 of all your accusations. However, just consider your charge that I have wronged you. It was I who gave you all your greatest pleasures, prestige, precedence, crowns of honour, and every sort of luxury. Through me you were admired, famous, and courted. And if you suffered at the hands of flatterers, that's not my fault. In fact, it's I who have been wronged by you, when you so basely handed me over to vile men who praised and cajoled and plotted against me in every way. And as to what you said last, that I betrayed you, on the contrary I could charge you with driving me off in every possible way and kicking me headlong out of your house. That's the reason Poverty, so dear to your heart, has exchanged your soft cloak for this leather jacket. So, Hermes here is my witness how I begged Zeus that I needn't visit you again after such hostile behaviour towards me.

39 HERMES. But can't you see how changed he has now become, Wealth? So don't be afraid to spend time with him. You keep on digging, Timon; and you, Wealth, put Treasure under his fork: Treasure will come at your call.

TIMON. I must obey, Hermes, and become rich again. For what can you do when the gods insist? But consider all the troubles you are throwing a luckless man into. Up to now I was leading a life of bliss; and all of a sudden, though I've done no wrong, I'm to get a heap of gold and take on heaps of cares.

40 HERMES. Put up with it, Timon, for my sake, even if it is harsh and intolerable, in order that those flatterers may burst with envy. And now I must be flying up to heaven by way of Etna.

WEALTH. He's gone, I suppose, to judge from the beating of his wings. But you stay here, while I go and send Treasure to you; or rather, strike the earth. I say, Treasure of gold, pay heed to Timon here and let him grub you up. Dig away, Timon, with good deep strokes. I will leave you two together.

41 TIMON. Come, my fork, show me your strength now and don't tire as you call up Treasure from the depths to the light of day. O Zeus, god of wonders! O favouring Corybants!* O Hermes, god of gain! Where did all this gold come from? This must be a dream. I fear I'll wake up and find nothing but ashes.* But yes, it is coined gold, red and heavy and most sweet to look upon.

O gold, to mortals fairest gift.*

Indeed, you shine out like blazing fire* both night and day. Come to me, O most beloved and desirable. Now I do believe that Zeus once turned into gold: for what girl would not receive with open

42 bosom so beautiful a lover pouring through the roof?* O Midas and Croesus and treasures of Delphi, how you fade away compared with Timon and Timon's wealth! Not even the Persian king can rival me.

My fork and my beloved leather coat, it is fitting to dedicate you to Pan here. As for me, I'll now buy the whole area, and I'll build a tower over the treasure, sufficient for me to live in alone, and to serve for my tomb when I'm dead.

'Let it be resolved as a binding law for the rest of my life that I shall avoid, ignore, and despise all men. Friend, guest, comrade, the Altar of Pity,* these shall just be empty words. To pity someone in tears and to help the needy shall be to transgress the law and the code of behaviour. My life shall be solitary like the wolves, and Timon my only friend. All others shall be enemies and plotters; to 43 associate with them shall be pollution. If I so much as see them, that makes the day unlucky. In short, they shall be to me just like statues of stone or bronze. I shall receive no herald from them and make no treaty with them: my solitude shall be the boundary between us. Tribesmen, clansmen, demesmen, even native land shall be cold and useless terms—the pride of fools. Timon shall enjoy his wealth alone, despise everyone, live in luxury alone, free from flattery and vulgar praise. He shall sacrifice and feast alone, his own neighbour and associate, shaking himself free of all others. And once for all be it resolved that he will pay the due honours to himself when he dies, and put on his own funeral wreath. Let his 44 own favourite name be Misanthrope, and the distinguishing marks of his character to be peevish, harsh, awkward, wrathful, and inhuman. If I see anyone being destroyed in a fire and begging for it to be quenched, I am to quench it with pitch and oil. And if a winter torrent is sweeping somebody away and he is stretching out his hands and begging me to grab him, I am to push his head right under so he cannot come up again. So shall they get fair repayment. Law proposed by Timon, son of Echecratides, of Collytus; put to the vote of the assembly by the said Timon.'

Very well: let that be resolved by us and let us stick to it firmly. 45 All the same, I would have given a lot for everyone somehow to find out that I am enormously rich: that would make them want to hang themselves. But what's this? Goodness, what a rush! People running up from all sides, panting and covered in dust: somehow they got a whiff of the gold. Now, shall I climb up this hill and drive them away with a shower of stones from above, or shall I break the law to the extent of talking to them just this once, to make them suffer even more by being despised? Yes, I think that's better. So, let me stand my ground and receive them. Well then, who is this I see first? Gnathonides the flatterer. When I asked him the other day for a loan he offered me a noose, though he has often vomited up whole jars of wine at my house. Well done in coming here: he'll be the first to suffer.

46 GNATHONIDES. Didn't I tell you the gods would not neglect a good man like Timon? Greetings, Timon, most handsome, most good-natured, and jolliest of fellows.

TIMON. Greetings to you, Gnathonides, greediest of all vultures, most rascally of men.

GNATHONIDES. You'll always have your little joke. But where's the party? I've brought you a new song from one of the shows that's just been produced.

TIMON. Indeed, it's a lament you'll be singing, and very feelingly too thanks to this fork of mine.

GNATHONIDES. Here, what's this? Hitting me, Timon? Witnesses, please. O lord, ow! ow! I'll summon you before the Areopagus* for assault.

TIMON. If you just stick around a bit longer maybe I'll be summoned for murder.

GNATHONIDES. No, no! At least heal my wound by dressing it with a little gold—it's marvellous for stanching blood.

TIMON. You still here?

GNATHONIDES. I'm going, but you'll be sorry you stopped being kind and became so surly.

47 TIMON. Who's this coming up, going bald on top? It's Philiades, the most loathsome of the flatterers. He had a whole farm from me and a dowry of two talents for his daughter, as payment for praising me to the skies when I'd sung a song that everyone received in silence: he swore I sang more sweetly than a swan. But when he saw me ill the other day and I approached him for some help, all the noble fellow gave me was blows.

48 PHILIADES. O for shame! Now do you all recognize Timon? Now is Gnathonides his friend and drinking partner? Then he has got his deserts for being so ungrateful. But we who have been old established intimates and fellow students and neighbours are more restrained, so as not to seem too pushy. Greetings, sir. Do be on your guard against these foul flatterers, who are only interested in your dinners and otherwise no different from ravens. You can't trust anyone nowadays: everybody is ungrateful and wicked. I was coming to bring you a talent to help you for your pressing needs, when I heard on the way not far off that you had come into an

enormous amount of wealth. So I've come to offer this word of warning; but as you're so wise you probably don't need to listen to me—you could tell even Nestor* what to do.

TIMON. True enough, Philiades; but come here so I can welcome you with my fork.

PHILIADES. Help! The thankless wretch has broken my head because I gave him some useful advice.

TIMON. Look, here comes a third, the orator Demeas, with a decree 49 in his right hand, and claiming to be a relative of mine. This man had sixteen talents from me on one day to pay to the city: he had been condemned to a fine and imprisoned for not paying it, so I took pity on him and got him freed. But the other day, when it was his turn to distribute the show-money to the Erechtheis tribe,* and I went up for my share, he said he didn't know me as a citizen.

DEMEAS. Greetings, Timon, great supporter of your clan, bulwark of 50 Athens, defender of Greece. The assembly and both the councils* have long since met and await your presence. But first hear the decree which I have drawn up on your behalf:

'Whereas Timon of Collytus, son of Echecratides, who is not only a man of the highest character but wiser than any other in Greece, never ceases to offer the highest services to the city, and has been victorious at Olympia in boxing and wrestling and running, all in one day, as well as in the chariot races, both the full-grown teams and the colt-pairs . . .'

TIMON. Actually I've never even been to see the Olympics.

DEMEAS. So what? You will one day: it looks good to put in a lot of that sort of thing. 'And he distinguished himself last year fighting for the city of Acharnae, where he cut to pieces two Spartan divisions . . .'

TIMON. How could I? I wasn't even on the service-list because I had 51 no armour.

DEMEAS. You are too modest, but we would be ungrateful if we didn't remember you. 'And furthermore he has done notable service to the state in proposing decrees, giving counsel, and serving as general. For all these reasons be it resolved by the Council and the Assembly and the Supreme Court, tribe by tribe, and the demes, both separately and in common, that a golden statue of Timon be set up beside Athena on the Acropolis, with a thunderbolt in his hand and a crown of rays on his head, and that he be decked with seven golden wreaths which shall be granted him by proclamation today at the Dionysia when the new tragedies are performed; for this day's Dionysia must be held in his honour. Moved by Demeas the orator, his next of kin and pupil; for Timon excels in oratory and in everything else he chooses.'

52   That's the resolution for you. I also wanted to bring my son to see you: I've called him Timon after you.

TIMON. How so, Demeas, when so far as I know you aren't even married?

DEMEAS. Well, I shall marry next year, god willing, and have a child, and I hereby call him Timon, for he'll be a boy.

TIMON. I don't know if you'll be marrying, my friend, when you've had this wallop from me.

DEMEAS. Ow! What's that for? You're trying to be a tyrant, Timon, and beating up free men when it's not clear that you are a free citizen yourself.* But you'll soon pay for everything, including setting fire to the Acropolis.

53 TIMON. It's not been set on fire, you brute: that proves you're an informer.

DEMEAS. Well, you got your wealth by breaking into the Treasury.

TIMON. That's not been broken into either, so that is another lie.

DEMEAS. It'll be broken into later; but you already have all the contents of it.

TIMON. All right then, take that as well.

DEMEAS. Oh, my back!

TIMON. Stop yelling or I'll give you a third. It would be utterly ridiculous if unarmed I could cut to pieces two divisions of Spartans, and not thrash one filthy little wretch. In vain would I have won the boxing and wrestling matches at the Olympics.

54   But what's this? Do we have Thrasycles the philosopher here? So it is. There he comes, with bushy beard and eyebrows lifted, giving himself airs, eyes flashing like a Titan, hair thrown back from his forehead, the very picture of a Boreas or a Triton as painted by Zeuxis.* He cuts a neat figure, with orderly gait and cloak decently worn. In the morning he discourses endlessly about virtue, attacking pleasure-lovers and praising contentment with little. But when he's had his bath and comes to dinner, and the boy hands him a large goblet—and the stronger the wine the better— it's as if he had drunk the water of Lethe, the way he behaves exactly opposite to his morning precepts. He snatches the meat like a kite, elbowing his neighbour aside, and covers his beard with

gravy as he gobbles his food like a dog. He crouches over his dishes
as though he expects to find virtue in them, carefully wipes the
bowls with his finger to leave not a drop of the sauce, and he's 55
always complaining even if he has a whole cake or a whole boar to
himself. He is supreme in greed and gluttony, and when he drinks
he's not just inebriated enough to sing and dance: he turns wrathful and abusive. Moreover, he has a lot to say in his cups—in fact he
is then at his most eloquent—about moderation and decorum, and
that too when he is by now in a bad way from unmixed wine and
stuttering like a clown. Then he vomits, and finally has to be picked
up and carried out of the dining-room, grabbing at the music-girl
with both hands. But even when sober he yields the palm to none in
lying, effrontery, or greed. He is your supreme flatterer and the
readiest of perjurers. He is led by imposture and followed by
shamelessness; in a word, he is a creature of all craft and subtlety in
every detail and accomplished in artfulness. So, he's about to suffer
for being such a worthy fellow. Why, dear me, Thrasycles, it's a
long time since we met.

THRASYCLES. I haven't come, Timon, for the same reason as all these 56
others. They are dazzled by your riches, and they've come running
up hoping for gold and silver and rich dinners, and meaning to
heap flattery upon a man as simple-hearted and generous with his
money as you. As for me, you know that barley-cake is sufficient
dinner for me, and the sweetest relish is thyme or cress or, if I spoil
myself, a bit of salt; my drink is water from the Nine Springs.*
I prefer this old cloak to the purple you fancy; and as for gold, it's
worth no more to me than pebbles on the beach. It's for your sake
that I've come, to prevent your being ruined by that most evil and
treacherous possession, wealth, which has been the cause of fatal
disasters many times to many people. Take my advice and throw
the whole lot of it into the sea: a good man has no need whatever of
it, for his eyes are open to the riches of philosophy. But don't throw
it in too deep, my good fellow; just wade in up to your waist and
throw it a bit beyond the breakers—with only me as witness. Or 57
if you don't want to do this, there is another better way to get it
quickly out of the house, leaving not an obol for yourself. Just give
it away to all the poor and needy, five drachmas to this one, a mina
to that one, half a talent to another. If there's a philosopher around,
he ought to get a double or triple share. As for me, I'm not claiming
for myself, but to distribute to colleagues who need it, and it will be

43

ample if you just give me what will fill this pouch: it holds a bit less than two Aeginetan bushels.* One who claims to be a philosopher should be moderate and content with little, and not have aspirations beyond the limit of his pouch.

TIMON. Quite right, Thrasycles; but instead of your pouch do let me fill your head with wallops, measured out by my fork.

THRASYCLES. O Democracy! O Laws! I'm being assaulted by the scoundrel in a free city.

TIMON. What are you complaining about, my friend? Surely I haven't cheated you? Here, then, take four more measures over the amount. But what's this? Here's a crowd coming: there's Blepsias and Laches and Gnipho, and a whole battalion who are going to suffer at my hands. So why don't I get up on this rock, give my long-suffering fork a rest, collect all the stones I can, and send a hailstorm onto them from a distance?

BLEPSIAS. Don't throw, Timon: we're going.

TIMON. But not without shedding blood and suffering wounds, I can tell you.

58

ICAROMENIPPUS OR HIGH
ABOVE THE CLOUDS

THIS dialogue is a piece of fantasy which illustrates two of Lucian's favourite motifs: an attack on the pretensions of professional philosophers and an exploratory journey by someone between the earth and the upper or the lower world. Among other examples we can compare *Charon*, in which the ferryman of the dead comes up to earth to see what the life of man is like; and *Menippus*, where the third-century BC Cynic philosopher goes to the underworld to consult the prophet Tiresias because he cannot make head or tail of what the philosophers on earth are telling him. In *Icaromenippus* the same Menippus goes up to heaven from a similar motive, as the only way of learning the truth, when all he hears around him are conflicting and contradictory theories from the philosophers. Another example of a journey to the heavens, with a different motive, can be seen in *A True History*.

The title of this piece derives from the story of the archetypal craftsman Daedalus and his son Icarus. Daedalus constructed wings for them both to fly away from Crete, but Icarus flew too close to the sun, which melted the wax on his wings so that he fell into the sea and drowned. The point here may simply be that Menippus also returned to earth (though more safely) without his wings.

MENIPPUS. So my first stage was 3,000 furlongs from the earth to the 1 moon; from there up to the sun was about 1,700 miles; and from the sun to heaven itself and Zeus' citadel, this again would be another day's ascent for an eagle in good training.

FRIEND. In the name of the Graces, Menippus, why are you acting the astronomer and quietly reckoning it all up like this? I've been following you around for a long while, listening to your outlandish babble about suns and moons, and even those threadbare items, stages and miles.

M. Don't be surprised, my friend, if my talk seems airy-fairy and high-flown: you see, I'm just totting up to myself the full length of my recent travels.

F. So you followed the Phoenicians, old fellow, and worked out your journey by the stars?

M. Certainly not: I was making my travels actually among the stars.

F. Good heavens! You're talking about a long dream, if you really weren't aware that you were sleeping for miles and miles.

M. What do you mean, dream? I've just returned from visiting Zeus. 2

F. Come again? My Menippus here, fallen from the sky after visiting heaven?

M. Yes, here I am, back today from the actual presence of Zeus himself, the real Zeus, and I've seen and heard marvellous things. And if you don't believe me, I am absolutely delighted that my good fortune is beyond belief.

F. O you divine, you Olympian Menippus, how could a mere mortal groundling like me not believe a cloud-man and, in Homer's phrase, a heaven-dweller? But please tell me this, how you were carried up, and where you got yourself such a long ladder? For you don't seem in looks at all like the Phrygian boy,* for us to imagine that you too were snatched up by the eagle to become a wine-waiter.

M. You've obviously been making fun of me all this time, and it's not surprising if you think my strange tale is like a fairy story. But I did not need a ladder for my ascent, nor to become the eagle's favourite, since I had my own wings.

F. From your account you've done better than Daedalus,* if apart from everything else you have changed from a man into a hawk or a jackdaw without our noticing it.

M. A good guess, my friend, which hits the mark. I did in fact make myself wings, based on Daedalus' clever device.

3 F. You must be the rashest man in creation! Weren't you then afraid that you too would fall into the sea somewhere, and give your name to a Menippean Sea like the Icarian?

M. By no means: for Icarus had his wings stuck together with wax, so that as soon as that melted in the sun he lost his feathers and of course fell down. But my feathers were not waxed.

F. What are you saying? I don't know why it is, but you're beginning to make me believe you are telling the truth.

M. What I'm saying is this. I got hold of a good-sized eagle, and a strong vulture too; and cutting off their wings along with the wing-bones—but let me tell you the whole device from the beginning, if you can spare the time.

F. Of course I can. Your words have put me into a state of suspense, and I'm now agog to hear the end of the story. For Friendship's sake, don't let me stay hanging by the ears in the middle of your tale.

4 M. Well then, listen to it. For abandoning a friend who is agog is not a pretty sight, especially if, as you say, he is hanging by the ears.

As soon as I discovered, in the course of surveying life's various elements, that all human affairs are absurd, trivial, and fickle—I mean wealth and office and power in the state—I despised these things, and assumed that exerting oneself to get them was a hindrance to acquiring things that are really worth while; and so I tried to look upwards and contemplate the universe. In doing this I was much puzzled, first by what philosophers call the cosmos, since I couldn't find out its origin or who created it, or its first principle or its ultimate purpose. Then, as I examined it in its various parts, I was forced into even greater perplexity. I saw the stars scattered at random over the sky, and I wanted to know the nature of the sun itself. Especially did the behaviour of the moon seem odd and completely strange to me, and I reckoned that her manifold shapes had some hidden cause. What's more, the flash of lightning, the crash of thunder, and rain or snow or hail pelting down—all these were baffling and hard to make out.

So, in this frame of mind I thought my best plan was to learn 5 about all these things from our friends the philosophers, as I assumed that they at any rate could tell me the whole truth. I chose the best of them, so far as I could judge from their bad-tempered expressions, pale complexions, and long beards, for they were the ones who immediately struck me as impressive in speech and knowledgeable about the heavens. To these I entrusted myself, paying down a large deposit on the spot, and agreeing to pay the rest later on the completion of my course in philosophy; and I expected to be taught how to talk of things on high and to learn about the orderly arrangement of the cosmos. But they were so far from ridding me of my long-standing ignorance that they actually threw me headlong into greater puzzlements, by deluging me every day with first principles, final causes, atoms, void, matter, forms, and suchlike. But to me at least the biggest difficulty of all seemed to be that, though they all disagreed with one another and everything they said was conflicting and inconsistent, they still expected to convince me, and tried to win me over each to his own creed.

F. How strange that wise men should be at odds with one another in their creeds and not have the same beliefs about the same things!

M. Well, my friend, you'll certainly laugh when you hear their pre- 6 tentiousness and their fantastic talk. To begin with, they had their feet on the ground, in no way superior to the rest of us earthlings; in fact they couldn't see more clearly than the next man, and some were even bleary-eyed from old age or lethargy. Yet they still claimed they could distinguish the boundaries of heaven, they measured the sun, they visited places beyond the moon; and as if they themselves had fallen from the stars, they described their sizes and shapes; and often, maybe, though not even knowing clearly how many miles Megara is from Athens, they presumed to tell you how many cubits is the distance between the moon and the sun. They measure the height of the air and the depth of the sea and the circuit of the earth; and what's more they draw circles, and super-impose triangles on squares, and construct intricate spheres, and thus, they claim, they measure the heavens themselves.

7 Secondly, too, was it not senseless and utterly crazy of them, when speaking of things so unclear, to say nothing at all conjec-turally, but to strain their assertions to the limit and outdo everyone else in exaggeration, almost swearing that the sun is a red-hot lump of metal, that the moon is inhabited, and that the stars drink water, as the sun draws up moisture from the sea in a bucket and distributes it around to them all to drink?

8 It's easy to grasp all the inconsistencies in their theories. Just consider, I ask you, whether their beliefs hang together and are not utterly discrepant. Take first their differing views about the universe. Some think it had no beginning and will have no end; while others have made bold to name its creator and describe its construction. The latter caused me the most astonishment, since they posited some god as the creator of the universe, but didn't tell us further where he came from or where he stood when he fitted it all together. Yet it is impossible to conceive of time and place before the creation of the universe.

F. The men you describe are certainly audacious charlatans, Menippus.

M. My good fellow, what if you were to hear all their discussions about forms and incorporeals, and their theories about finite and infinite? Indeed, in this very area they dispute mightily, some of them putting a limit to the universe, others supposing it to be unlimited. What's more, they have claimed that there are very many worlds and censured those who talk as though there is only one. Another, not known for his peaceful tone, has supposed that war was the father of the universe.*

9 Why indeed talk about the gods at all, when we find that to some god was a number, while others swore by geese and dogs and

plane-trees?* Then, too, some banished all the other gods and assigned the rule of the universe to one only, so that it annoyed me somewhat to hear that there was such a dearth of gods. On the other hand, others generously declared that there were many gods, and distinguished between what they called the first god, and others they ranked second and third in divinity. Again, some believed the divine was without body or form, and others supposed it to be body itself. Furthermore, they did not all believe that the gods show an interest in our affairs; but some absolved the gods of any responsibility at all, just as we usually relieve the elderly of public duties. In fact they assign them roles just like extras in comedies. Some, taking the most extreme view, didn't believe in the gods at all, but left the world to carry on without ruler or guide.

That was the reason why, hearing all this, I didn't venture to 10 doubt the 'high-thundering' men with their 'fine beards';* but I was at a loss where to turn to find some argument of theirs which wasn't open to criticism, and couldn't somehow be refuted by somebody else. So I experienced exactly what Homer describes: many times I made an effort to believe one of them—

But another thought drew me back.*

Being utterly at a loss in all this, I despaired of learning any truth about these things while I was on earth, and I thought the only escape from all my difficulties would be somehow to acquire wings and go up to heaven. My eagerness chiefly gave me this hope, and also the fabulist Aesop, who opens up heaven to eagles and beetles, and sometimes even to camels.* Now, it seemed quite impossible for me to grow wings myself; but if I put on the wings of a vulture or an eagle—for only these would sustain the weight of a human body—perhaps my venture would succeed. So, I caught the birds and carefully cut off the right wing of the eagle and the left wing of the vulture; then tying them together I fitted them to my shoulders with strong straps, and contrived grips for my hands at the ends of the quill-feathers. Then, first I tested myself by jumping up and down, making use of my arms, and, as geese do, lifting myself and flapping along the ground on tiptoe. As my device began to succeed I worked at the experiment more boldly; and going up to the citadel I let myself fall down by the cliffside straight into the theatre. Since I flew down without coming to grief I set my thoughts now 11 on the heights, and rose on my wings, flying from Parnes or

Hymettus to Geraneia, from there up to Acrocorinthus, and then over Pholoe and Erymanthus as far as Taygetus.*

So, now that I was fully experienced in my enterprise and an expert in high flying, I put aside fledgling thoughts, rose up to Olympus, and taking as few supplies as possible proceeded to make my way straight to heaven. To start with I was dizzy from the height, but in time even this did not bother me. But when I was far above the clouds and near to the moon, I realized I was getting tired, especially in my left wing, which was the vulture's. So I made for the moon, and sitting on it I had a rest, gazing down on the earth from on high, and like Zeus in Homer looking now at the land of the horse-keeping Thracians, now at the land of the Mysians,* and soon, as the fancy took me, Greece, Persia, and India. All this filled me with a lot of varied pleasure.

F. Well, you must tell me all about it, Menippus, so that I don't miss any details at all of your excursion, and I can also learn what you may have found out incidentally on your way. I'm really looking forward to hearing a lot about the shape of the earth and about everything on it, as it appeared to you seeing it from above.

M. You certainly won't be disappointed, my friend. So come up to the moon as best you can in imagination, and share my journey and my view of the whole state of things on the earth. First of all, you must imagine that you are looking at a very small earth, I mean much tinier than the moon; so that when I suddenly looked down I couldn't make out for a long time where the large mountains and the great sea were. If I hadn't seen the Colossus of Rhodes and the lighthouse on Pharos,* you can be sure I would have missed the earth altogether. But as in fact they were tall and prominent, and the ocean was shining gently in the sun, they showed me that what I was seeing was the earth. And once I had fixed my gaze intently, the whole life of man was revealed to me, not just in nations and cities, but clearly as individuals—sailors, soldiers, farmers, litigants, women, animals, and, in short, all that the bountiful earth nurtures.*

F. Your story is utterly incredible and inconsistent. Just now you said you were searching for the earth, Menippus, because it was shrunk through the intervening space, and that if the Colossus hadn't given you a clue you might have thought you were seeing something else. How can you now have suddenly become a Lynceus* and can distinguish everything on earth—men, animals, and almost mosquitoes' nests?

M. Ah, you've done well to remind me. Somehow I left out the most 13 essential point. When I saw and recognized the earth itself, but couldn't distinctly see any details because my vision did not reach so far down, the thing annoyed me intensely and caused me great perplexity. I got depressed and was close to tears, when the philosopher Empedocles appeared behind me, looking as if burnt to a cinder and baked in ashes.* I must tell you that when I saw him I was somewhat startled, and thought I was seeing some moon spirit; but he said 'Don't worry, Menippus:

> I am no god: why think me like the immortals?*

You see before you Empedocles the scientist. The fact is, when I threw myself headlong into the crater, the smoke snatched me out of Etna and carried me up here; and now I live on the moon, walking the air a lot and feeding on dew. So here I am to help you out of your present difficulty. I gather you are annoyed and tormented because you cannot clearly see what's happening on earth.' 'That's kind of you, my dear Empedocles,' I replied, 'and as soon as I fly back down to Greece I shall remember to pour an offering to you at the chimney, and at the start of every month to face the moon and open my mouth three times in prayer.' 'No, by Endymion,'* he said, 'I'm not here for payment: but my heart was a bit moved when I saw you so sad. Do you know what you must do to become keen-sighted?' 'No,' I replied, 'unless you can somehow 14 remove the mist from my eyes. For at the moment my vision seems exceedingly blurred.' 'Indeed,' he said, 'you have no need of my help, for you yourself have brought from earth the means to keen-sightedness.' 'What's that, then, as I'm quite unaware of it?' I said. 'Don't you know', he said, 'that you are wearing an eagle's right wing?' 'Of course,' I replied, 'but what has a wing got to do with eyes?' 'The fact', he said, 'that the eagle has the keenest sight of all creatures, so that he alone can look straight at the sun; and the sign of the true royal eagle is that he can stare into its rays without blinking.' 'So they say,' I replied, 'and I'm now regretting that when I came up here I didn't replace my own eyes with those of the eagle. As it is, here I am in a half-finished state and not equipped royally in every respect: instead, I'm like those bastard and disowned eagles you hear about.' 'None the less,' he said, 'it is possible for you immediately to have one royal eye. If you're willing to stand up for a moment, keep the vulture's wing still, and flap only with the other one, your right eye will become keen-sighted to correspond with that wing. There is no way of avoiding your other eye being dimmer as it is on the worse side.' 'It's enough for me,' I said, 'if even the right one can see like an eagle: that would be quite sufficient, as I'm sure I've often seen carpenters doing better with one eye when planing timbers to a straight-edge.'

15   Saying this, I followed Empedocles' suggestion, and he gradually moved away and slowly dissolved into smoke. And as soon as I had flapped the wing, a tremendous light shone around me, revealing everything that had previously been hidden. Bending forward to the earth I could clearly see cities and people and all that was going on, not only in the open, but what they were up to in their homes when they thought they couldn't be seen. I saw Ptolemy sleeping with his sister; Lysimachus' son plotting against him; Seleucus' son Antiochus slyly making eyes at his stepmother Stratonice; Alexander of Thessaly being killed by his wife; Antigonus committing adultery with his son's wife; and Attalus' son pouring out poison for his father. Elsewhere I saw Arsaces killing the woman and the eunuch Arbaces drawing his sword against Arsaces; and Spatinus the Mede was being dragged by his leg from the banquet by the guards, with his forehead broken by a golden cup.* I could see similar things happening in Libya and in royal palaces among the Scythians and the Thracians—adulterers, murderers, plotters, plunderers, perjurers, men living in fear, and men betrayed by their next of kin.

16   Well, such was the entertainment which the activities of the kings gave me; but those of the ordinary people were far more hilarious. For they were visible too: Hermodorus the Epicurean perjuring himself for a thousand drachmas; the Stoic Agathocles taking a pupil to law for his fee; Clinias the orator stealing a cup from the temple of Asclepius; and the Cynic Herophilus asleep in a brothel.* Need I mention the others—burglars, litigants, usurers, beggars? It was, in a word, a varied and motley spectacle.

F.   Indeed, Menippus, you really should talk about that too, as it seems to have given you no ordinary pleasure.

M. To give you a complete account, my friend, would be impossible, when even to see it was quite a job. However, the main activities were like those which Homer portrays on the shield.* In one place there were banquets and weddings; in another, court cases and assemblies; elsewhere someone was sacrificing, while next door another man was mourning. Whenever I looked towards the country of the Getae I saw them at war. When I turned to the Scythians, they could be seen roaming around on their waggons. If I shifted my gaze away slightly, I noticed the Egyptians working their land; the Phoenicians were travelling on business, the Cilicians practising piracy, the Spartans lashing themselves,* and the Athenians going to law. As all this was happening at the 17 same time, you can readily imagine what a hotchpotch it seemed to be. It was as though you were to set up a lot of choral singers, or rather a lot of choirs, and then instruct each singer to forget about harmony and sing his own tune; then, when each was doing his own thing in rivalry, and eager to outdo his neighbour in loudness of voice, in heaven's name what do you imagine the song would sound like?

F. A complete jumble, Menippus, and quite ridiculous.

M. Well, my friend, that's what all the singers on earth are like, and of such a discord is the life of men composed. Not only do they sing out of harmony, but they dress differently, move in opposite directions, and have no common purpose, until the producer drives each of them off the stage, saying he has no more need of them. Then they all alike become quiet, no longer singing that tuneless and unrhythmical medley. But in the theatre itself, with its diverse and changing scenes, everything that happened was really and truly ludicrous.

The ones who gave me the biggest laugh of all were those who 18 were disputing about boundary-lines, and those who prided themselves on farming on the plain of Sicyon, or owning land around Oenoe in Marathon, or having a thousand acres in Acharnae. In fact, since from up there the whole of Greece then looked to me four fingers in size, I reckon proportionately Attica was a very tiny fraction. So I thought how little was available for these men to pride themselves on: for it seemed to me that the biggest landowner among them had just about one of Epicurus' atoms to cultivate. And when I turned my gaze to the Peloponnese and saw Cynuria, I thought to myself what an insignificant region, in no way bigger than an Egyptian bean, had caused the deaths of so many Argives and Spartans in one day.* Then, too, if I saw someone priding himself on his gold, because he possessed eight rings and four cups,

I had a good laugh at him too: for the whole of Pangaeum* along with its mines was the size of a grain of millet.

19 F. O Menippus, weren't you lucky in that incredible sight! But in heaven's name, what about the cities and the people: how big did they look from up there?

M. I suppose you've often seen a colony of ants, where some are swarming around the mouth of their nest and running their affairs in public, while some are going out and others coming back to their city; one is carrying out dung, while another has grabbed a bean-husk or half a wheat-grain from somewhere and is running off with it. Probably, too, according to the pattern of their lives, ants have builders, politicians, magistrates, musicians, and philosophers. Anyway, the cities and their inhabitants resembled ant-hills more than anything else. And if you think that likening men to the commonwealth of ants is a demeaning comparison, have a look at the old stories about the Thessalians, and you'll find that the most warlike of races, the Myrmidons, were changed from ants into men.*

Anyway, when I'd seen everything and had my fill of laughter, I shook myself and flew up—

to the palace of Zeus of the aegis, to join all the other immortals.*

20   Before I had risen two hundred yards, the Moon, speaking with a woman's voice, said, 'Menippus, I'd be so grateful if you would do me a favour with Zeus.'

'Say what it is,' I replied, 'it will be no trouble, unless you're asking me to carry something.'

'Carry a simple message from me,' she said, 'and a request to Zeus. I've become tired, Menippus, of listening to all the extraordinary things the philosophers are saying. They have nothing better to do but meddle with me, asking what I am, and how big, and why I become a half-moon or gibbous. Some of them claim that I'm inhabited; others that I hang over the sea like a mirror, others attribute to me anything that occurs to them. Most recently they've even been saying that my very light is stolen and illegitimate and comes from the sun above; and they never cease deliberately causing strife and discord between us, though he is my brother. For they were not content with describing Helios himself as a stone and a red-hot lump of metal.

21   'And yet don't I know perfectly well all the shocking and

54

abominable things people get up to at night, who by day are grave of countenance, with a manly look and solemn bearing, and are looked up to by ordinary folk? Yet, though I see all this I say nothing, as I don't think it seemly to expose and bring to light these nocturnal activities and every individual's life in bed. In fact, if I see one of them committing adultery, or stealing, or doing some other audacious nocturnal deed, I straightaway cover myself in a veil of cloud, so as not to let ordinary people see old men bringing disgrace on their long beards and on virtue. But they lose no opportunity to pick me to pieces in their talk and to insult me in every possible way; so that (Night is my witness) I have often made up my mind to remove myself as far as possible to escape their meddlesome chatter.

'So remember to tell Zeus all this, and say also that I can't possibly remain in my place unless he crushes the natural philosophers, gags the logicians, destroys the Stoa, burns down the Academy, and stops the peripatetic lectures. Only then could I get any peace, and have a rest from being measured every day by them.'

'It shall be done', I said, and with that I pressed on with my   22
journey on the path up to heaven,

> From where there was nothing to see of the labours of cattle
> and men.*

For soon even the moon looked small to me and the earth was lost to view.

Having the sun on my right and flying on through the stars, on the third day I arrived close to heaven. At first I decided just to go straight in as I was, as I thought I would easily escape notice being half-eagle, and I knew that Zeus had long been accustomed to eagles. But then I considered that they would very soon catch me out, as my other wing was a vulture's; so I decided it was best not to take any risks and I went up and knocked on the door. Hermes answered my knock, asked my name, and hurried off to tell Zeus. Soon I was admitted in great fear and trembling, and I found them all sitting together and showing signs of concern themselves. For my unexpected visit had caused them mild anxiety, and they were expecting that almost any minute the whole human race would arrive similarly equipped with wings. But   23
Zeus, giving me a fierce look like a Titan's, said in a really terrifying voice:

What is your name among men, and where are your city and
parents?*

Hearing this I nearly died of fright, but I stood my ground,
though stupefied and thunderstruck by his tremendous voice. After
a while I pulled myself together and told him everything clearly
from the beginning: how I was anxious to learn all about celestial
matters; how I'd gone to the philosophers; how I'd heard their
contradictory arguments; how I'd got sick of being pulled in different ways by their theories; then about my device of the wings
and so on, until I got to heaven. And after all that I added the
message from the moon. Zeus smiled and relaxed his frown a bit,
with the words, 'What can you say about Otus and Ephialtes,*
when even Menippus has ventured to come up to heaven? Well, be
our guest now; but tomorrow, when we have dealt with the reasons
for your visit, we shall send you away.' So saying he got up and
went to the part of heaven that was the best listening-post, as it was
his time for sitting and dealing with prayers.

24   On the way, he questioned me about matters on earth: first the
usual topics about the current price of wheat in Greece, whether
our last winter had been particularly severe, and whether our
vegetables needed more rain. Then he asked whether Pheidias* had
any descendants surviving; why the Athenians had abandoned the
Diasia* for so many years; whether they were planning to complete
the Olympieion* for him; and whether the men who had robbed his
temple at Dodona had been caught.*

When I had answered these questions, he said, 'Tell me,
Menippus, what views do men have about *me*?' I replied, 'My lord,
what view could they have but the most pious, that you are king of
all the gods?'

'You will have your fun,' he said, 'but I am fully aware of their
love of novelty, even if you don't tell me. There was a time when
they thought me a prophet and a healer, and I was everything to
them:

> And all the streets were full of Zeus,
> And all men's assemblies . . .*

In those days Dodona and Pisa were famous and universally
admired, and I couldn't even see anything for the smoke of the
sacrifices. But ever since Apollo established his oracle at Delphi,

and Asclepius his healing shrine in Pergamum, and the temple of Bendis* was founded in Thrace, the temple of Anubis* in Egypt, and the temple of Artemis* in Ephesus, everyone goes flocking to these, and they hold their festivals there and set up their hecatombs and offer their gold ingots; while they think I'm past my best and they've done their duty if they sacrifice once every four years to me at Olympia. So you can see that my altars are more frigid than the *Laws* of Plato or the *Syllogisms* of Chrysippus.'*

While we were discussing all this we came to the place where he 25 was due to sit and listen to prayers. There was a series of holes, like the openings of wells, with lids on them, and next to each was a golden seat. Zeus sat down by the first one, took off the lid, and applied himself to the supplicants. The prayers were of all sorts and kinds and came from all over the earth; for I too leant over and listened to them with him. Here are some examples: 'O Zeus, may I become a king.' 'O Zeus, make my onions and my garlic grow.' 'O gods, let my father die soon.' Or someone would say, 'May I inherit my wife's estate'; 'May my plot against my brother go undiscovered'; 'May I win my law suit'; 'Grant me victory in the Olympic games.' From sailors came prayers for the north wind, or the south wind; a farmer was praying for rain; a fuller was praying for sunshine.

Zeus listened to each prayer and assessed it carefully, without promising everything:

But one thing the Father did grant and another rejected.*

The fact is he accepted the just prayers coming up through the opening, and stored them away on his right; but the unholy ones he ignored and dismissed, blowing them back down, so that they wouldn't even come near to heaven. In the case of one prayer I noticed that he was in a quandary. Two men offered conflicting prayers and promised equal sacrifices, so he didn't know which one to favour, and found himself in the predicament of the Academics: he couldn't come to a decision, so, like Pyrrho,* he put it off while he pondered the matter.

When he had dealt sufficiently with the prayers, he moved on to 26 the next seat and the second hole, and bending down he gave his attention to oaths and those who swear them. Having dealt with these too and crushed Hermodorus the Epicurean,* he changed to the next seat to attend to omens and prophetic sayings and augury from birds. From there he went next to the sacrifice hole, through which the smoke came up and revealed to Zeus the name of each sacrificer. Then when he had left the holes he issued instructions to the winds and the seasons on what they must do: 'Today it must rain in Scythia; there must be lightning in Libya and snow in Greece. North Wind, you must blow in Lydia. South Wind, you must ease off. The West Wind must stir up the waves in the Adriatic; and about a thousand bushels of hail must be scattered over Cappadocia.'

27   By now he had sorted out just about everything and we went to the dining-room, as it was time for dinner. Hermes took charge of me and seated me beside Pan and the Corybantes and Attis and Sabazius*—foreign gods of ambiguous status. Demeter supplied me with bread, Dionysus with wine, Heracles with meat, Aphrodite with myrtle-berries, and Poseidon with sprats. But on the quiet I also tasted ambrosia and nectar, as Ganymede, bless him, whenever he saw Zeus looking the other way, in his kind-heartedness poured me out a cup or two of nectar. The gods, as Homer says somewhere (and I imagine that like me he was there and saw for himself), 'eat not bread nor drink of sparkling wine',* but have ambrosia set before them and get drunk on nectar. They particularly enjoy feeding on the savoury smoke of sacrifices which comes up to them and on the blood of the victims, which sacrificers pour around the altars.

    During the meal Apollo played his lyre, Silenus* gave us a comic dance, and the Muses got up and sang us an extract from Hesiod's *Theogony* and the first song from Pindar's *Hymns*.* When we'd had enough of that, we settled ourselves to sleep just as we were, being pretty tipsy.

28   The rest of the gods and the men who marshal their chariots
    Did sleep through the night, but I was not held by sweet sleep;*

For I was pondering many things, especially how in all this time Apollo had not grown a beard, and how there can be night in heaven when the sun is always there, sharing their meals.

    Anyway, I had a little sleep then, and at dawn Zeus arose and
29 ordered an assembly to be summoned. When everyone was present, he began to speak: 'The reason for summoning you is the visitor here who arrived yesterday; but for some time I've been wanting to have a discussion with you about the philosophers, and now I'm

particularly urged on by the moon and her complaints, so I've decided no longer to put off our debate.

'There is a certain class of men who became widespread in the world not long ago, lazy, quarrelsome, conceited, quick-tempered, gluttonous, stupid, demented, full of arrogance, and as Homer puts it, "a useless burden on the land".* Well, these men have divided themselves into schools, and invented elaborate and tortuous jargon, calling themselves Stoics, Academics, Epicureans, Peripatetics, and other things much more ridiculous than these. Then, clothing themselves in the impressive title of Virtue, raising their eyebrows, wrinkling their foreheads, growing long beards, they go around hiding disgusting habits under a false appearance. They most resemble actors in tragedy: if you take off their masks and gold-spangled robes all you have left is a laughable little creature hired for the show for seven drachmas.

'But, such as they are, they still despise the whole human race, 30 and make absurd statements about the gods. They gather round them youths who are easily misled, and rant on about their much-vaunted Virtue, and teach them their logical conundrums. To their pupils they are always praising endurance and temperance and self-sufficiency, and abhorring wealth and pleasure; but when on their own by themselves how could you describe how much they eat, how much they indulge in sex, how they lick the dirt off obols?*

'But worst of all is that, while they themselves do nothing worthwhile in public or in private, but stand around useless and superfluous,

Having no value in war or in council,*

yet they accuse everyone else, and pile up bitter phrases, and carefully rehearse novel forms of abuse to censure and rebuke their neighbours. And he is thought the finest performer who shouts the loudest and is the boldest and most insolent in his abuse. And yet, 31 if you asked the man who is straining himself in yelling and accusing everyone else, "What about you? What are you achieving, and what, in the name of the gods, are you contributing to humanity?", he would reply, if he felt like saying what was right and truthful, "I think it's unnecessary for me to be a sailor or a farmer or a soldier or to ply a trade. I shout, I'm squalid, I wash in cold water, go barefoot in winter, wear a filthy cloak, and like Momus* find fault with everything other people do. If one of my neighbours has spent a lot of money on a dinner or has a mistress, I make it my business and show my annoyance; but if a friend or companion of mine is ill in bed, needing help and treatment, I pay no attention."

32   'So there you have these creatures, gods. And what's more, some of them, called Epicureans, are exceedingly insolent and attack us violently, saying that the gods have no care for human affairs and pay no attention whatever to what is happening. So now is the time for you to be considering that if they once manage to persuade the world, you will be extremely hungry. For who would go on sacrificing to you if he didn't expect a return for it?

    'As to the moon's complaints, you all heard the stranger telling us yesterday. In response, you must decide on whatever will be most helpful to men and most in our interests.'

33   When Zeus finished the assembly was in an uproar, and they all began shouting out at once: 'Thunderbolt them!', 'Burn them up!', 'Crush them!', 'Into the pit!', 'Off to Tartarus!', 'To the Giants with them!' Zeus called for silence again and said, 'Just as you wish: they shall all be crushed, along with their logic. But it is not appropriate to punish anyone just now, for as you know it is the four-month festival season, and I have already sent around proclaiming the truce from hostilities.* So next year, at the start of spring, those horrors shall die horribly by the fearful thunderbolt.'

So spoke the son of Cronus and nodded dark brows to confirm it.*

34   'Regarding Menippus,' he went on, 'my decision is this: he is to be stripped of his wings, so that he can never come back here, and then escorted down to earth today by Hermes.'

    With these words he dissolved the meeting, and Hermes, lifting me up by my right ear, carried me down to the Potters' Quarter* yesterday evening.

    You've heard it all, my friend, all that happened in heaven. So now I'm off to take this good news to the philosophers who wander around the Painted Hall.*

NIGRINUS

LUCIAN recounts a visit he paid to the Platonist philosopher Nigrinus in Rome and the spellbinding effect Nigrinus' discourse had upon him. Much of the piece consists of a highly unfavourable picture of Rome compared with Athens, and this anti-Roman attitude is clearly a satirical commonplace which we find elsewhere in Lucian, notably in *On Salaried Posts*. There is an obvious comparison here with Juvenal's mordant picture of life in Rome (*Satire* 3), and satirical passages in Horace and Martial also suggest themselves; but it is not at all clear whether Lucian knew and was influenced by any of these writers. It is safest to say that a traditional *topos* has surfaced in several diverse writers.

Nothing is known of Nigrinus, but we need not assume that Lucian invented him. It is more important to observe that the label Platonist is irrelevant to what he actually says, and that his discourse is essentially a rhetorical show-piece in praise of Athens at the expense of Rome.

The formal setting shows one of Lucian's variations in the structure of his pieces, an introductory letter and a dialogue that frame the central exposition. The letter and the opening words between Lucian and his friend give an emphatic build-up to Nigrinus' discourse and the electrifying effect it had on Lucian himself.

Letter to Nigrinus

Greetings from Lucian to Nigrinus.

There is a proverb 'An owl to Athens'* meaning that it would be silly to take owls there since they have plenty already. If I wished to display my rhetorical skills by writing a book and sending it to Nigrinus, I'd become a laughing-stock as really and truly trading in owls. But as I only want to show you my state of mind—my present feelings and how totally I was gripped by your eloquence—I may fairly evade even the charge contained in Thucydides' maxim,* that men are bold through ignorance, whereas reflection makes them cautious. For obviously it is not just ignorance that leads me to such temerity as this, but love for reasoned debate.

Farewell

The Wisdom of Nigrinus
(A dialogue between Lucian and a friend)

1 FRIEND. How lordly and dignified you are returning to us! You don't bother to notice us any more or keep company with us or take part in our conversations: you've altered suddenly, and in a word seem supercilious. I'd dearly like to hear from you why you're behaving so oddly and what's the cause of all this.

LUCIAN. My dear fellow, it's simply good fortune.

F. How so?

L. A by-product of my journey is that I return to you happy and elated, and as they say on the stage, 'thrice-blest'.*

F. Heavens! In so short a time?

L. Yes, indeed.

F. But what's this great experience on which you give yourself such airs? Let us not just enjoy a hint at it but learn details of all that happened.

L. Don't you think it extraordinary, in heaven's name, that instead of a slave I am now free, instead of poor I am truly rich, instead of witless and deluded I am tolerably sane?*

2 F. Well, that's great news; but I'm still not clear what you mean.

L. I went off straight to Rome, wishing to see an oculist—the trouble in my eye was getting worse.

F. I know all about that and I was hoping you would find a good man.

L. Well, I had decided to pay a long overdue visit to Nigrinus, the Platonist philosopher, so I got up early and went to his house. I knocked at the door, the servant announced me, and I was invited in. I found him inside with a book in his hands and surrounded by a lot of statues of ancient philosophers. Before him was placed a tablet inscribed with some geometrical figures, and a sphere made 3 of reeds which seemed to represent the universe. Well, he greeted me very hospitably and asked how I was getting on. I gave him full details, and of course wanted to know in turn how he was getting on and whether he had decided to visit Greece again.

Once launched on these matters, my friend, and explaining his intentions, he poured such verbal ambrosia over me as made the Sirens (if they ever existed) and the nightingales and the lotus* 4 of Homer all out of date—so divine was his eloquence. For he was led on to praise philosophy itself and the freedom it offers, and to pour scorn upon what are commonly called blessings,

wealth, reputation, kingship and honour, gold too and purple—all
that seems wholly admirable to most people, myself included until
then. All this I took in with a rapt and receptive soul, and to start
with I couldn't imagine what was happening to me: I was a prey to
every sort of feeling. One moment I was hurt because all that was
dearest to me was treated with contempt, wealth, money, renown,
and I almost wept at their loss. The next, they seemed to me petty
and ridiculous, and I was rejoicing to be looking up as it were from
the foggy atmosphere of my previous life into a sky that was bright
and clear. And this had the strangest result that I actually forgot
about the trouble in my eye, but gradually became more sharp-
sighted in my soul, which till then I had been carrying around
unawares in a state of blindness. So I went on, and ended up in this 5
state you reproached me with just now. His words made me feel
proud and buoyant, and I have altogether banished petty thoughts.
I suppose philosophy has had the same sort of effect on me as wine
is said to have had on the Indians when they first drank it. Being
naturally quite warm-blooded, when they drank such strong liquor
they at once became quite frenzied and the manic effect was
doubled because they were drinking it neat. So too, you see, I'm
going about feeling possessed and drunk with intoxicating words.

F. Indeed, that's not drunkenness, but soberness and temperance. 6
But I'd like, if possible, to hear his actual words. I don't think it's all
right to be grudging with them, especially if it's a friend who wants
to hear, and one who shares your interests.

L. Don't worry, my good fellow: you are urging on someone who is
already keen, as Homer* says, and if you hadn't got in first I would
have asked you to listen to my story. I want you to be my witness to
the world that my madness has reason behind it. Moreover, I much
enjoy frequently recalling all this, and already practise doing so
regularly. Even if there's nobody around I repeat his words to
myself two or three times a day. Lovers, when their darlings are 7
absent, recall some word or act of theirs, and so beguile the time by
cheating this lovesickness into thinking they are really there. Some
in fact even believe they are talking to them, take delight in things
they previously heard as if just then spoken to them, and by this
mental clinging to the memory of the past they leave themselves no
time to be distressed by their immediate circumstances. So in my
case too, in the absence of Philosophy I get a great deal of comfort
in putting together the words I heard then and revolving them

within myself. To sum it up, it's as if I were drifting out at sea on a dark night. I keep that man in view like a beacon fire, imagining him beside me in whatever I'm doing, and always seeming to hear him repeating his message to me. Sometimes, especially if I am concentrating strongly, I seem to see his face too, and the sound of his voice lingers in my ears. It is indeed true of him, as the comic poet said, 'he left his sting behind in all who heard him'.*

8 F. Hold on, my fine fellow: pull back a bit and tell me from the beginning what he said. I find it very exasperating the way you beat about the bush.

L. Well said—I must do as you say. But look, my friend, you must have seen in your time bad tragic actors, and surely comic ones too: I mean those who are hissed and finally driven off the stage for murdering their pieces, even though the plays are often excellent and have won prizes?

F. I know many such: so what?

L. I fear that as we go along you'll think that I am making the same sort of fool of myself, stringing things together haphazardly, and sometimes even spoiling the sense by my inadequacy, with the result that you'll gradually be induced to condemn the play itself. That doesn't bother me much on my own account, but I would naturally be greatly upset if my drama suffered failure and disgrace 9 because of me. So do remember through all my speech that we cannot hold the poet responsible for such faults. He is sitting far away from the stage, quite unconcerned with any of the action in the drama; it is of myself you are to make trial—my powers of memory as an actor, for so far as anything else is concerned I am no different from a messenger in tragedy. So if there seems to be anything inadequate in my lines, you can have this ready excuse, that the poet probably said something different and better. And even if you hiss me off I won't be hurt in the least.

10 F. By Hermes,* what a fine rhetorical preamble, all according to the rules! I suppose you are going on to say that you had only a brief conversation, that you have come unprepared to speak, and that it would be better to hear him saying these things himself as you have only managed to store up a few points in your memory. Weren't you about to say that? Well, don't bother on my account: as far as that is concerned consider your introduction completed. I am ready to cheer and applaud; but if you keep on delaying, I'll be resenting it all through your performance and I'll hiss you loud and clear.

L. Yes, I should like to have made all the points you have listed, and 11
also that I do not intend to make a long speech, quoting in detail
all he said: that would be quite beyond me. Nor will I assume
his identity in what I say, in case I become in another way like
those actors I talked about, who, when they are acting the part of
Agamemnon or Creon or even Heracles himself, are often dressed
in cloth of gold, with fierce gaze and wide-open mouth, but the
voice that emerges is thin, squeaky and womanish, much too feeble
even for Hecuba or Polyxena. So, in order not to invite criticism by
wearing a mask much too big for my head, and disgracing my
costume, I wish to talk to you with my face uncovered, so I don't
involve the hero I am playing in my own fiasco.

F. Will the fellow never stop going on to me about all that stage and 12
tragedy?

L. Yes, I will stop, and turn now to my theme. He began his talk with
praise of Greece and the people at Athens, because philosophy and
poverty are their foster-brothers, and they don't look with favour
on anyone, citizen or foreigner, who tries to force luxury into their
lives. If anybody comes among them with this in view they gently
correct and reform him, and so convert him to a simple style of
living.

For instance, he mentioned a certain rich man, conspicuous for 13
his vulgarity, who came to Athens with a crowd of retainers and
gold and garish clothes. He thought he would be the envy of all the
Athenians and be gazed upon as a happy man; but they thought
the poor fellow an unlucky creature, and proceeded to educate
him—not harshly nor forbidding him outright to live as he wished
in a free city. But when he behaved offensively in the gymnasia
and the baths, jostling people he met and crowding them out with
his retainers, somebody would say quietly and calmly, as if in
an aside not directed at the man himself: 'He must think he is going
to be killed in his bath. Yet all is peaceful in the baths: no need
for an army here.' And he heard the truth and picked up some
instruction on the way. They also had a witty way of stripping him
of his garish clothes and purple robes, by making fun of their
bright floral colours. 'Is it spring already?' they would say, or
'Where did this peacock come from?', or 'Maybe it belongs to his
mother', and so on. In the same way they jeered at his other
excesses, his mass of rings, his elaborate hairdo, and his extravagant
life-style. The result was that he gradually learnt moderation,

and departed much improved by the public education they gave him.

14   As an indication that they are not ashamed to admit to poverty, he told me of a remark he had heard everyone utter unanimously at the Panathenaic festival. A citizen had been arrested and taken to the steward of the games because he was watching the show in a coloured robe. The onlookers felt sorry for him and pleaded for him, and when the hearld declared that he had acted illegally in wearing such clothes at the show they all cried out in unison, as if it were preconcerted, that he should be pardoned for dressing like that as he had nothing else to wear.

Well, he commended this and also the freedom there, the unpretentious life-style, and the tranquil leisure, all of which they have in abundance. He declared that life among such people is in harmony with philosophy and can keep the character pure, and that if a man is serious and has been trained to despise wealth, and chooses a life devoted to what is intrinsically noble, then living at
15 Athens will suit him perfectly. But anyone who loves wealth and is beguiled by gold, who measures happiness by purple and power, who has not tasted liberty or known freedom of speech or observed truth, who has been nurtured entirely in flattery and servility, or gives up his soul completely to pleasure, determined to serve no other, who is addicted to elaborate meals and to drinking and sex, and is steeped in chicanery, deceit, and falsehood, whose ears delight in twangings and twitterings and licentious songs—all such
16 as these, he said, should dwell in Rome. For all its streets and all its squares* are full of what they like best, and they can receive pleasure by every door, through the eyes, the ears, the nose, the throat, the sex organs. Pleasure's ever-flowing turbid stream widens every road: adultery and greed and perjury—all that tribe of pleasures— troop along together, flooding the soul and sweeping away every trace of modesty and virtue and righteousness. Without them the ground is a desert, perpetually parched, where lusts blossom like a crop of weeds.

That was his picture of Rome, teacher of all these good things.
17 'As for me,' he said, 'when I first returned from Greece, as I was approaching Rome I stopped and asked myself the reason for coming here, quoting those words of Homer*

Why did you leave, O hapless one, the light of day?

meaning Greece, and all that happiness and freedom— "and come to see" the turmoil here—informers, insolent greetings, lavish dinners, flatterers, murders, legacy-hunting, false friendships? And what do you actually plan to do here, since you can't either escape or endure these practices?

'So I deliberated and drew myself out of the line of fire, as Zeus 18 drew Hector

Away from the slaughter, the bloodshed and the din.*

I decided henceforth to stay at home, and choosing this life which most think spiritless and womanlike I hold converse with Philosophy herself and Plato and Truth. I seat myself as it were right at the top of a theatre full of thousands and observe the scene before me, which offers much entertainment and cause for laughter—and can also be a test of a man's real resolution.

'For if one must commend even what is bad, don't imagine that 19 there is any better school for virtue or truer test for the soul than this city and living here. It is no easy matter to resist such desires, such sights and sounds that grip you and pull you in all directions. You simply have to follow Odysseus' lead* and sail past them, not with your hands tied (that would be cowardly) or your ears stopped with wax, but unfettered and listening openly and with unfeigned contempt. Indeed, contemplating all that folly leads you to admire 20 philosophy, and you can despise the gifts of fortune when you see, as on the stage in a play with many characters, how one man's role changes from servant to master, another's from rich to poor, another's from poor to a governor or a king, and he in turn has a friend here, an enemy there, and a third whom he has exiled. And really the most dreadful thing of all is that while Fortune declares that she makes sport of human life and admits that nothing is secure here, and while men see this every day, they still long for wealth and power, and they all go around full of impossible hopes.

'But I did say that there is room for laughter and entertainment 21 in the life here, and I will now explain. The rich are obvious figures of fun, as they flaunt their purple clothes and show off their rings and betray their teeming vulgarity. The most outrageous fad is to greet people they meet through another's voice,* expecting them to be satisfied with a passing glance. There are others even more arrogant, who demand an obeisance, and not from a distance or in the Persian style. You have to go up close and make a low bow, and prove the abasement of your soul by a similar posture of your body, kissing his chest or his hand—and this performance is admired and envied by those who aren't allowed even that. And there he stands for hours exposing himself to this hypocrisy. At least I approve of that part of these people's unsociability which denies us their lips.

22   'But much more ridiculous than these men are those who pay court to them and flatter them, getting up at midnight and rushing around the city, only to have servants shut the doors on them and to put up with being called names like "dog" and "toady". The reward for this hateful round is the hoped-for dinner—a vulgar occasion and the cause of many woes. They stuff themselves, they drink more than is wise, they talk recklessly, and at last they depart grumbling and aggrieved, either criticizing the dinner or accusing their host of arrogance or meanness. They fill the alleyways, vomiting and fighting outside brothels; and by daylight most of them have retired to bed, giving their doctors cause to make their own rounds. Some, however, believe it or not, haven't time even to be ill.

23   'Mind you, I think that the toadies are far more pernicious than those they toady to, and are themselves responsible for the others' arrogance. When they admire their abundant resources, and praise their goldware, crowd their doorways at crack of dawn, and approach them with servile addresses, what do they expect them to think? If by general agreement they refrained for a while from this voluntary slavery, don't you think that the reverse would happen and the rich would come to the doors of the poor, begging them not to let their prosperity go unwitnessed and unattested, or their fine tables and great houses be idle and unused? It isn't wealth they love so much as being congratulated on it. And it is true that the man who lives in a gorgeous house gets no benefit from it, or from his gold and ivory, if nobody admires it. So what we should do is to cheapen and demolish the domination of these people by attacking their wealth from a fortress of contempt. As it is, the servility shown to them is what drives them mad.

24   'If it were just ordinary men, who make no secret of their lack of culture, who were acting like this, we would no doubt think it not so bad. But when many who claim to be philosophers behave still more ludicrously than the others, that is the most disgusting thing of all. How do you think my mind reacts to the sight of one of these, especially if he is getting on in years, joining a crowd

of sycophants, or dancing attendance on some man of standing, or hobnobbing with those who might invite him to dinner? And it is his philosopher's dress that distinguishes him and makes him more conspicuous. What really irritates me is that they don't change their costume for the parts they act so well in other respects. Look 25 at their performance at dinner parties: does it resemble any of their philosophical ideals? Don't they stuff themselves more vulgarly, get drunk more publicly, leave the table after everyone else, and aim to carry off more scraps than anyone? Often the more sophisticated of them have even ventured to sing.'

All this he regarded as ridiculous; but he had most to say about paid philosophers who offer virtue for sale like any other market produce. In fact he called their schools factories and shops; for he maintained that one who proposed to teach contempt for wealth should first show himself superior to profit. Certainly he always 26 observed this principle, not only teaching all who wanted it without payment but assisting those in need and despising all profit. He was so far from grasping at other men's property that he took no thought for his own, even when facing ruin himself. He had a farm not far from the city, but he didn't bother to set foot on it for many years, even disclaiming any right to it at all. I suppose he thought that we have no natural claim to ownership of these things, but that custom and inheritance give us the use of them for an unspecified time, and for a brief while we are considered their owners: when our appointed time is up someone else takes over and enjoys the title.

He also sets an important example in other ways to those who wish to emulate him—his plain diet, moderate exercise, modest expression, simple dress, and above all his finely-tuned mind and gentle character. He urged his pupils not to put off seeking the 27 good, which many people do by setting themselves a festival or holiday as a deadline, after which they will stop telling lies and start doing their duty. In his view the urge towards virtue must not be delayed. He also made it obvious that he despised those philo-sophers who think the right course of training in virtue for the young is to make them endure a lot of physical ordeals and sufferings, many of them prescribing cold baths, while others inflict whippings, and the more refined sort scrape their pupils' skins with a knife-blade. He believed that such toughness and 28 endurance should be produced rather in the soul, and that if you want to offer men the best sort of education you must keep in view their soul, body, age, and previous training, to avoid the charge of taxing them beyond their strength. Indeed he claimed that many had died as a result of being subjected to such unreasonable strains. I saw one student myself who had tasted the rigours of those masters, but as soon as he heard the words of truth he deserted and fled to Nigrinus without a backward glance—and was obviously the better for doing so.

29   He then turned from the philosophers back to men in general, and talked about the uproar in the city, the jostling, the theatres, the racecourse, the charioteers' statues, the names of the horses, the gossip about all this in the side streets. For there is a real mania for horses there, and many even supposedly serious people have caught it.

30   He turned next to the drama staged by those who are perpetually concerned with the next world and with wills, adding that Romans speak the truth only once in their lives, meaning in their wills, to avoid reaping the fruits of their truthfulness. I had to laugh when he was saying that they insist on having their stupidities buried with them, while allowing a written record of their insensitivity: some leave instructions that those clothes they had valued in life should be burnt with them; others that servants are to stay by their graves; others that their tombstones must be wreathed with

31   flowers. They remain idiots up to the end. He reckoned he could guess what they had done in this life when they gave such instructions about the next. They were the ones who bought expensive delicacies, and served their wine at banquets along with saffron and perfumes, who covered themselves with roses in midwinter, prizing them because they are rare and out of season, while despising what is natural and in season because it is cheap; these were the ones who even drank myrrh. That was where he really tore a strip off them, because they don't even know how to cope with their desires, but act outrageously in them and blur their boundary-lines, surrendering their own souls to be trampled underfoot by luxury, and, to quote both tragedy and comedy, forcing their way in beside the door.* Pleasures like that he thought resembled absurdities in speech.

32   Taking the same attitude he made another comment which exactly recalled the words of Momus,* who criticized the god who created the bull for not putting his horns in front of his eyes; and

Nigrinus similarly accused people who wear garlands of not
knowing where to put them, saying 'If they want to enjoy the scent
of violets and roses they should have put the garland right under
their noses, as close to inhalation as possible, so they could have got
the most pleasure from breathing the scent.'

He also made great fun of people who put such a prodigious 33
effort into their dinners, with all their varied sauces and elaborate
cakes, saying that they too endure a great deal of trouble to enjoy
a brief and fleeting pleasure. He declared that all their efforts were
directed to a measure of four fingers' breadth—the length of the
longest human throat. They cannot enjoy anything they've bought
before eating it, and after a meal their feeling of repletion is no
pleasanter because the food was more expensive. It follows that all
that expenditure has simply bought them the pleasure of swallowing. And he said it served them right for being boorish and not
appreciating the truer pleasures, to all of which philosophy can lead
those who choose to work hard.

About the way people behave in the baths he also had a lot to 34
say—the crowd of their attendants, their insolence, the way they
are carried by their servants almost as if they were being taken out
for burial. But the thing he seemed to loathe most of all, which is
much in evidence in the city, and in the baths, is the practice of
certain slaves having to go ahead of their masters, and calling out to
warn them to watch their step if they are about to walk over some
obstacle or hollow in the ground—actually having to remind them,
would you believe it, that they are walking! His complaint, you see,
was that they don't need another's mouth or hands for eating, or
another's ears for hearing, but having perfectly healthy eyes they
need others to see ahead for them, and they allow themselves to be
spoken to as if they were unfortunates and cripples. And this is all
happening in broad daylight, in our public places, and the people
involved are those who are running our cities.

These were the points he made and many others like them, 35
and then he ceased talking. All the while I was listening to him
awestruck, fearful that he would become silent. And when he did
cease I felt just like those Phaeacians.* For a long while I gazed at
him spellbound; then I was seized by a fit of confusion, my head
swam, sweat poured from me, I tried to speak but stumbled, and
my words were cut off as my voice gave up and my tongue failed
me. At last I just cried helplessly, for his words had made no slight

or casual impression on me: the blow was deep and accurate, and his well-aimed speech, if I can so express it, had cut through my very soul. If I too can now exploit the language of philosophers, this is how I see it. The soul of a man of good natural capacities is like a very sensitive target, and throughout his life many bowmen, with quivers full of varied and subtle arguments, take a shot at it. They don't all shoot well, but some draw the string too hard and let fly with too much force, so that the aim is right but the shafts don't stick in the target. Their momentum takes them through it and onwards, leaving only a gaping wound in the soul. Others on the contrary are too weak and their bows too slack, so that the arrows don't even reach the target, but often spend their force and hit the ground halfway. If they do reach it they just scratch the surface,* without causing a deep wound, because they were not discharged with any strength. But a skilful bowman like Nigrinus first observes the target carefully, to make sure it is not too soft or too tough for the arrow. For naturally there are targets which are impenetrable. Having taken note of this, he smears his arrows not with poison like the Scythians, or with the acid juice of the Curetes,* but with a sweet and mildly pungent drug, and then carefully lets fly. The arrow's momentum and force is exactly right for it to puncture and just pass through the soul before sticking there and diffusing the drug, which of course spreads around and completely fills the soul. This is why people listen to him with both pleasure and tears, as I myself did while the drug was quietly pervading my soul. That prompted me to quote Homer to him:

Shoot thus and bring perhaps salvation.*

Not all become frenzied when they hear the Phrygian pipe, but only those who are possessed by Rhea* and whose excitement is triggered by the music. So too, not all those who listen to philosophers go away inspired and stricken, but only those with a natural kinship with philosophy.

38 F. What an impressive and marvellous, yes and divine, account you have given, my friend. I hadn't realized how full you really were of ambrosia and lotus. The result is that as you were talking I felt emotion stirring in my soul, and now you have finished I feel vexed and, in your own words, stricken. This shouldn't surprise you. You know that people who are bitten by mad dogs don't only go mad themselves, but if they similarly treat others in their madness they

too lose their wits. Something of the condition is passed on with the bite, the disease spreads, and there follows a long transmission of madness.

L. Then you admit to a passionate longing?

F. Of course, and what is more I beg you to devise some treatment for both of us.

L. We must follow the example of Telephus.*

F. What do you mean?

L. Go to the man who wounded us and ask for a cure.

THE DEATH OF PEREGRINUS

THIS is an attack on the Cynic philosopher Peregrinus of Parium, also known as Proteus, who cremated himself on a pyre at the Olympic games of 165. As a satiric invective it can be compared with the *Alexander*, though it lacks the concentrated venom which characterizes that work. Lucian hits Peregrinus hard, but the picture here is a more dispassionate one of a character who literally stopped at nothing in his frenzy for notoriety. An element of deliberate disengagement in the narrative can be seen in the fact that though himself present at the actual cremation, Lucian earlier employs the device of a double in the person of the unnamed character who gives an account of Peregrinus' life, which takes up a large section of the piece (8–30), and which Lucian could have given us himself. These biographical details are almost the only source of our knowledge of Peregrinus' life. As in the *Nigrinus* and the *Alexander*, a letter is the vehicle for the narrative, the addressee here being one Cronius, a minor Platonist whom we hear of from other sources.

The treatise has a particular interest in its extensive references to the Christians, with whom Peregrinus involves himself. These allusions seem to us not unfriendly, if a little dismissive, but they caused great offence to later church leaders, so that the *Peregrinus*, along with the spurious *Philopatris*, was proscribed by the Papal Index of 1559. (Subsequently, in 1590, the Index put a total ban on Lucian's works.)

Greetings from Lucian to Cronius.

1 Ill-starred Peregrinus, or as he liked to call himself, Proteus, has suffered exactly the same fate as the Homeric Proteus.* After turning himself into all things for the sake of notoriety and adopting umpteen changes of shape, he has at long last turned into fire: such, it seems, was his passion for notoriety. And now your fine friend has been burnt to a cinder, like Empedocles;* except that the latter tried to avoid notice when he threw himself into the crater, whereas this noble fellow waited for the most crowded of the Greek festivals, piled up a most enormous pyre, and jumped into it in front of all those witnesses. He even made a speech about it to the Greeks a few days before his escapade.

2 I seem to picture you convulsed with laughter at the drivelling old fool—or rather, I can hear you crying out, as you well might: 'Oh, the stupidity! Oh, the thirst for renown! Oh—', all the other things we

74

tend to say about them. Well, you can say all this at a distance and much more safely; but I said it right by the fire, and even before that in a large crowd of listeners. Some of these became angry, the ones who were impressed by the old man's lunacy; but there were others who laughed at him too. Yet I can tell you I was nearly torn to pieces by the Cynics, like Actaeon by his dogs or his cousin Pentheus by the Maenads.*

This is how the whole performance was set up. You know the sort 3 of playwright he was, and the extraordinary spectacles he put on all his life, far beyond Sophocles and Aeschylus. Well, as soon as I arrived in Elis, while lounging around the gymnasium I listened to a Cynic yelling out in their usual street-corner style invocations to virtue in a harsh, loud voice, and abusing everyone indiscriminately. Then his ranting ended with Proteus, and I'll try my best to quote to you from memory exactly what he said. But of course you will recognize it, as you've often stood by while they were ranting.

'Does anyone', he said, 'dare to call Proteus vainglorious, O Earth, 4 O Sun, O rivers, O sea, O Heracles, god of our fathers!—Proteus, who was imprisoned in Syria, who gave up five thousand talents to his native land, who was exiled from Rome, who is more in men's eyes than the sun, who can rival Olympian Zeus himself? Is it because he has decided to depart from life through fire that they accuse him of vainglory? Did not Heracles do so? Did not Asclepius and Dionysus, through a thunderbolt?* Did not Empedocles end by throwing himself into the crater?'

After these words of Theagenes*—that was the ranter's name—I 5 asked one of the bystanders, 'What does he mean about fire, and what have Heracles and Empedocles to do with Proteus?' He replied, 'Proteus is shortly going to cremate himself at the Olympic festival'. 'How?', I asked, 'and why?'

Then he attempted to tell me, but the Cynic was yelling so that you couldn't hear anyone else. So I listened to him as he drenched us with the rest of his speech, delivering himself of wonderful hyperboles regarding Proteus: not stooping to compare him with the man from Sinope, or his teacher Antisthenes,* or even Socrates himself, he summoned Zeus to the contest. But then he decided to keep them on a sort of level, and ended his speech thus: 'The two finest works of art 6 the world has seen are the Olympian Zeus and Proteus. The artist who created the one was Pheidias,* the other, Nature. But now this ornament of ours will be leaving the world of men for the gods, borne upon flames and leaving us bereft.'

Thus he sweated his way through his oration, wept in a most ludicrous way, and tore his hair—but making sure not to pull it too hard. At last he was led away still sobbing by some Cynics, who tried to console him.

7   Immediately after him another man went up, without waiting for the crowd to disperse, and poured a libation on the previous sacrifice while it was still burning. And first he laughed for a long while, clearly very heartily; then he began in something like these words: 'Since that scoundrel Theagenes ended his abominable speech with the tears of Heraclitus, I shall do the opposite and begin with the laughter of Democritus.'* Again he laughed for a long while, so that he caused us to do the same.

8   Then turning to us he said, 'What else can you do, gentlemen, when you hear such ludicrous utterances, and see old men almost standing on their heads in public for the sake of a bit of contemptible notoriety? So you can know just what is this "ornament" which is to be burned, listen to me, for I have kept a close eye on his character and watched his career from the beginning. I have also learnt a few things from his fellow-citizens, and from people who must have known him through and through.

9   'Well, this work of art of nature's creation, this canon of Polyclitus,* when he first arrived at manhood was caught in adultery in Armenia, got a thoroughly good beating, and eventually managed to escape by jumping down from a roof, with a radish plugging his anus.* Next he seduced a good-looking youth, and bribed the lad's poverty-stricken parents with three thousand drachmas not to bring him before the governor of Asia.

10   'This behaviour and anything like it I intend to pass over; for his clay was still unmoulded, and our "ornament" was not yet perfected. But you really must hear what he did to his father, though you all know it, and you've heard how he strangled the old fellow because he couldn't bear him living past 60. Then, when that episode became common talk he condemned himself to exile, and wandered around from one place to another.

11   'That was when he learnt the remarkable wisdom of the Christians, by getting to know their priests and scribes in Palestine. And—naturally—in a short time he made them look like children, being himself prophet, fraternity-leader, convener of synagogues, all in one

person. Some of their books he interpreted and expounded, and many he wrote himself; they honoured him as a god, employed him as a lawgiver, and entitled him a protector, though naturally coming after him whom they still worship—the man who was crucified in Palestine for introducing this new cult into the world.

'Then to be sure Proteus was arrested for this activity and put in 12 prison, and this in itself won him no little reputation for his subsequent career, and the miracle-working and thirst for renown that possessed him. Well, the Christians regarded his imprisonment as a disaster, and did everything they could to rescue him. Then, when this proved impossible, they showed every other form of care towards him, not just casually but in real earnest. From early dawn you could see elderly widows and orphan children waiting by the prison, while officials of the Christians even bribed the guards and slept inside with him. Again, elaborate meals were taken in, their sacred books were read to him, and our excellent Peregrinus, which was still his name, was called by them "the new Socrates".*

'Indeed, people arrived even from the cities of Asia, sent by the 13 Christians and paid for out of their joint funds, in order to help, defend, and encourage the man. They move with extraordinary swiftness when any such corporate action is undertaken, and at a moment's notice they spend their all. Well, at that time too they sent a lot of money to Peregrinus on the occasion of his imprisonment, from which he derived no small income. The poor fools have persuaded themselves above all that they are immortal and will live forever, from which it follows that they despise death and many of them willingly undergo imprisonment. Moreover, their first lawgiver taught them that they are all brothers of one another, when once they have sinned by denying the Greek gods, and by worshipping that crucified sophist himself and living according to his laws. So, they despise all things equally and regard them as common property, accepting such teaching without any sort of clear proof. Accordingly, if any quack or trickster, who can press his advantage, comes among them, he can acquire great wealth in a very short time by imposing on simple-minded people.

'However, Peregrinus was released by the then governor of Syria, a 14 man who was keen on philosophy, and who being aware of Peregrinus' lunacy and that he would welcome death for the reputation he would acquire for it, released him as not being even worthy of punishment. When he returned home he found that the question of his father's murder was still a burning issue, and that many people were threatening him with prosecution. During his absence most of his possessions had been seized, and only his farms were left, valued at about fifteen talents. For the whole property left by the old man was worth perhaps thirty talents, and not five thousand, as that totally ridiculous Theagenes claimed. Not even the whole city of Parium* together with the five neighbouring ones, and including the inhabitants with their cattle and the rest of their belongings, could be sold for that much.

15   'But still, the prosecution and the charge were still being hotly pursued, and it seemed likely that before too long someone would appear against him. The people themselves were particularly angry with him, as they grieved for a fine old man (as those who had seen him said), who had been so heartlessly murdered. But note how our crafty Proteus dealt with all this and managed to escape the danger. He appeared before the assembly of the Parians, with his hair now grown long, wearing a dirty cloak, a pouch at his side and a staff in his hand,* got up altogether in a very dramatic fashion. Presenting himself thus to them, he stated that he was relinquishing to the public all the property which his blessed father had left him. When the people heard this, poor fellows all gaping for handouts, they at once shouted out, "The one and only disciple of Diogenes and Crates!"* His enemies were muzzled, and if anyone even tried to mention the murder he was immediately stoned.

16   'So he went forth a second time on his wanderings, being adequately funded by the Christians, and under their patronage he lived in clover. For a time he supported himself like that; but then he managed to transgress even one of their laws—I think he was seen eating some food forbidden among them—and as he was no longer accepted by them and in dire straits, he thought he'd better recant and demand his property back from the city. He submitted a formal request and expected he would recover it by the emperor's orders. But then the city made counter-representations, and he lost his claim and was told to stick to what he had once for all decided under compulsion from nobody.

17   'After that he went on his travels a third time, to Egypt, to see Agathoboulos,* where he underwent that extraordinary training in asceticism, shaving half of his head, smearing his face with mud, demonstrating what they call an "indifferent" act* by masturbating in the middle of a large crowd, as well as giving and receiving blows on

the rump with a fennel cane, and acting the charlatan in many other audacious ways.

'After these preparations he sailed from there to Italy, and as soon 18 as he had disembarked he began abusing everyone, especially the emperor,* knowing that he was very mild and placid and he could venture to do so with impunity. As you would imagine, the emperor paid little attention to his profanities, and didn't think it worth punishing for his words a man who just wore philosophy as a mask, and particularly one who made abuse into an art. But even this caused Peregrinus' reputation to increase, at least among the uneducated people, and he was admired for his lunacy; until the city prefect, an intelligent man, sent him away for flaunting his profession beyond any reasonable bounds, saying that the city did not need a philosopher like that. Yet even this brought him fame, and everyone talked about him as the philosopher who had been banished for his outspokenness and for exercising too much freedom; so that in this way he approached Musonius, Dio, Epictetus,* and anyone else in a similar situation.

'And so he arrived in Greece, where at one time he abused the 19 Eleans; at another he advised the Greeks to take up arms against the Romans; at another he insulted a man of outstanding culture and renown* because of his benefactions to Greece, which included bringing a water supply to Olympia and so preventing those attending it from dying of thirst. He had just made the Greeks effeminate (so ran the charge), when the spectators ought to endure their thirst— and to be sure, death too, many of them, from the dangerous diseases which until then spread through the huge crowd because of the dryness of that area. And all this he said while drinking that very water.

'When they all made a rush at him and were on the point of killing 20 him by stoning, our fine friend managed to avoid death by taking refuge at Zeus' sanctuary; and at the next Olympiad he delivered a speech to the Greeks which he had composed in the intervening four years, praising the man who had built the aqueduct and defending himself for running away on the previous occasion.

'But by now he was ignored by everyone and no longer the centre of attention: all he did was stale, and he could no longer think up anything novel to startle those who met him and win their wonder and admiration, which was what he had always longed for passionately. So he finally contrived this exploit involving the pyre, and spread the word among the Greeks immediately after the last Olympics that he was going to cremate himself at the next one. And now, they say, he is plotting just that piece of quackery, digging a pit, collecting faggots, and promising us an awesome feat of endurance.

21   'In my view he should ideally have waited for death and not run away from life; but if he had decided at all costs to take himself off, he should not have used fire or any such device from the tragic stage, but have chosen to depart by some other of the thousands of ways of dying. But if he is keen on fire because it has a touch of Heracles to it, why not quietly choose a well-wooded mountain and cremate himself there in solitude, taking with him just one person, like Theagenes here, to act as his Philoctetes?* But no, it is at the crowded festival of Olympia, and virtually in the theatre, that he is going to roast himself—and serve him right too, by Heracles, if parricides and atheists deserve to suffer for their shameless crimes. And in that connection he seems to be leaving it very late: he should long ago have been thrown into the bull of Phalaris* to pay the penalty he deserved, rather than just opening his mouth once to the fire and dying in a moment. For lots of people tell me that no other form of death is quicker than by fire: you just have to open your mouth and you're immediately dead.

22   'Of course I imagine the purpose of the spectacle is to be impressive, a man being cremated in a holy place, where it is wrong even to bury others who die. But you must have heard that long ago someone who wished to become famous, and couldn't find any other way to do it, set fire to the temple of Artemis at Ephesus.* Our man too is contriving something similar, such is the passion for fame which has filled his being.

23   'Yet he claims he is doing it on behalf of humanity, so he can teach men to despise wealth and endure suffering. But I would like to ask, not him but you, whether you would want criminals to become his disciples in this sort of hardihood, and to despise death and burning and suchlike terrors. I know very well that you would not. So how does Proteus make this distinction, and benefit the good without making the wicked more reckless and daring?

24   'However, grant that it is possible that only those will be present at this event who will benefit from witnessing it. Again I shall ask you: would you wish your children to emulate such a man? You would not say so. Yet why did I ask that, when not even any of his own disciples would emulate him? Indeed, what you would most blame Theagenes

for is that, while he imitates the man in everything else, he doesn't follow his master and join him on his journey, as he says, to Heracles; though he could speedily acquire complete blessedness by leaping headlong into the fire with him!

'Emulation does not lie just in having a pouch and staff and cloak: all that is safe and easy and open to all. You must emulate the sum and substance, build a pyre of fig-wood logs as green as possible, and stifle yourself in the smoke. For fire itself is not for Heracles and Asclepius alone but for temple-robbers and murderers, whom you can see suffering it by sentence of the law. So it is better to endure smoke, which would be appropriate, and peculiar to you people.

'Anyway, if Heracles really did endure such a fate, he did it because 25 of his sufferings, when the Centaur's blood was eating into him, as the tragic poets tell us.* But what's the pretext for this fellow throwing himself bodily into the flames? To be sure, to prove his physical endurance, like the Brahmins; for Theagenes thought him worthy of comparison with them—as if there couldn't be fools and attention-seekers among the Indians too. All right then, let him imitate them. They do not leap into the fire, according to Onesicritus, Alexander's helmsman, who witnessed Calanus in the flames;* but when they have heaped up their pyre, they stand motionless beside it, enduring a roasting, and then stepping onto it they cremate themselves in a dignified manner, without moving a muscle as they lie there.

'But what great deed will this fellow achieve if he just jumps in and dies in the grip of the fire? It's on the cards that he will jump out half-burnt unless, as people say, he is preparing a pyre deep within a pit. And there are those who say he has even changed his mind, 26 and is recounting dreams in which Zeus forbids his holy place to be polluted. But he can be reassured on that count: I would swear a great oath that none of the gods would be distressed if Peregrinus came to a bad end. Nor indeed could he easily back out now, for his fellow Cynics are all inciting and propelling him into the fire, and keeping his resolution kindled, to prevent him from being a coward. If he would only drag a couple of these along with him when he jumps into the fire, that would be the one gracious act in his performance.

'I've heard that he no longer chooses to be called Proteus, but has 27 changed his name to Phoenix, because the phoenix, an Indian bird, is also said to mount a pyre when it is very old. Moreover, he even

81

invents stories and quotes oracles, supposedly ancient, to the effect that he is fated to become a guardian spirit of the night; and he is obviously yearning for altars and expecting to be set up as a golden image.

28   'And indeed, it's not unlikely that among all the crowds of idiots some would be found to claim that he had caused them to be relieved of quartan fever, and that by night they had met the guardian spirit of the night. And I imagine that these ghastly disciples of his will also be setting up an oracular shrine and sanctuary on the site of the pyre, because the well-known Proteus, son of Zeus, the founder of his name, was himself a seer. I give you my word too that priests will be appointed for him, with whips or branding-irons or some such mind-boggling equipment, or even, by heaven, that some nocturnal rite will be established in his name, with a torch-procession on the site of the pyre.

29   'One of my friends has told me that Theagenes recently said the Sibyl predicted these things, quoting the lines from memory:

But when Proteus, the greatest by far among all the Cynics,
Shall kindle a fire in the precinct of thundering Zeus,
And leaping into the flames shall arrive at lofty Olympus,
Then this is my bidding to all who consume the fruits of the land,
To honour that greatest of heroes who wanders abroad in the night,
And shares a throne with Hephaestus and also with lord Heracles.

30   'That is what Theagenes claims to have heard from the Sibyl. But I will quote him an oracle of Bacis* on the same subject, who speaks as follows, expressing it admirably:

Whenever the Cynic who has many names shall into the fire
Hurl himself bodily, stirred in his soul by a frenzy for glory,
Then it is right for the others, the jackals who like to attend him
To mimic the death of the wolf who has now gone his way and
    departed.
But if there's a coward among them who flees from the might of
    Hephaestus,
Then speedily must he be pelted with stones by all the Achaeans,
To teach the cold-hearted never to indulge in fiery speeches,
Stuffing his wallet with gold from plentiful practice of usury,
And storing away fifteen talents in the beautiful city of
    Patrae.*

What do you think, gentlemen? Is Bacis a worse soothsayer than the Sibyl? So now is the time for these admirable disciples of Proteus to look around for somewhere to vaporize themselves—that's what they call cremation.'

When he had finished speaking the bystanders all shouted out, 'Let 31 them be burned now: they deserve the fire!'

And the man got down laughing; but 'Nestor noticed the shouting':* I mean Theagenes, who when he heard the uproar came at once, mounted the platform and began bawling and uttering countless slanders about the man who had got down from it—I don't know that excellent fellow's name. I left Theagenes bursting his sides and went off to see the athletes, as the Hellanodicae were said to be now in the Plethrium.*

So now you know what happened at Elis. When we got to Olympia, 32 the back chamber was full of people either criticizing Proteus or praising his resolution, so that many of them were even coming to blows. At last Proteus himself arrived, with an innumerable escort, after the contest of the heralds, and gave some account of himself, describing the sort of life he had led, the dangers he had endured, and the troubles he had borne for the sake of philosophy. It was a long speech, though I heard little of it because of the crowd around me. After a while, afraid that I might be crushed by such a large mob, which I saw happening to many people, I left, saying a long farewell to the death-loving sophist who was delivering his own funeral oration before his departure.

However, I did overhear this much. He said he wanted to put 33 a golden tip on a golden bow:* for he who had lived the life of Heracles should die the death of Heracles and be mingled with the ether. 'And I wish', he said, 'to be of benefit to men by showing them how one should despise death. Therefore all men ought to act Philoctetes to me.'

The more stupid of the people present began to weep and to cry out, 'Save yourself for the Greeks!', while those of stronger fibre yelled, 'Carry out your purpose!' The latter greatly upset the old man, as he was hoping they would all take hold of him and not abandon him to the fire, but force him—unwillingly of course— to go on living. That 'Carry out your purpose' striking him so unexpectedly made him turn still paler, though his colour was already deathlike, and even start to tremble, so that he ended his speech.

34   I imagine you can guess how I laughed; for no man deserved pity who was so disastrously in love with glory, beyond all others who are hounded by the same Fury. Anyway, there he was being escorted by a crowd, taking his fill of glory as he looked around at the multitude of his admirers, not realizing, poor fool, that a great many more attend those being led to the cross or in the hands of the public executioner.

35   And now the Olympic games were over, the finest Olympics I have ever witnessed, and that was the fourth time for me. But I couldn't secure myself a carriage, as many were leaving at the same time, so I reluctantly stayed behind. Peregrinus had kept putting things off, but at last he announced the night when he would display his cremation. One of my friends asked me to go with him, so I got up around midnight and went straight to Harpina, where the pyre was. This is fully 2¼ miles from Olympia as you go eastwards past the hippodrome. As soon as we arrived we found the pyre piled up in a pit about six feet deep. It was constructed mainly of pinewood, stuffed with dry kindling so as to catch fire quickly.

36   When the moon rose—for she too had to witness this glorious performance—he came forward dressed as usual, and attended by the leading Cynics, notably our noble friend from Patrae, holding a torch—no bad supporting actor in this drama. Proteus too was carrying a torch. Then from all sides men came up and lit the pyre into a mighty flame, fed by the pinewood and kindling. And he—now pay close attention—putting aside his pouch and cloak and that famous Herculean club, stood there in a shirt that was utterly filthy. Then he asked for incense to throw on the fire, and when someone produced it he did so, and said, looking towards the south (for the south too was an element in the spectacle): 'Spirits of my mother and father, receive me favourably.' With these words he jumped into the fire; nor indeed could he be seen, but he was enveloped by the towering flames.

37   I see, my good Cronius, that you are laughing again at the climax of the drama. As for me, I certainly didn't criticize him seriously for calling on the spirits of his mother; but when he invoked his father's too, I remembered what had been said about his murder and couldn't contain my laughter. The Cynics surrounding the pyre were not weeping, but showed some silent grief as they looked at the flames, until choking with rage at them I said, 'Let us be off, you idiots. It is not a pleasant sight, watching an old man being roasted and inhaling a

foul stench of burning. Or are you waiting for some painter to come and portray you, as the companions of Socrates are pictured with him in prison?'

They became angry and abused me, and some even made a grab at their sticks. Then, when I threatened to seize some of them and pitch them into the fire, so they could follow their master, they left off and held their peace.

As I came back, my friend, I was pondering a variety of things, and reflecting on the nature of the love of glory: how this is the only passion which can't be evaded even by those who seem to be wholly admirable, let alone that man whose life in other respects had been reckless and unstable, and not undeserving of the flames. Then I met a lot of people coming over to see the spectacle themselves; for they thought they would find him still alive. The fact is, it had been given out on the previous day that before mounting the pyre he would greet the rising sun, as indeed the Brahmins are said to do. So I turned back most of them, explaining that the deed was finished and done, those at least who were not particularly interested just in seeing the actual place and in collecting some remnant of the fire.

Therein, my friend, I must say I had a deal of trouble describing what happened to everyone who asked me questions and wanted full details. Faced by anyone sophisticated, I would give him an unadorned account of the events. But when it came to the thick-witted, agog to hear the story, I souped it up a bit with my own inventions: that when the pyre was lit and Proteus threw himself onto it, first there was a tremendous earthquake and rumbling of the ground; and then a vulture flew up from the midst of the flames* and went off to the heavens, saying loudly and in human language:

The earth I have left and I mount to Olympus.

They were astonished, and bowed down shuddering, and they asked me whether the vulture had rushed away to the east or the west. I told them in answer anything that occurred to me.

Returning to the festival I encountered a grey-haired man, whose countenance, as well as his beard and his generally dignified appearance, really made him seem trustworthy. He was talking all about Proteus, and how after his cremation he had recently observed him clad in white, and had just now left him cheerfully walking around the Colonnade of the Seven Echoes,* wearing a crown of wild olive. Then on top of all this he added the vulture, swearing he had personally seen it flying up from the pyre, when I myself had just sent it flying off to make a mockery of the stupid and the witless.

41   You can imagine what's likely to happen to him from now on, what swarms of bees will not settle on the site, what cicadas will not sing over it, what crows will not fly to it, as they did to Hesiod's tomb*— and all that sort of thing. Then, too, I know there will be lots of statues set up very soon by the Eleans themselves and by the other Greeks, to whom he said he had written. It is alleged that he sent letters to almost all cities of note—his testaments, as it were, and exhortations and statutes. For this purpose he also appointed envoys from among his companions, calling them 'messengers of the dead' and 'couriers from the underworld'.

42   Such was the end of the ill-starred Proteus, a man who* (not to beat about the bush) never gazed steadily at the truth, but whose words and deeds were always without exception aimed at glory and popular praise, to the point of even leaping into the fire, though destined not to enjoy the praise for that since he couldn't hear it.

43   Let me tell you one more story to give you a good laugh, and then I'll stop. For you've long known that other one which you heard me tell as soon as I returned from Syria: how I sailed with him from Troas,* and how he indulged himself throughout the voyage, particularly in converting a handsome young lad to become a Cynic, so as to furnish himself with an Alcibiades;* and how during the night in mid-Aegean we were hit and tossed about by a dark storm which stirred up enormous waves, and this admirable character, who seemed superior to death, was to be heard shrieking along with the women.

44 Well, a short while before his death, nine days or so, having eaten more than he should, I imagine, he was sick during the night and seized with a violent fever. I learnt this from Alexander, the doctor who was sent for to see him. He told me he had found him rolling about on the ground, unable to bear the fever, and desperately pleading for cold water, but that he had not given it to him. Furthermore, the doctor said he had told him that if he really and truly wanted death, it had come to his door unbidden, and he would do well to follow along without asking help from the fire. Proteus' reply was: 'But that way would bring less renown, being common to everyone.'

45   That was Alexander's story. Not many days earlier I myself saw Proteus having smeared himself with ointment, so that the pungency of the unguent would clear his eyes by making them water. Get the point? Aeacus* is very unwilling to receive anyone with weak eyes.

Just as if a man about to be crucified should nurse a sore finger! How do you think Democritus would have reacted to seeing this? Wouldn't he have roared with laughter at the man, as he deserved? But where could he have got that much laughter? Well, my good friend, you too can have a laugh—especially when you hear other people admiring him.

HERMOTIMUS OR ON
PHILOSOPHICAL SCHOOLS

THIS is Lucian's longest piece, and here he is again taking up one of his favourite themes, philosophy and philosophers. Under his often assumed name Lycinus he presents himself in conversation with an ageing student of Stoicism, who has not yet been able to work himself to the final goal of happiness as seen by the Stoics. The question-and-answer technique used here is very much that of the Platonic dialogue, in which Socrates' seemingly innocent questions eventually push his opponent into a corner where he is forced to throw in his hand. Here Lycinus is concerned, at great length and in unremitting detail, to ask Hermotimus how he can possibly be sure that only the Stoics, and no other school, have the right answer to the goal of life and the nature of happiness. In the end Hermotimus, like Socrates' opponents, gives up and agrees with Lycinus that all his years of philosophical study have been a waste of time.

Hermotimus is not otherwise known, but the dialogue contains some biographical references to Lucian which we can probably accept. At the time of the conversation he is about 40 (section 13) and highly critical of philosophy and its pretensions; but at about 25 (section 24) he had shown some interest in it and was offered instruction, but 'being then young and foolish' he had not pursued it. So, we may infer, he might have profited by it as a young man, but now at 40 he knows better—and so should Hermotimus.

1 LYCINUS. To judge from your look and your rapid walking, Hermotimus, you must be hastening to your teacher. At any rate, you were thinking about something as you went along: you were moving your lips and muttering under your breath, and waving your hand as if organizing a speech to yourself, composing some intricate question or thinking over a sophistical speculation. Even when out for a walk you don't relax, but you're always busy at something serious which might be useful for your studies.

HERMOTIMUS. Indeed, that's about right, Lycinus. I was thinking over yesterday's class and reviewing all that he said. You should, I fancy, never miss an opportunity, but recognize the truth of what the Doctor from Cos* said: 'Life is short but art is long'. He, however, was referring to medicine, an easier subject; philosophy is unattainable even if you spend a long time over it, unless you are constantly very wide awake and keep your gaze fixed intently on it; and the stakes are high—whether to perish wretchedly among the teeming rabble of the common people, or to win happiness through philosophy.

L. That's an extraordinarily fine prize you speak of, Hermotimus, and 2 I really think you can't be far off it, to judge by the time you spend studying philosophy, and also all the tremendous vigour you seem to have long been devoting to it. If I remember, it's nearly twenty years since I've been seeing you solely occupied in attending your teachers, and usually poring over a book and making notes on the lectures, always pale and thin from studying. I imagine you don't relax even in your dreams; you are so totally involved in it. So, observing all this, I'd guess you'll soon be grasping happiness, unless you've had it for ages and we haven't noticed.

H. How could I, Lycinus, since I'm only beginning to glimpse the road ahead? Hesiod* tells us that Virtue lives very far off, and the way to her is long and steep and rough, causing much sweat for the travellers.

L. Haven't you travelled and sweated enough, Hermotimus?

H. No: for once I'm at the top nothing can keep me from complete happiness. As it is, Lycinus, I'm still just beginning.

L. But the same Hesiod* says that the beginning is half of the whole, 3 so we wouldn't be wrong if we said you were halfway up.

H. No, I'm not even there yet: if I were, I would have achieved a great deal.

L. Well, where can we say you are on the road?

H. Still down in the foothills, Lycinus, just now struggling to go forward. But it's rough and slippery and needs a helping hand.

L. Surely that's for your teacher to do, letting down his teaching from the top, like Zeus' golden rope in Homer,* by which clearly he can draw and lift you up to himself and to Virtue—he got up there himself long ago.

H. You're absolutely right, Lycinus: so far as he is concerned, I should have been drawn up long ago and joined them, but my own efforts are still falling short.

L. Well, cheer up and don't lose heart; keep your eye on the end of 4 the road and the happiness up there, especially as he is seconding your enthusiasm. But what hopes does he offer you concerning when you'll get up there? Did he guess that you'll be at the top next year, say after the Great Mysteries, or the Panathenaea?*

H. Too soon, Lycinus.

L. Well, the next Olympiad?

H. That's also too soon for a training in virtue and the achievement of happiness.

L. Then after two Olympiads, at any rate? Or could you people be accused of great laziness if you can't make it even in that time? You could easily travel from the Pillars of Heracles to India three times and back again in that time, even if you didn't always go directly, but made detours to visit nations on your way. But how much higher and smoother would you have us put this peak, where your Virtue lives, than Aornos, which Alexander took by storm in a few days?*

5 H. There's no comparison whatever, Lycinus, of the sort you are trying to make. It cannot be captured or taken in a short time, even if a host of Alexanders attacked it. If it could, many would have scaled it. As things are, not a few make a very valiant start and achieve a certain amount of progress, some very little, others rather more. But when they get halfway and meet a lot of difficulties and hardships, they give up and turn back, panting and sweating and unable to bear the exhaustion. But those with lasting endurance get to the top, and thereafter enjoy wonderful happiness for the rest of their lives, observing other men from this height as if they were ants.

L. Gracious me, Hermotimus! How tiny you make us; not even pygmies, but creeping around close to the surface of the earth. That's not surprising, as your thoughts are already way up there; and all of us, the rabble who cleave to the earth, will pray to you people among the gods, when you are above the clouds, having gained the heights you've long been striving for.

H. If only I can get up there, Lycinus! But there's an awfully long way still to go.

6 L. You still haven't said how long, in terms of time.

H. I don't even know accurately myself, Lycinus; but I guess not more than twenty years, after which I'll surely be at the top.

L. Heavens! That's a long time.

H. Yes, Lycinus; for great prizes will reward my labours.

L. That may be so, but has your teacher promised you that you will live for those twenty years? Is he not only wise, but a prophet or diviner or an expert in the lore of the Chaldeans? They claim to know such things. For if it is not clear that you will live to reach Virtue, then it's unreasonable for you to undertake all this toil and to wear yourself out day and night, not knowing whether, when you are near the top, fate will appear and dash your hopes by dragging you down by the foot.

H. Off with you and your ill-omened words, Lycinus! May I live long enough to become wise and be happy even for one day!

L. Would one day be sufficient reward for all your toils?

H. Even a moment would be enough for me.

L. How can you be sure that there is happiness up there and the sort 7 of things which it is worth enduring everything to gain? After all, you've not been up there yourself.

H. Well, I trust what my teacher says. He is right at the top and fully informed.

L. In heaven's name, what did he say about things there, and how did he describe the happiness which is there? I suppose it is some sort of riches and glory and superlative pleasures?

H. Hush, my friend! Those things have nothing to do with a virtuous life.

L. Well, what blessings does he say those who complete their training will achieve, if not those?

H. Wisdom and courage and nobility itself and justice, and the confident certainty of knowing the real nature of everything. Riches and glories and pleasures and bodily concerns are all cast off and left below as you climb up, as we are told happened to Heracles when he was cremated on Mount Oeta and became a god.* He cast off the mortal elements he derived from his mother, and flew up to the gods with his divine element sifted by the fire to become pure and undefiled. So these too are stripped by philosophy, as by a fire, of all those things that other men wrongly judge to be admirable. They climb to the peak and achieve happiness, no longer even remembering wealth and glory and pleasures, and laughing at those who believe in them.

L. By Heracles on Oeta, Hermotimus, you give a manly and happy 8 account of them. But tell me, do they ever come down from the peak, if they wish, to make use of what they have left down below? Or do they have to stay there once they've climbed up, and live with Virtue, laughing at wealth and glory and pleasures?

H. It's not just that, Lycinus; but anyone who has achieved perfect virtue cannot be a slave to anger or fear or desires; he cannot suffer grief or, in short, any other such emotion.

L. Well, to speak the truth without hesitation—but I suppose I'd better shut up, as it's not permitted to enquire about what wise men get up to.

H. By no means: please say what you want to say.

L. Just see, my friend, how terrified I am!

H. Don't be afraid, my good fellow: you're talking only to me.

9 L. Well, Hermotimus, I followed and I believed the rest of what you said about them becoming wise and brave and just and so on—I was even sort of spellbound by your account. But when you said that they despise wealth and glory and pleasures, and don't feel anger or grief, then I stopped short (we are alone), as I remembered what I saw someone doing recently—shall I say who? Or is it enough not to name him?

H. By no means: do tell me who it was.

L. This very teacher of yours, a man who on the whole deserves respect, and is now pretty old.

H. So, what was he doing?

L. You know the stranger from Heraclea who was his pupil in philosophy for a long time, the quarrelsome fellow with blonde hair?

H. I know the one you mean: his name is Dion.

L. That's him. I gather that he didn't pay his fee on time, so the other day the teacher, shouting with anger, pulled his cloak round his neck and dragged him before the magistrate. If some of the young fellow's friends hadn't intervened and pulled him out of his clutches, the old man would certainly have hung on to him and bitten off his nose, he was so furious.

10 H. That fellow, Lycinus, has always been a knave and careless in paying his debts. There are lots of others to whom the old man lends money, and he has never treated them like that. But they do pay him his interest on time.

L. But, my dear fellow, suppose they don't? Does it matter to him now he has been purified by philosophy and no longer needs what he left behind on Oeta?

H. Do you think it's for his own sake that he's shown such a concern for these things? He has young children and he's anxious that they shouldn't live in poverty.

L. He should bring them too up to Virtue, so that they can share his happiness and despise wealth.

11 H. There's no time to talk to you about this, Lycinus: I'm rushing off to hear his lecture, or I'll fall behind before I know where I am.

L. Don't worry, old fellow. A holiday has been announced for today, so I can save you the rest of your journey.

H. How do you mean?

L. You won't find him now, if we can trust the notice. There was a little board hanging over the gate proclaiming in large letters, 'No philosophy class today'. Report has it that he dined with the great Eucrates yesterday, who was celebrating his daughter's birthday. He had a long philosophical discussion at the party, and was a bit sharp with Euthydemus the Peripatetic, taking issue with him about their usual arguments against the Stoics. Apparently the din went on until midnight, and it gave him a headache and made him sweat a lot. I expect he had also drunk more than he should, as the loving-cup made the usual rounds, and had dined too well considering his age. And so, they say, when he got home he was violently sick; and as soon as he had counted and carefully marked the bits of meat he had given to the lad who was standing behind him at dinner, he gave orders to admit nobody and has been sleeping ever since. All this I heard his servant Midas telling some of his pupils, a lot of whom were themselves coming away from there.

H. Who won the argument, Lycinus, my teacher or Euthydemus? Did 12 Midas say anything about that?

L. Apparently they were level to start with, Hermotimus, but eventually victory went to your side and the old man was way ahead. At any rate, they say Euthydemus didn't escape unscathed, but he had a bad wound in his head. He was boastful and argumentative, he wouldn't be persuaded, and he didn't allow himself readily to be criticized; so your peerless teacher knocked him down with a cup as big as Nestor's* from his couch near by, and so gained the victory.

H. Good for him! That's the way to deal with people who don't respect their betters.

L. That's well said, Hermotimus. What got into Euthydemus to provoke an old man who is placid and not easily roused, but with such a heavy cup in his hand? But since we are at leisure, why not tell me 13 as a friend how you first took up philosophy, so that if possible I too can start from there and join your group on your journey? For as we are friends you surely won't exclude me.

H. Please do, Lycinus: you'll soon see how much you surpass other people. You'll certainly regard all of them as children compared to you, with all your superior wisdom.

L. It'll be enough if in twenty years I could be as you are now.

H. Don't worry: I was your age when I started philosophy, about 40—which I guess is your age now.

L. Correct, Hermotimus. So take me too along the same road: that would be fitting. But first, tell me this: do you allow pupils to argue against anything they disagree with, or do you not let the young do this?

H. Certainly not. But, if you like, *you* can ask questions and make objections as we go along. That way you'll learn more easily.

14 L. Good, by Hermes himself, from whom you are named, Hermotimus. Well, tell me, is your Stoic path the only one that leads to philosophy? Or is it true, as I've heard, that there are many others?

H. A great many—the Peripatetics, the Epicureans, those who have enrolled as Platonists; also the devotees of Diogenes and Antisthenes, the Pythagoreans, and a host of others.

L. You're right: that is a lot. Do they say the same things, Hermotimus, or different things?

H. Very different.

L. But at least one of their creeds must surely be true, though they can't all be, if they are different.

H. Quite right.

15 L. Well then, my friend, answer me this. When you first began to study philosophy and there were many doors open to you, you passed by the others and came to the Stoic door, which you entered on your way to virtue, believing it was the one true door which opened up the straight path, while the others led to blind alleys. What made you believe this? What signs then guided you? And don't think of yourself as you are now: whether you are half-wise or fully wise, you can now make better judgments than we the masses can. Answer as the complete layman you were then and I am now.

H. I don't see what you are getting at, Lycinus.

L. My question wasn't very involved. There have been a lot of philosophers, Plato, Aristotle, Antisthenes, your own school founders, Chrysippus and Zeno, and all the others. So, what persuaded you to ignore the others and to decide to choose the creed you did to guide your studies? Did Pythian Apollo treat you like Chaerephon,* and send you to the Stoics as the best of all? His practice is to direct different people to different philosophies, as he knows each individual's requirements.

H. Nothing like that, Lycinus: I didn't even ask the god about this.

L. Didn't you consider it worth a divine consultation, or did you think that you could make the best choice on your own without the god?

H. I did.

L. Well, do explain to me first, how we can distinguish right at the start which is the best and the true philosophy, the one we should choose, ignoring the others. 16

H. I'll tell you. I saw most people going for it, so I assumed it was the best one.

L. How many more are there than Epicureans, Platonists, or Peripatetics? You must have counted them as we do when people vote.

H. I didn't count: I made a guess.

L. So, you don't want to explain things to me. You're just hiding the truth from me and cheating me with your talk of deciding about all this by guesswork and majorities.

H. Not only that, Lycinus. I also heard everyone saying that the Epicureans were self-indulgent and pleasure-loving; the Peripatetics were avaricious and argumentative; and the Platonists arrogant and vainglorious. But many said that the Stoics were manly and understood everything, and that the man who followed their path was the only king, the only rich man, the only wise man, and the only everything.

L. But these were obviously other people's views about them. You surely wouldn't have trusted them praising their own qualities. 17

H. Of course not: this was what other people said.

L. But presumably not their rivals.

H. No.

L. Then these were laymen's views?

H. Yes, indeed.

L. You see how you're still deceiving me and not telling the truth. You think you're talking to a Margites,* who would believe that Hermotimus, an intelligent man of 40, trusted the views of laymen on philosophy and philosophers, and on that basis made his choice of the better school. I just don't believe you when you talk like that.

H. But you must know, Lycinus, I did trust my own judgment as well 18 as that of others. I used to watch the Stoics, with their dignified way of walking, their neat dress, always looking thoughtful, with a manly expression, usually short-haired, and neither effeminate

95

nor showing that totally exaggerated indifference of your lunatic Cynic. Theirs is a state of moderation, which everyone agrees is best.

L. Then did you see them also doing the things I told you just now I myself saw your master doing, Hermotimus—lending money, angrily demanding repayment, disputing contentiously in conversation, and showing off in their usual way? Or do you not much mind these things, provided they dress neatly and have long beards and short hair? So from now on we are to have this strict rule and standard for such matters, according to Hermotimus, and we must recognize the best men by their appearance, their deportment, and their haircut; and anyone who doesn't pass these tests, and doesn't look sullen and deep in thought, is to be dismissed and rejected?

19 Now look here, Hermotimus, you must be making fun of me, to see if I'm aware that I'm being hoodwinked.

H. Why do you say that?

L. Because, my good fellow, this test you propose from appearance applies to statues. They at least are far more elegant and dignified in their dress if a Pheidias or Alcamenes or Myron* has created them in the best-looking style. But if such features are to be the essential criteria, what is a blind man to do if he is eager to learn philosophy? How does he recognize the one who has chosen the better creed, when he cannot see either appearance or deportment?

H. I'm not talking about the blind, Lycinus, and I'm not concerned with them.

L. But, my good fellow, there has to be some generally accepted token in a field that is so important and useful to everyone. But if that is your view, let us say the blind must stay out of philosophy, since they cannot see—though such people have the greatest need of philosophy to help them not to be totally oppressed by their affliction. But as to those who can see, however keen their sight,

20 what can they detect in the soul from this outer covering? What I'm trying to say is, were you not attracted to these men by love of their minds, and didn't you expect to improve your own mental qualities?

H. Certainly.

L. Then using the characteristic features you described, how could you distinguish the true philosopher from the false? Such qualities don't usually appear like that: they are secret and outwardly invisible, though revealed in conversation and social intercourse and actions connected with these, even if it takes time and trouble to grasp them. I expect you've heard about the faults Momus found in Hephaestus,* but if not, I'll tell you. The story is that Athena, Poseidon, and Hephaestus were quarrelling about which was the best artist. Poseidon fashioned a bull, Athena designed a house, and Hephaestus apparently constructed a man. They had appointed Momus as judge, and when they came to him he examined the handiwork of each. His criticisms of the others do not concern us, but the fault he found in the man and his censure of the craftsman Hephaestus, was that he had not made windows in his chest, which could be opened to show everyone his desires and thoughts, and whether he is lying or telling the truth. Of course Momus was short-sighted and that's why he had these ideas about men; but you have keener sight than Lynceus,* and you seem to see through the chest to what is inside, and everything is open to you, so that you know not only what everyone desires and thinks, but also whether he is better or worse.

H. You're making fun of me, Lycinus. I chose with divine help, and I don't regret my choice. At any rate, it's good enough for me. 21

L. But won't you tell me too, my friend, or will you abandon me to perish among the rabble?

H. No, for nothing I say satisfies you.

L. The fact is, my good fellow, that you refuse to say anything to satisfy me. But since you are deliberately being secretive and grudge my becoming a philosopher on your level, I shall try my best to discover for myself what is the accurate test in this field and the safest choice to make. Now you please listen to me.

H. Willingly, Lycinus: you might say something worth knowing.

L. Pay attention, then, and don't make fun of me if my investigation is completely unprofessional. That is unavoidable, since you're not willing with your superior knowledge to explain things more clearly.

Let me imagine virtue to be a sort of city, whose citizens are 22 happy (as your teacher would say, having come from there, wherever it is), totally wise, all of them brave, just, reasonable, almost godlike. All that goes on among us, robbery, violence, fraud, they say you would see no one daring to do in that city. They live together in peace and concord, as is very natural: for what I imagine in other cities stirs up strife and contention and the causes of mutual plotting, is completely absent there. They no longer regard gold or pleasures or glory as things worth quarrelling about, but banished them long ago from their city as unnecessary to their corporate life. The result is that they live calm and totally happy lives, with good laws, equality, freedom, and every other blessing.

23 H. Well, Lycinus, is it not therefore worth while for everyone to long to become a citizen of such a city, without worrying about the laborious journey involved or giving up because of the time it takes, if having arrived they too will be enrolled and share the privileges of the city?

L. Of course, Hermotimus: this must be our most earnest endeavour, to the neglect of everything else. If our country here has a claim on us, we must pay little regard to it; if we have children or parents who cling to us weeping, we must stand firm. Indeed, we should do our best to encourage them to take the same road; but if they don't want to or cannot, we must shake them off and go straight to that all-blessed city, even casting off our cloak if they hold on to it to drag us back as we hasten there: for there's no fear of being shut out even if you arrive naked.

24   I did once earlier hear an old man reporting how things were there, and exhorting me to follow him to the city. He would lead me himself, and when I got there he would enrol me to be a fellow-tribesman and a fellow-clansman, so I might enjoy the universal happiness. 'But no heed did I pay',* being then young and foolish— it was about fifteen years ago: perhaps I would now be actually in the suburbs and even at the city gates. He told me a lot about the city, as I recall, and especially the fact that they were all strangers and foreigners, without a single native. There were many aliens too with citizens' rights, as well as slaves, cripples, dwarfs, and paupers—in short, anyone who wished to have a share in the city. For the legal requirements for enrolment did not include property, dress, height, beauty, or birth. These things did not count: but it was enough for a man to become a citizen if he had intelligence, a longing for what is noble, toughness, perseverance, and would not yield or show weakness in the face of all the hardships he met on his journey. Whoever showed these qualities and completed his journey to the city, at once became a citizen with the same privileges as everyone else. Superior or inferior, well-born or low-born, slave or free, just did not exist nor were they spoken of in the city.

H. So you see, Lycinus, I am toiling not in vain nor for trivial ends 25
    when I long to be a citizen myself of such a noble and happy city.

L. Why, yes, Hermotimus, and I too desire the same things as you,
    and there is nothing I would pray for more. If the city were near by
    and clearly visible to all, be assured that without any hesitation I
    would have got there and become a citizen long ago. But since,
    as you and the poet Hesiod* both say, it is built a very long way off,
    we have to look for the road that goes there, and the best guide to
    take us. Don't you think we have to do this?

H. How else could you get there?

L. Well, as for promises and claiming to know, there's no lack of
    would-be-guides. Many are standing ready, all of them saying they
    are natives of the place. But there is no one identical road in sight,
    but many different ones, not in the least similar. One seems to go
    west, another east, another north, another straight southwards.
    One leads through meadows and orchards and shady places; it is
    well watered and pleasant, with nothing to cause stumbling or hard
    going. Another is rough and rocky, offering much sun and thirst
    and exhaustion. But all these roads are said to lead to the city,
    though it's only one city, yet they finish up in completely opposite
    directions.

    There you have the whole of my problem. For whichever I 26
    approach, there's a man at the beginning of every path I take, who
    stands at the starting-point, a very convincing figure, stretching his
    hand and urging me to go down his road. Each one says that he
    alone knows the direct way, and that the others go astray because
    they have neither been there themselves nor followed others
    who could lead them. If I go to the next one, he makes the same
    promises about his own road and abuses the others. The next one
    to him does the same, and so on with the rest of them. So, the
    multiplicity of roads and the differences between them, and above
    all the guides over-exerting themselves in praising what they each
    have to offer, cause me not a little bother and bewilderment. I don't
    know which way to turn, or which one to follow to come to the city.

H. Well, I'll release you from your bewilderment. Trust those who 27
    have gone before you, Lycinus, and you can't go wrong.

L. Which do you mean? What road did they travel? Which guides did
    they follow? I seem to have the same problem again in a different
    form, involving not circumstances but people.

H. How do you mean?

99

L. That the man who chose Plato's path and travelled with him will obviously praise that route, and similarly with Epicurus' path, and so on with the others, as you will with yours. Surely, Hermotimus? Isn't that right?

H. Naturally.

L. So, you haven't released me from my bewilderment, and I'm still just as uncertain which of the travellers to trust. I can see that each of them, including the guide himself, has tried one path and praises that one and says that it alone leads to the city. But I can't know if he is telling the truth. Perhaps I'll grant that he has arrived at some point and seen some city; but whether he has seen the right one, where you and I want to become citizens, or when he should have gone to Corinth he ended up in Babylon and thinks he has seen Corinth, I still don't know. For just because you've seen a city doesn't mean you've necessarily seen Corinth, since Corinth is not the only city. But my biggest problem is knowing that only one road can possibly be the right one: only one road goes to Corinth, and all others go anywhere except to Corinth, unless you're so half-witted as to think that the road to the Hyperboreans and the road to India lead to Corinth.

H. Impossible, Lycinus: different roads lead to different places.

28 L. Well then, my good Hermotimus, it takes no little deliberation to choose roads and guides, and we won't be doing as the saying has it, and going where our feet take us.* That way, before we know it we shall be off on the road to Babylon or Bactra instead of Corinth. For it doesn't do to trust to fortune in the hope that we might choose the best road, if we set out on any one at random without asking first. That might happen, and perhaps has happened on occasion over a long period; but in cases of such importance I don't think we ought to take a reckless risk or limit our hopes so completely, being prepared, as the proverb goes, to cross the Aegean or Ionian Sea on a mat.* We would then have no right to blame fortune, if with her arrow and spear she didn't quite hit the one true target among the myriad false ones: not even Homer's archer (Teucer, I think) managed that, as he cut the cord when he should have hit the dove.* In fact it was much more reasonable to expect that one of the many others would be wounded and fall by the arrow than that particular one. I think one can guess that there is no little danger involved, if in our ignorance we rush into one of the paths that go astray instead of the straight one, leaving it to fortune to choose

better on our behalf. For it isn't easy to turn round and return safely, once you have cast off your cable and are running before the wind. You're bound to be carried adrift on the sea, usually frightened and seasick, with a headache from being tossed about, when you ought in the beginning, before setting sail, to have climbed to some look-out point to see if the wind was fair and favourable for those wishing to sail to Corinth. Indeed you should have chosen the best navigator of all, and a good sound ship capable of withstanding such rough water.

H. That's much the best way, Lycinus. But I'm sure that if you went 29 the rounds you'd find no other better guides or more experienced navigators than the Stoics. If you want to get to Corinth some day, you'll have to follow them, tracking the footsteps of Chrysippus and Zeno. There is no other way.

L. Don't you see, Hermotimus, that your claim is common to everyone? The fellow-traveller of Plato, the follower of Epicurus, and all the others would each say the same thing, that I would not get to Corinth without him. So that I must either believe them all (which is quite absurd), or disbelieve them all alike. The latter is much the safest policy until we find one who offers us the truth.

Well, then, suppose that in my present state of not knowing 30 which of them all knows the truth, I were to choose your way, trusting in you, a friend, but one who knows only the Stoic teaching, and has travelled that route alone; then suppose some god brought back to life Plato, Pythagoras, Aristotle, and the others, and they stood around and questioned me, or even, Heavens! took me to court on a charge of personal injury, each saying, 'My good Lycinus, what's got into you? Who persuaded you to esteem Chrysippus and Zeno more highly than us, who are much older than they—creatures of yesterday or the day before—not giving us a chance to speak and not testing any of our claims?' Suppose they said this, what could I reply? Would it be sufficient to say that my good friend Hermotimus persuaded me? I know they would say, 'Lycinus, we don't know this Hermotimus, whoever he is, and he doesn't know us. So you had no right to condemn us all and pass judgment in default against us, trusting a man who knows only one way in philosophy, and perhaps not even that one properly. Lawgivers do not prescribe this procedure for jurymen, Lycinus, or let them hear one side but not allow the other to say what it thinks is in its own interest. They must listen to both sides equally, so that by comparing the arguments they can more easily discover what is true and what is false; and if they do not follow this procedure the law grants an appeal to another court.'

31   That's more or less what they would reply. One of them might even ask me as well: 'Tell me, Lycinus: imagine an Ethiopian who had never travelled abroad and so had never seen other men like us, but who stated firmly in an assembly of the Ethiopians that nowhere in the world were there men who were white or yellow or any other colour than black, would they believe him? Or wouldn't one of the older Ethiopians say to him, "Now this is very bold of you: how do you know it? You've never been away from us, and you can't possibly have seen what life is like among other peoples." ' Personally, I would say the old man had asked a fair question. What's your view, Hermotimus?

H. Agreed: I think his rebuke was just.

L. So do I, Hermotimus. But I don't know if you'll also agree with what follows. I certainly think that this too is just.

H. What's that?

32 L. The man will certainly add another point, and say to me something like this: 'By the same token, Lycinus, let us suppose someone who knows only the Stoic creed, like your friend Hermotimus, who has never travelled abroad to Plato's abode, or Epicurus', or indeed anyone else's. Well, if he were to say that there was nothing so fine and so true to be found in all the others as the beliefs and statements of the Stoics, would you not rightly think him over-bold in this sweeping statement, especially when he knows only one creed, and has never set foot outside Ethiopia?' What answer should I give him?

H. Obviously the truest one: that we certainly make a thorough study of Stoicism, as this is our chosen school; but we are not ignorant of what the others have to say. For our teacher deals with all that in the course of his expositions, and refutes it with his own arguments.

33 L. Do you really imagine that at this point the followers of Plato and Pythagoras and Epicurus and the rest will keep quiet, and not roar with laughter, saying to me, 'What is your friend Hermotimus up to, Lycinus? Does he think it right to believe our adversaries in their views about us, and to accept their account of our doctrines, when either they don't know the truth or they hide it? In that case, if he sees an athlete training before a match, kicking the air, or

shadow-boxing as though hitting an opponent, will he as referee announce him to be unbeatable; or will he regard this child's play as easy and safe when he has no opponent, and judge him the victor only when he has beaten down and defeated an actual antagonist and the latter has yielded, and not otherwise? So don't let Hermotimus imagine from the shadow-boxing his teachers indulge in against us in our absence, that they are winning and that our beliefs can be easily swept aside. Such an assumption would be like the houses children build: they make them flimsy and knock them down at once. Or indeed it is like archers practising: they tie twigs together and stick them on a pole, and setting this up not far away they take aim and shoot at it. If they happen to hit it and pierce the twigs, they immediately give a loud shout, as if it's a great achievement that their arrow has gone through the sticks. But you won't find the Persians or the Scythian archers doing this. First of all, they generally shoot from a moving position on horseback; and secondly, they think that their targets should be moving too, and not motionless and waiting for the arrow to hit them, but running around as fast as they can. They usually shoot at wild animals, and some of them hit birds. If they ever want to test the power of the arrow's impact on a target, they set up a tough piece of wood or a rawhide shield and shoot through it, thus acquiring confidence that their arrows will even penetrate armour. So you can inform Hermotimus from us, Lycinus, that his teachers are shooting at targets made of sticks and then claiming to have defeated armed men; and they are punching at dummies they have painted to look like us, so that having beaten them, as you'd expect, they think they've beaten us. We would each say to them in the words of Achilles about Hector,

> They do not see my helmet's front.*

Well, that's what they would all say in turn. I imagine Plato 34 would also quote one of the Sicilian stories of which he knows so many. It is said of Gelo of Syracuse that he suffered from bad breath, but was quite unaware of it for a long time, as no one dared to criticize a tyrant, until a foreign woman with whom he had been to bed dared to tell him about it. He went to his wife in a fury because she had not told him of his bad odour, though she was the one most aware of it. She begged his forgiveness on the grounds that, as she had never experienced being close to another man, she thought all men's breath was like that. 'So Hermotimus too,' Plato would say, 'only having experience of the Stoics, obviously doesn't know what other men's mouths are like.' Chrysippus too might say the same, or express himself even more strongly, if I abandoned him without hearing what he had to say and turned eagerly to Platonism, relying on someone who had followed only Plato's doctrines. Let me summarize by saying that, so long as it's not clear which philosophical system is true, choose none. Choosing one is an insult to the others.

35 H. In the name of Hestia,* Lycinus, let us leave Plato, Aristotle, Epicurus, and the others in peace: I'm no match for them. But let us enquire, just the two of us, whether engaging in philosophy is essentially the sort of thing I say it is. As for Ethiopians and Gelo's wife—why did you have to bring her from Syracuse into the argument?

L. Well, let them depart if you think they are unnecessary to the argument. It's your turn to talk now: you look as though you are about to say something marvellous.

H. It seems to me, Lycinus, perfectly possible by studying thoroughly the Stoic teaching to learn the truth from them, without making an extensive and detailed study of the other creeds. Look at it like this. If somebody simply tells you that two and two make four, must you then go around asking all the other mathematicians in case one of them says it's five or seven? Or would you know immediately that this man is right?

L. I'd know immediately, Hermotimus.

H. Then why do you think it impossible for a man encountering only the Stoics, who speak the truth, to believe them and no longer need the others, knowing that four could never be five, even if countless Platos and Pythagorases say so?

36 L. That's not relevant, Hermotimus. You are comparing what is agreed with what is disputed, and they are very different. Or what would you say? Have you ever met anyone who says that putting two twos together adds up to seven or eleven?

H. No, I haven't. Anyone would be mad not to say it came to four.

L. Well, then: have you ever met (and for the Graces' sake try to speak the truth) a Stoic and an Epicurean who didn't disagree about first principles and the goal of life?

H. Never.

L. Then make sure you aren't reasoning falsely with me, my good fellow, even though I'm your friend. For while we are still seeking those who have the true philosophy, you have anticipated the answer in choosing the Stoics, saying (which is by no means clear) that they are the ones who make twice two equal to four. For the Epicureans or the Platonists might say that they make it this, whereas you people call it five or seven. Don't you think that this is what they mean, when you believe that only the beautiful is good, while the Epicureans consider it is pleasure? And when you say that everything is corporeal, and Plato thinks that there is an incorporeal element in existing things? No, you have, as I said, most arrogantly seized upon the point at issue and given it to the Stoics, as if it unquestionably belonged to them. But when the others make counter-claims and say it is theirs, then I think we really have to make a judgment. If it becomes clear that it is a monopoly of the Stoics to think that twice two equals four, that will be the time for the others to be silent. But while they are disputing this very point, we must give them all an equal hearing or be accused of bias.

H. You don't seem to understand, Lycinus, what I'm getting at. 37

L. Then you should express yourself more clearly if your meaning is different from what I've said.

H. You'll soon grasp what I mean. Let us imagine that two people have entered the Asclepieion or the shrine of Dionysus, and that subsequently one of the sacred bowls has disappeared. Obviously it will be necessary to search both of them to see which has the bowl under his clothes.

L. Certainly.

H. One of them is bound to have it.

L. Clearly, if it has disappeared.

H. So, if you find it on the first, you won't be stripping the other, as he obviously hasn't got it.

L. Obviously.

H. And if we don't find it in the first one's clothing, the second must have it, and there's no need to search in this case either.

L. Yes, he has it.

H. Then, similarly, if we find the Stoics already have the bowl, we won't think we need to search the others, as we have what we've long been looking for. What's the point of taking any further trouble?

38 L. None at all, if you do find it, and having done so you can be sure that is what was missing, or you really can recognize it as the sacred vessel. But in our case, my friend, to start with, those who are going into the temple aren't just two, so that one or the other must have the spoil, but a very large number. Secondly, it is not obvious exactly what the missing object is—a bowl, a cup, or a garland. All the priests disagree about it and don't even concur in what it is made of, some saying copper, others silver, others gold, others tin. So you have to strip all the visitors, if you want to find the lost object. For even if you find a golden bowl on the very first, you still have to strip the others too.

H. Why, Lycinus?

L. Because it's not obvious that it was the bowl that was lost. And even if everyone agrees on this, they don't all say the bowl is golden, and if it is absolutely clear that a golden bowl is missing, and you find a golden bowl on the first person, not even then would you stop searching the others, because it wouldn't be certain that this was the god's. Don't you think that there are lots of golden bowls?

H. Yes, I do.

L. Then you'll have to go around searching everyone, and collecting everything you find on each, and then guess which of them is fit to be the god's property.

39   For this is the great difficulty you are up against: each of those who are stripped assuredly has something, one a cup, another a bowl, another a garland, and they may be of copper, gold, or silver. And you're still not sure if what each one has is the sacred object. So you cannot avoid the difficulty of whom to call a temple-robber, when even if all had similar articles it would not be clear who had taken the god's property—the things could be privately owned. I imagine that the reason for our uncertainty is that the missing bowl (assuming it is a bowl) is not inscribed, since if it had been inscribed with the name of the god or the dedicator, we would have had less of a problem, and having found the inscribed bowl we would have stopped stripping and bothering the others. I suppose, Hermotimus, you've often watched athletic contests?

H. You suppose correctly: many times and in many places.

L. Well, have you ever sat next to the judges themselves?

H. Indeed I have. At the Olympics the other day I was on the left of the chief judges. Euandrides from Elis kept me a seat among his fellow-citizens, as I was eager for a close view of everything that took place among the judges.

L. Well, are you also aware how they draw lots for the pairs in the wrestling matches and the pancratium?

H. I am.

L. So, as you've seen it from close at hand you could describe it better than I could.

H. In the old days, when Heracles was presiding, bay leaves— 40

L. Don't give me your 'old days', Hermotimus: tell me what you saw from close at hand.

H. They put out a silver urn, dedicated to the god, into which are thrown small lots, the size of beans, engraved with letters. There are two marked alpha, two beta, two gamma, and so on with the rest, if there are more entrants, two lots always having the same letter. Each athlete comes up, prays to Zeus, and puts his hand into the urn to take one of the lots. After him comes another man, and there is a guard standing by each who holds his hand and doesn't allow him to read the letter he has drawn. When they all have their lots the chief officer, I think, or one of the judges themselves (I can't remember), goes round and inspects the lots of the entrants, who are standing in a circle, and thus he matches the two who have drawn the alpha lots for the wrestling or the pancratium, and so likewise with the two betas and the other matching letters. This is the procedure if there are an even number of entrants, like eight or four or twelve; but if they are an odd number, five or seven or nine, he adds an extra lot with an odd letter on it which has no matching letter. Whoever gets this has a bye, and waits until the others have competed, for he has no matching letter. This indeed is a considerable advantage to the athlete, as he will be competing fresh against tired opponents.

L. Hold on. That's just what I needed. Let's say there are nine in all, 41 holding the lots they have drawn. Now, you go round and inspect the letters—I want to make you a judge instead of a spectator. I don't imagine you would know in advance who is the reserve, unless you go to all of them and pair them off.

H. What are you getting at, Lycinus?

L. You cannot immediately find the letter that tells you the bye; or maybe you might find the letter, but you wouldn't know if that was it, as there is no advance statement that K or M or I is the one that selects the bye. But when you find A you look for the man who has the other A, and having found him you've already matched them. Then, when you find beta, you look for the other beta which corresponds to the one you've found, and likewise with all of them, until you are left with the man who has the only letter without a match.

42 H. Suppose you find that one first or second: what will you do?

L. It's not a question of what I shall do: you are the judge, and I'd like to know what you will do. Will you immediately say that this man is the bye, or will you need to go round all of them to see if there is a matching letter anywhere? If you didn't inspect everyone's lots you wouldn't find the bye.

H. Oh yes, Lycinus, I could easily find him. If there are nine entrants and I find E first or second, I know that the man with this one is the bye.

L. How, Hermotimus?

H. Like this. Two of them have A and likewise two of them have B, and of the other four two must have drawn C and two D, and four letters have now been used up on eight entrants. So, clearly, only the following letter E can be odd, and the one who has drawn it is the bye.

L. Shall I applaud your intelligence, Hermotimus, or do you want me to give my own contradictory view of this?

H. Please tell me. But I'm at a loss how you could reasonably contradict such a statement.

43 L. You've spoken as though all the letters are written in sequence, that is, alpha first, beta second, and so on in order, until the number of the competitors finishes at one of them. I agree that this is the procedure at the Olympics. But what if we choose five letters at random, chi, sigma, zeta, kappa, and theta, and write four of them twice on eight lots, but zeta only on the ninth, which will tell us the bye. What will you do if you find the zeta first? How will you distinguish the man holding it as the bye unless you go round all the others without finding a matching letter? You cannot, as you did before, judge from the order of the letters.

H. That's a difficult question to answer.

44 L. Well then, consider the same question from a different angle. Suppose we didn't write letters on the lots, but signs and symbols, like all the ones the Egyptians use instead of letters—men with dogs' heads and lions' heads. But let's forget them as they're so

outlandish. Let us inscribe simple, uniform figures, making the best likenesses we can: men on two lots, two horses on two others, two cocks and two dogs, and on the ninth let a lion be stamped. Now, if you find this lion-marked lot first, how can you tell that this is the one that assigns the bye, unless you go around comparing them all to see if another one has a lion too?

H. I can't answer that, Lycinus.

L. Of course you can't: there's no convincing answer. So, if we want 45 to find the man with the sacred bowl or the bye or our best guide to that city of Corinth, we shall have to approach everyone and make a careful trial and examination by stripping and comparing them. Even so we shall have difficulty finding the truth; and if anyone is going to give me trustworthy advice on which philosophy I should follow, he will be the only one who knows what they all say. The others will be useless, and I wouldn't trust them as long as they are ignorant of even one philosophy, because that might be the best one. If anyone produced a handsome man and told you he was the handsomest of all men, we'd certainly not believe him unless we knew he had seen all the men there are. This man might indeed be handsome, but he couldn't know he was the handsomest of all if he hadn't seen all. And we are trying to find not just the beautiful, but the most beautiful; and if we don't find it, we won't think we've got anywhere. We shall not be satisfied with just any kind of beauty: we are seeking that consummate beauty, of which there can only be one sort.

H. That's true. 46

L. Well, can you give me anyone who has tried every philosophical path, who knows the teachings of Pythagoras and Plato and Aristotle and Chrysippus and Epicurus and the rest, and has ended up choosing one of all these paths, having tested its truth and learnt by experience that it alone leads straight to happiness? If we could find someone like that our difficulties will be over.

H. It's not easy to find such a man, Lycinus.

L. Then what are we going to do, Hermotimus? I think we shouldn't 47 give up just because we find we have no such guide at present. The best and safest course is for everyone to start by making his own way through every philosophical system and to study critically what each says.

H. That seems to follow. But there is this difficulty which you spoke of a while ago, that once you have committed yourself and spread your sails it's not easy to retreat. As you say, how can you try out all the paths if you get stuck in the first?

L. I'll tell you. We'll imitate that ploy of Theseus, and taking a thread from Ariadne, as in the play, we'll go into every labyrinth, and by unwinding it find our way out again without difficulty.

H. Well, who'll be our Ariadne and where shall we get the thread?

L. Don't worry, my friend. I think I've found what to hold on to in order to get out.

H. What's that?

L. I'll tell you, though it's not mine but comes from a wise man: 'Stay sober and remember to be sceptical'.* For if we are not too quick in believing what we hear, but like a good judge we allow others their turn to speak, perhaps we'll easily get out of the labyrinth.

H. Well said: let's do that.

48 L. Very well. Which path should we first go along? Or will it not matter? If we begin at random, say with Pythagoras; how long do we think it will take to learn all his doctrines? And please don't ignore those five years of silence.* If we include them I suppose thirty years will be sufficient, or twenty at least.

H. Let's agree to that.

L. After that we clearly must allow the same number to Plato, and of course not less to Aristotle too.

H. Agreed.

L. I won't now ask you how many to give to Chrysippus, as I know from what you said that forty would scarcely be enough.

H. True.

L. Then there's Epicurus and the rest of them. And you can tell that I'm not exaggerating these figures if you consider how many octogenarians there are among the Stoics, the Epicureans, and the Platonists, who all admit that they don't know the full range of their sect's teaching, so as to have a complete grasp of its doctrines. If they didn't admit this, then Chrysippus and Aristotle and Plato would do so; and all the more would Socrates, who was in no way inferior to them, and who used to tell the world loudly not only that he didn't know everything, but that he knew nothing at all, except that he knew nothing. So let's reckon up from the beginning. We allotted twenty to Pythagoras, the same number to Plato, and the same to all the others in turn. What would that all add up to if we assume only ten schools of philosophy?

H. Over two hundred years, Lycinus.

L. Shall we subtract a quarter, to make a hundred and fifty years enough, or a round half?

H. You would be a better judge. What I see is this, that few would get 49 through them all at this rate, even if they began right from birth.

L. Well, if that is the situation, Hermotimus, what can one do? Should we abandon what we've already agreed, that you can't choose the best out of many if you haven't tried them all? Didn't we say that choosing without testing is to seek the truth by divination rather than judgment?

H. Yes.

L. Then it is absolutely necessary for us to live all that time, if we are to test them all and make a good choice, to practise philosophy after we have chosen, and to be happy after practising philosophy. Until we do that, we shall, as they say, be dancing in the dark,* stumbling over anything we come upon, and assuming that whatever first comes to our hands is what we are seeking, because we don't know the truth. And if we do happen by good fortune to encounter it, we won't be able to be certain it is what we are seeking. There are a lot of very similar things, each claiming to be the absolute truth.

H. Lycinus, you seem to me to be making a reasonable point; but to 50 tell you the truth, you really irritate me, going through everything in such detail and with such needless nit-picking. It does seem to have been a big mistake for me to leave home today and then meet you. I was almost realizing my hopes, and then you threw me into a quandary by showing that the search for truth is impossible, as it requires so many years.

L. It would surely be much more fair, my friend, if you blamed your father Menecrates, and your mother, whose name I don't know, or, going back a lot further, our human nature, for not giving you many years and a long life, like Tithonus,* and for limiting human life at most to a hundred years. I just helped you to examine and discover the logical outcome of the argument.

H. Not so. You're always being high-handed; and I don't know what 51 makes you hate philosophy and jeer at philosophers.

L. What is truth, Hermotimus, you sages are better qualified to say —you and your teacher. But at least I know this much, that it is not altogether pleasant to the ears and therein is far surpassed by false-hood. Falsehood is more fair to look upon and therefore pleasanter, while truth knows no dishonesty and speaks freely to men, and so causes offence. Just look at us: you are now offended with me for helping you to find the truth in this matter, and for pointing out that what you and I are longing for is not at all easy. It's as if you were in love with a statue, and supposing it to be human thought you could win it; but I saw it was stone or bronze, and explained to you out of kindness that your love was impossible. In that case too you would think I was being unfriendly, because I didn't let you deceive yourself by hoping for something hopeless and unnatural.

52 H. So what you are saying is this, Lycinus, that we shouldn't study philosophy, but surrender ourselves to idleness and spend our lives as ordinary laymen?

L. When did you hear me say that? My point is not that we shouldn't study philosophy, but that since we should and since there are many paths, each claiming to lead to philosophy and virtue, and the true one is not obvious, we have to make a careful choice. But it became clear to us that, with many alternatives being offered to us, it was impossible to choose the best without going and testing them all. Then we saw that the testing would be a long process. So what do you think? I'll ask you again: will you follow the first philosopher you meet and join him in his studies, while he treats you as a gift from the gods?

53 H. How can I answer that now, when you tell me that no one can judge for himself, unless he lives as long as the phoenix and goes the rounds testing all of them, and when you don't think it right to trust those who have previously tested them, or the many who praise and bear witness to them?

L. Who are the many you refer to who know and have tested them all? If such a one exists, one is enough for me and there'll be no need for many. But if you mean those who don't know, their numbers won't make me trust them, so long as they are making assertions about all the systems when they know none or just one.

H. But you alone have seen the truth, while all the other students of philosophy are fools!

L. You do me a wrong, Hermotimus, if you say that I am somehow putting myself forward in preference to others, or in general classing myself among those who know. You don't remember what I said. I did not claim to know the truth more than others do: I admitted that along with everyone else I was ignorant of it.

54 H. Well, Lycinus, it may be quite reasonable to have to go round everyone, testing what they say, and that no other way of choosing would be better than this; but it is absolutely ridiculous to devote so

many years to each test, as if it were not possible to grasp a whole system from a small part of it. My own view is that such a procedure is very easy and doesn't take much time. Why, they say that some sculptor, Pheidias, I think, from seeing just the claw of a lion could calculate the size of the whole lion, assuming it was fashioned in proportion to the claw. And you too, if someone showed you just the hand of a man, while concealing the rest of the body, would know at once, I guess, that the hidden body was a man, even if you couldn't see the whole of it. So it is easy to grasp, in a small fraction of a day, the principal points of all the systems, and this over-exact procedure, involving an extensive examination, is quite unnecessary for choosing the better one: you can decide from those principal points.

L. Good heavens, Hermotimus, how confidently you speak when   55
you claim to know the whole from the parts! Yet I can remember hearing just the opposite, that knowing the whole you know the part too, but knowing only the part you don't yet know the whole.

H. I've heard that.

L. And tell me this too. When Pheidias saw the lion's claw, would he have known it was a lion's if he had never seen a whole lion? If you saw a man's hand, could you have said that it was a man's if you'd never before seen or known a man? Why are you silent? Shall I give your only possible answer for you, that you *couldn't* have said so? So it seems likely that Pheidias has retired frustrated, and modelled his lion in vain: he is obviously saying nothing that concerns Dionysus.* Or what sort of comparison is there here? for you and Pheidias there was no other way of recognizing the parts than knowing the whole, that is, the man and the lion. But in philosophy, Stoicism for example, how can you judging from one part know the other parts as well or prove that they are noble? For you don't know the whole of which they are parts.

As for your saying that it is easy to pick up the principal points   56
of every philosophy in a small fraction of a day—that is, their first principles and ends, their view of the gods and the soul, who state that everything is corporeal, and who claim that there are immaterial entities too, the fact that some identify pleasure and others nobility with goodness and happiness, and so on—if you have picked up all this, it is easy and straightforward to describe them. But to decide which is telling the truth surely requires not a fraction of a day but many days. Otherwise, what induced them all

to write hundreds and thousands of books on these very subjects, which I suppose are intended to prove the truth of those few elements which you think straightforward and easily learnt? As it is, I think you'll need a prophet here too to help choose the best, unless you can bear to spend the time on making a careful selection, after personally inspecting everything in detail. It would in fact be a short cut, avoiding complications and delays, if you sent for a prophet, listened to the principal points of all the systems, and offered a sacrifice for each. The god will relieve you of a huge amount of trouble by revealing the right choice for you in the sacrificial victim's liver.

57   If you like, I can also suggest another way, which is less trouble-some, and doesn't involve slaughtering victims and making sacri-fices and employing some expensive prophet. Put some tablets into an urn, each having on it the name of one of the philosophers, and tell a boy—a youth with both parents alive*—to go to the urn and pick up the first tablet that comes to his hand. Then you just follow the philosopher whose name is on the tablet he picked.

58 H. That's just buffoonery, Lycinus, and not worthy of you. You tell me this: have you yourself ever bought wine?

L. Yes, frequently.

H. Well, did you go the rounds of all the wine-merchants in the city, tasting and comparing and testing the quality of the wines?

L. Certainly not.

H. I imagine it's sufficient for you to take the first one you find that is good quality and value for money.

L. Of course.

H. And from that brief tasting could you tell the quality of the whole?

L. I could.

H. Now, if you had gone to the wine-merchants and said, 'I want to buy half a pint; so will each of you please give me a whole jar to drink, so that having drained them all I can tell who has the best wine and which one I must buy'—if you had said this, don't you think they would have laughed you to scorn, and if you persisted in being a nuisance you might have been drenched in water?

L. I agree, and I would have deserved it.

H. Well, think of philosophy in the same way. Why must you drain the jar when you can taste a little and so learn the quality of the whole?

L. How slippery you are, Hermotimus, the way you escape my 59
clutches! But you have given me some help: you thought you'd
escaped, but you've fallen into the same trap.

H. What do you mean?

L. You take something which is self-evident and familiar to everyone,
wine, and compare with it things that are totally dissimilar and that
everyone argues about because they are so obscure. For myself, I
can't say how you think philosophy and wine are alike, except in
this one respect, that philosophers sell their doctrines, as wine-
merchants their wines—many of them diluting and adulterating it
and giving short measure. But let us examine your reasoning. You
say that all the wine in the jar is exactly the same, and there's
certainly nothing odd in that. Also, it follows, as you say, and I
certainly would not deny it, that if you draw off and taste the tiniest
amount of it, you can tell at once the quality of the whole jar. Now
take the next point: do philosophy and philosophers like your
teacher say the same things to you on the same subjects every day,
or different things on different days?

H. Many different things.

L. Obviously, my friend, you would not have stayed with him,
wandering around uncertainly for twenty years like Odysseus, if he
had repeated the same things, but you would have been satisfied
having heard him once.

H. Yes, of course. 60

L. Then how could you have known everything from the first taste? It
was not the same thing being said, but always a succession of new
things, unlike the wine, which was always the same. So, my friend,
unless you drain the whole jar, you must have been walking around
drunk to no purpose. God seems to me to have well and truly
hidden the benefits of philosophy at the bottom, right under the
lees. You will need to drain it all completely, or you'll never find
that divine drink for which you seem to have been thirsting for a
long time. But you believe that it is such that you have only to draw
and taste ever so little of it, in order to become all at once completely wise; just as they say the prophetess at Delphi becomes
divinely inspired to give responses to her consultants as soon as she
drinks from the sacred spring. But it doesn't seem to work like this:
at any rate, you had drunk more than half the jar and you said you
were still at the beginning. But perhaps this is a better analogy for 61
philosophy. Let's keep your jar and your dealer, but instead of the

wine a mixture of seeds—wheat on top, then beans, then barley, and under that lentils, then chick-peas and an assortment of others. You arrive and want to buy some of the seeds, and he has taken a sample of wheat from where it was and put it in your hand for you to inspect. Now, could you tell by looking at it whether the chick-peas were sound, the lentils tender, and the beans not hollow?

H. Of course not.

L. Well then, neither could you learn the nature of the whole of philosophy from the first thing that anyone says. For it is not of one consistency, like the wine you compared it to when you said it was similar to your sample-tasting. For we have seen that it varies in itself and a superficial test is not sufficient. You may lose a couple of obols if you buy bad wine; but to be lost yourself among the rabble, as you said yourself at the beginning, is no minor disaster. Besides, if you insist on drinking the whole jar just to buy half a pint, you will cause the merchant to suffer loss through all your sceptical tasting, whereas philosophy would not suffer such a loss, because however much you drink of it, the jar never gets less and the merchant loses nothing. As the proverb says, the more you empty the fuller it is*—quite the opposite to the jar of the Danaids, which didn't hold what they put in, but let it run out at once. If you take anything from philosophy, all the more is left behind.

62 But I'd like to make another similar point about sampling philosophy, and don't think I'm slandering it if I say it is like a deadly poison, hemlock, say, or aconite or some such. Now, though fatal, not even these will kill you if you scrape off a tiny bit with your finger-nail and taste it. If the amount and the method of having it and the mixture are wrong, you won't die by taking it. But you claimed that the smallest amount was enough to give you a complete grasp of the whole.

63 H. I grant you that, Lycinus. So what? Do we have to live a hundred years and put up with all that trouble? Is there no other way to study philosophy?

L. No, Hermotimus: nor is it so awful, if what you said at the beginning is true, that life is short but art is long. And I don't know what makes you so vexed if you can't become Chrysippus or Plato or Pythagoras before today's sunset.

H. You're penning me in, Lycinus, and driving me into a corner, though I've done you no harm. You're obviously jealous because

I've got further in my studies, while you've neglected yourself in spite of your age.

L. Well, you know what you can do. Ignore my frenzied raving, and let me chatter away foolishly; and you continue as you are on your own journey, and finish the job according to your original decision.

H. But you are so forceful you don't allow me to choose anything unless I've tried everything.

L. Well, be assured I'll never say anything else. But in calling me forceful you seem to be blaming the blameless, as the poet says,* for I myself am now being forced along, unless you can find some other argument to remove the force. But observe that the argument may have some much more forceful things to tell you, though perhaps you will ignore it and blame me.

H. What things? I'd be surprised if it had anything more to say.

L. It says that to choose the best it is not enough to make a detailed 64 investigation of everything: the most important thing is still missing.

H. What's that?

L. A critical and enquiring faculty, my good sir, along with a sharp mind and a keen and unbiased intelligence. That's what you need in order to make a decision on such matters as these, or you will have seen everything in vain. The argument says that the time devoted to such an enquiry must not be stinted, and having placed everything in front of you open to view, you must take your time and delay your decision, making frequent reviews and having no regard for the age of each speaker, or for his appearance or reputation for wisdom. You must act like the court of the Areopagus,* which gives judgments at night in the dark, so as to attend not to the speakers but only to what is said. *Then* you will be able to make a sound choice and study of philosophy.

H. When I'm dead, you mean. From your account of it, no mortal could live long enough to cover everything and examine every detail precisely, and after examining make a judgment, and after judging choose, and after choosing study philosophy. For you say that only in this way, and in no other, can the truth be discovered.

L. I hesitate to tell you, Hermotimus, that even this is not sufficient. 65 We seem to be in a fool's paradise, thinking we'd found something secure though really we had found nothing. We are like fishermen who often let down their nets, and when they feel something heavy draw them up, thinking they have caught a great number of fish.

Then when they are worn out with hauling in, all that appears is a stone or a jar full of sand. You must consider whether we too have drawn up something similar.

H. I don't see the point of these nets of yours. You have certainly got me in their toils.

L. Well then, try to slip out. With god's help you know how to swim as well as anyone. Now, even if we visit all the sects and eventually get through the business of testing them, I don't think even then we will know for sure if any of them has what we are looking for, or if they are all alike in their ignorance.

H. What do you mean? Not one of them has it?

L. It's uncertain. Do you think it impossible that they are all deceived, and that the truth is something different and that none of them has yet found it?

66 H. How could that be?

L. Like this. Suppose, for example, we have a true number, twenty, and someone takes twenty beans in his hand, which he then closes, and he asks ten people how many beans he has in his hand. Suppose one guesses seven, another five, another thirty, yet another ten or fifteen, in a word everyone a different number. Yet, it's possible that someone might happen to guess correctly, isn't it?

H. Yes.

L. However, it's not impossible that all may guess different numbers and that all of these are wrong, and no one says that the man has twenty beans. Agreed?

H. It's not impossible.

L. By the same token then, all who study philosophy are seeking to learn what happiness is, and each gives a different answer, one saying it is pleasure, another beauty, and whatever else they say about it. It's quite likely that happiness is one of these things, but it's not unlikely that it is something different altogether. We seem to have done this the wrong way round, rushing on to the end before we have found the beginning. We should first have made sure that the truth has been discovered, and that one of the philosophers really does know it. Having done that, the next step would be to discover whom to believe.

H. So this is what you mean, Lycinus, when you say that even if we make our way through every philosophy we won't necessarily be able to find the truth.

L. Don't ask me, my dear fellow: once again, you must ask the argument itself. It may reply that we cannot yet do so, as long as it is not clear whether truth is one of the things they are saying.

H. From what you're saying, we shall never find it or practise 67 philosophy; but we'll have to give up philosophy and live the lives of laymen. At least, the inference from what you're saying is that for an ordinary mortal philosophy is impossible and unattainable. You claim that someone who is going to study philosophy must first choose the best one, and you think the choice would only be correct if we chose the truest after reviewing every philosophy. Then you reckoned up the number of years each one needed, exceeding all bounds as you extended the process into other generations, so that the search for truth lasted longer than any single lifetime. Finally, you declared that even this is not beyond doubt, suggesting that it's not clear whether the philosophers of old did discover the truth or not.

L. But how could you, Hermotimus, state on your oath that they have found it? I certainly couldn't; and yet what a lot of other points I have purposely omitted which also require lengthy scrutiny!

H. Like what? 68

L. Do you not hear some Stoics or Epicureans or Platonists saying that some of them know some particular doctrines, while others do not, though in other respects they are completely trustworthy?

H. That's true.

L. Then don't you think it's a very troublesome task to separate and distinguish those who know from those who don't but say they do?

H. Yes, very.

L. So, if you are going to know the best Stoic, you will have to go and test most of them, if not all, and choose the best as your teacher, after first training yourself to acquire a critical capacity in such things, so that you don't without realizing it choose one who is inferior. Just imagine how long this takes! I didn't mention it on purpose in case you got annoyed, and yet I think this one point is of the greatest and most essential importance in matters of this kind, I mean where we have uncertainty and doubt. And this is the only safe and secure hope you can have for discovering the truth. There is no other hope at all apart from being able to judge and distinguish truth from falsehood, and like assayers of silver to separate the genuine and unadulterated from the counterfeit, and if you can come to test the doctrines equipped with that sort of capacity and skill. If you can't, you can be sure that nothing will stop you being dragged by the nose by all of them, or following like sheep a leafy twig held in front of you. I'd go further and say you will be like water spilt on a table, moving in whatever direction somebody draws you with the tip of his finger; or indeed like a reed growing on a river bank, which bends to every breath of air, however mild the breeze that blows and stirs it.

69   So, if you can find an experienced teacher who can train you in exposition and in deciding matters which are disputed, you'll certainly solve your problems. The best will immediately become obvious to you, and the truth too, subjected to this art of demonstration, and falsehood will be found out; and having made a sound choice and judgment you will practise philosophy and achieve your much longed for happiness, living with her and having all good things in this one single package.

H. Oh good, Lycinus! What you are saying is much better and offers a good deal of hope. It seems we must find a man who can make us capable of selecting and distinguishing, and above all of expounding. The rest will now be easy and trouble-free and won't take much time. I'm really grateful to you for finding us this excellent short-cut.

L. Well, you have no good reason yet to be grateful to me. I haven't found or shown you anything that will bring you nearer to your hope. We are actually much further away than before, and, to quote the proverb, 'after all our toil we are just where we were'.

H. How do you make that out? That seems a distressing and pessimistic remark.

70 L. Because, my friend, even if we find someone who claims to know the art of exposition and to be able to teach it, I don't think we shall believe him straightaway, but we shall be looking for another man who can tell if the first is speaking the truth. And even if we find him, we still won't be sure if this arbiter knows how to distinguish if a man is judging correctly or not, and I think we'll need yet another arbiter for him. For how could we know how to judge the one with the best judgment? You see how this regresses to infinity and cannot be checked and stopped? You will note that all the proofs you can find are open to question and offer no certainty. Indeed, most of them try to force us to accept them by means of questionable arguments; while others link the most obscure and irrelevant suppositions with quite self-evident ones, and then claim

that the former are thereby proved, as if someone thought he could prove the gods exist because we can see their altars. So, Hermotimus, it looks as though we've been running in a circle, and have returned to our starting-point and our original difficulty.

H. See what you've done to me, Lycinus, proving that my treasure 71 is but ashes,* and all these years of heavy toil are likely to be wasted.

L. Well, Hermotimus, you'll be much less grieved if you reflect that you aren't the only one left out of your longed-for blessings. All practising philosophers are, as it were, fighting over a donkey's shadow.* Who could bear to go through all that I have described? You yourself admit that it is impossible. As it is, you seem to be behaving like someone who weeps and blames fortune because he cannot go up to heaven, or plunge deep into the sea off Sicily and come up off Cyprus, or fly away on wings from Greece to India in a day. The cause of his grief, I suppose, was basing his hopes on some such dream, or inventing the idea himself without first finding out if his wishes were attainable and humanly possible. So too you, my friend, while you were dreaming all your wonderful dreams, the argument gave you a nudge which made you start from your sleep. Then, with your eyes hardly open you are angry with it, and you are having trouble shaking off your sleep because you are so delighted with what you were seeing. People who imagine empty blessings for themselves feel just the same. There they are, rolling in wealth, digging up treasure, ruling as kings, and enjoying any other form of bliss—all that the goddess Prayer, who is rich in gifts and refuses nothing, easily achieves, whether they want to fly, or to be as big as a colossus, or discover whole mountains of gold. Then in the midst of their fantasizing, if a slave comes and asks about some household essential, for example, where's the money to buy the bread, or what is he to say to the landlord who has been waiting for ages for the rent, they are so annoyed at being deprived of all those blessings by his irritating questions, that they nearly bite off the lad's nose.

But don't feel that about me, my dear fellow, if as a friend I 72 didn't let you spend your whole life in a dream, sweet though it was, digging up treasure, flying on wings, imagining extraordinary visions, and indulging in unattainable hopes; and if I urge you to stir yourself and do some needful tasks, and stick to what will keep your mind for the rest of your life occupied with these ordinary everyday things. For what you have been recently doing and thinking about is just like Hippocentaurs and Chimaeras and Gorgons,* and all the other creations of dreams and the unfettered imaginings of poets and painters, things that never existed and couldn't exist. Yet most people believe them, and are charmed by seeing or hearing such things because they are strange and outlandish.

73   You too must have heard from some storyteller of a woman of extraordinary beauty, surpassing the Graces or Aphrodite; and even before finding out if he was telling the truth and whether this creature actually existed anywhere in the world, you immediately fell in love with her, as they say Medea fell in love with Jason in a dream.* But my guess is that what most of all attracted you to this love, and all the others who are in love with the same vision as you, was the fact that when he had first told you about the woman and got you to believe him, he went on to add the details. You all had eyes for nothing else, so once you had let him get a hold on you, he dragged you by the nose and led you to the beloved by what he claimed was a straight path. After that I suppose it was easy, and none of you turned back to the entrance to ask if it was the right one and whether you hadn't mistakenly gone in where you shouldn't have. Instead, you followed in the footsteps of those who had gone before, like sheep following their leader, whereas you should have considered right at the start, at the entrance, whether you should go in there.

74   You might grasp what I'm saying more clearly if you consider this analogy. Imagine one of these over-daring poets saying that there was once a man with three heads and six hands, and say that you blithely accepted this without enquiring if it were possible, but just believed it. He would straightaway continue by adding details: that this man had six eyes, six ears, three mouths which simultaneously uttered three voices and ate food, thirty fingers, not like us with ten on both hands; and if he had to fight, three of his hands held three shields, light, oblong or round, and the other three brandished an axe, a spear, and a sword. Who would not believe these further details, as they matched the original picture— which was the point when you should have considered if it was to be accepted and believed? Once you grant the first account, the rest comes in a flood over you, and cannot be stopped; and it is hard to be sceptical now, as it follows consistently on what you agreed to at

the beginning. Now, this is what has been happening to all of you. Because of your passion and your enthusiasm you didn't investigate the situation at each of the entrances, and you are going ahead, lured by consistency, and not realizing that something can be both consistent and false. For example, suppose someone told you that twice five is seven and you believed him without doing the calculation yourself; obviously he will carry on to say that four times five must be fourteen, and so on for as long as he wants. This is what that wonderful subject of geometry does: it offers us at the start some absurd axioms and requires us to accept them, though they are quite impossible, indivisible points, lines without breadth, and so on; and on these rotten foundations it builds all its system, and claims to establish truths though it starts from false beginnings.

In just the same way, all of you accept the premisses of the 75 different systems, and then you believe what follows from them, because you imagine that the consistency there, though false, proves the truth of it. Then some of you die still hoping, and before you see the truth and can condemn your deceivers; while others, even if they realize too late that they have been deceived, are by now grown old and hesitate through shame to turn back, if they have to acknowledge that at their age they didn't know they were acting so childishly. Consequently, they carry on in their course through shame, and praise what they have, and encourage anyone they can to follow them, so they won't be the only ones deceived, but can take comfort from the fact that many others are in the same boat. They also realize that if they speak the truth they won't be treated with respect as now above ordinary mortals, nor will they have the same honour. So they would not willingly speak out, knowing from what heights they will seem to have fallen to the level of the rest of us. You'll come across very few who are brave enough to admit that they were deceived, and to dissuade others from making a similar attempt. If you do meet one, you can call him a lover of truth and honest and just, and, if you like, a philosopher. For to him alone I wouldn't grudge the name. The rest of them either know nothing of the truth, though they think they do, or they know it but conceal it through cowardice and shame and the desire to be highly honoured.

However, in the name of Athena, let us forget all that I've said, 76 putting it aside and consigning it to oblivion like everything that happened before Euclides' archonship.* Let us assume that this philosophy of the Stoics, and no other at all, is the right one, and let us see if it is possible and attainable, or if those who long for it are wasting their efforts. For I hear some marvellous promises it makes about all the happiness in store for those who win to its heights, since only they will grasp and possess all true blessings. As to the next point, which you would know better than I: have you ever met a Stoic, even a perfect specimen of the sect, who does not feel pain, and is not dragged down by pleasure, and never gets angry, who is superior to envy and despises wealth, and, in a word, is a happy man? That has to be our rule and our standard for the virtuous life—for if he falls short in the least respect he is imperfect, even if he possesses everything in abundance—and if he doesn't match the standard he is not yet happy.

77 H. I've never seen such a person.

L. Well said, Hermotimus: you don't deliberately tell lies. So what is your aim as a philosopher when you see neither your teacher, nor his teacher, nor his teacher's teacher, right back to the tenth generation, truly wise and therefore happy? For you couldn't rightly say that it is sufficient to approximate to happiness: that's no use. A man standing just outside the door is as much outside the threshold and in the open as a man some distance off. The difference is that the former is more distressed because he has a better view of what he can't have. Then, in order to approximate to happiness (I don't dispute this), you take such pains and wear yourself out, while so much of your life has passed by in weariness and toil, bowed down through sleeplessness. And you will continue to toil, you say, for at least another twenty years, so that when you are 80 (if there's any guarantee that you'll live that long), you may still become one of those who are not yet happy—unless you think that you alone in your pursuit will find and grasp what a great many good and much swifter men before you have pursued without catching it.

78   Well, catch it if you fancy, and hang on to all of it when you've got it. But, firstly, I don't see what good you could ever imagine would compensate for all these toils. Then, how long will you have to enjoy it, as by then you'll be an old man, past it for any pleasures, and with one foot in the grave, as they say? Unless, my good friend, you are doing some advance training for another life, so that knowing how to live you can enjoy it more when you get there: like

someone who prepares and gets himself ready for a better dinner for so long that he unwittingly dies of hunger first.

What is more, I think you haven't yet grasped the fact that virtue 79 surely lies in deeds, in behaving justly, wisely, and bravely; whereas all of you (by which I mean you leading philosophers) ignore such things, and practise how to invent and construct your wretched phrases and your syllogisms and problems. You spend most of your lives on these, and whoever is best at them is your supreme champion. I imagine the reason you admire this old fellow, your teacher, is that he reduces his pupils to a state of perplexity, and knows how to entangle them inextricably with his questions and quibbles and knavish tricks. So, you simply cast away the fruit, which is concerned with actual deeds, and instead occupy your-selves with the husk, and shower each other with its leaves during your discussions. Isn't that exactly what you all do, Hermotimus, from morning till night?

H. Yes, exactly that.

L. So, would it not be correct to say that you are ignoring the sub-stance and hunting the shadow, or chasing the snake's slough and not attending to the coiling creature itself? Or rather, that you are like someone who pours water into a mortar and grinds it with an iron pestle, thinking he is doing something essential and useful, and not realizing that you can grind your arms off, as they say, and water stays water?

At this point, allow me to ask you whether, apart from his 80 arguments, you would wish to be like your teacher: he is so quarrel-some, so petty, so contentious, and, my goodness, so pleasure-loving, even if most people don't realize it. No reply, Hermotimus? Shall I tell you what I heard a very old man saying the other day, when he was expounding some philosophy, with a large group of young men attending him for the sake of his wisdom? He was angrily demanding his fee from one of his pupils, saying it was overdue, for by their agreement it was due on the last day of the month, sixteen days ago.

While he was thus carrying on angrily, the youth's uncle 81 appeared, a rustic fellow and a layman compared with all of you; and he said, 'My good sir, do stop saying you've been mightily ill-treated because we've bought some verbiage from you and not yet paid for it. Anyway, you still have what you sold us, and your store of knowledge is no less. And what about my own wishes when I first recommended the lad to you? He's shown no improvement through you: he carried off and raped my neighbour Echecrates' virgin daughter. He barely escaped an action for assault, but I paid Echecrates, who is a poor man, a talent in compensation for the wrong committed. And he struck his mother the other day, because she caught him carrying off the wine-jar under his shirt—his contribution, I suppose, to some entertainment. As for anger and passion and shamelessness and audacity and falsehood, he was much better last year than now. Yet I would have preferred you to help him in these characteristics, rather than he should know all those things he makes us listen to reluctantly every day at dinner: how a crocodile carried off a boy, and promised to return him if his father answered some question or other; or how it can't be night if it's day. Sometimes the fine fellow even makes us grow horns,* with his strange twists of language. All this makes us laugh, especially when he covers his ears, and practises to himself his "states" and "relations" and "perceptions" and "images", and goes through a catalogue of such terms. We hear him saying that god is not in heaven but pervades all things, like sticks and stones and even the humblest of creatures. And if his mother asks him why he talks such drivel, he just laughs at her and says, "If I learn this 'drivel' properly, nothing can stop me being the only rich man and the only king, and everyone else being reckoned slaves and outcasts compared to me." '

82   So said the man; note the philosopher's reply, Hermotimus, what a judicious one it was: 'Well, if he had not attended me, don't you think his behaviour would have been much worse, and indeed he might have been handed over to the public executioner? As things are, philosophy and his respect for it have put a curb on him, and therefore he is more moderate and still tolerable. For it disgraces him if he shows himself unworthy of his dress and title, which do indeed attend and help to train him. So it's right for me to claim my fee from you, if not for making him any better, at least for what he has avoided doing through his respect for philosophy. Nurses too say the same about children, that they must go to school: for even if they are too young to benefit from learning, at least they won't get into mischief while they are there. So, I think I've fulfilled all my obligations. If you'd like to come along tomorrow and bring anyone who is familiar with our teaching, you will see how he asks questions and gives replies, and all he has learnt, and

all the books he has already read on propositions and syllogisms, on perception, on duties, and all kinds of things. It's nothing to do with me if he has beaten his mother or carried off girls. You didn't make me his guardian.'

That was the old man's defence of philosophy. But would you 83 also agree, Hermotimus, that a sufficient reason for studying philosophy is to avoid bad behaviour? Or did we start out with other hopes that philosophy was worth studying, and not just to go around seeming better behaved than the laymen? Why don't you answer that too?

H. Just because I'm almost in tears. Such an effect does a true argument have on me, and I'm grieving for all the time I've been fool enough to waste, and, what's more, the high fees my labours have cost me. It's as though I've been drunk and I'm now sober again, and I can see what it was that I was longing for and all I suffered for the sake of it.

L. What need for tears, my good friend? I think there's a lot of good 84 sense in that fable Aesop tells,* in which a man is sitting on the sea-shore, where the waves are breaking, in order to count the waves. He gets angry and distressed when he can't do it, until a fox comes up and says to him, 'My good sir, why are you distressed about those that have gone by? You must forget about them and start counting again where you left off.' So it is with you: since this is your feeling, you'll do better for the future by resolving to share our ordinary life. Play your part in the affairs of the city along with many of your fellow-citizens, and give up bizarre and extravagant expectations. If you are sensible, you won't be ashamed to learn new ways in your old age, and to make a desirable change of direc- tion. Do not think, my friend, that all I have said has been aimed at 85 the Stoa, or that I've been actuated by a special hatred for the Stoics. My remarks applied to all alike. I would have said the same things to you if you had joined the school of Plato or Aristotle and condemned all the others untried. As things are, since you have preferred the Stoics, the argument has seemed to be aimed at the Stoa, though there was no special application to it.

H. You're quite right: I shall do just that, so as to make a change in 86 myself—including even my dress. So you'll soon see me without my present long and shaggy beard and the ascetic life-style: I'll be completely relaxed and easygoing. I might even change into some- thing purple, to show the world that I've given up all that rubbish.

If only I could disgorge all that I heard from them; and you can be sure that I wouldn't hesitate even to drink hellebore, for the opposite reason to Chrysippus*—to banish their doctrines from my mind. So I owe you a large debt of gratitude, Lycinus, because you came and pulled me out when I was being whirled along by a rough and turbid torrent, abandoning myself to being carried along with the stream. You appeared just like the *deus ex machina* in a tragedy. I'm thinking I could reasonably shave my head like men who are free and safe after shipwreck, as a thank-offering for deliverance today, now that I've shaken off such a mist from my eyes. And if I ever again even unintentionally meet a philosopher as I'm walking on the road, I'll turn round and avoid him like a mad dog.

ALEXANDER OR THE FALSE PROPHET

THIS is the longest of Lucian's personal attacks on an individual, and it may be the latest of his datable works. It is a deeply hostile account of Alexander of Abonoteichus, a self-styled prophet and mouthpiece of the snake-god Glycon, who is alleged to be a reincarnation of the healing god Asclepius. His home town Abonoteichus (later Ionopolis, now Ineboli) was on the southern shore of the Black Sea, in the area called Paphlagonia, which was part of the Roman province of Bithynia and Pontus, but he acquired enormous prestige throughout all the eastern Roman empire, and his influence extended through his son-in-law Rutilianus even to the court of Rome. Whether he really was the master of fraud, deceit, and chicanery which Lucian portrays is impossible to say, but this was an age in which oracles were extremely popular in all levels of society, and no doubt a great deal of dishonest exploitation occurred at some shrines. Lucian's motive for writing the attack is allegedly a request that he do so from his friend, the Epicurean Celsus, to whom the work is addressed and who had himself written a treatise against sorcerers (21). This man is generally agreed not to be identified with Origen's anti-Christian opponent, who was a Platonist; but however that may be it is this friend's Epicurean sympathies which account largely for the strength of Lucian's venom against Alexander, who hated the Epicureans, and the piece ends with a striking eulogy of Epicurus himself.

The cult of Glycon was quite widespread: his image and name are represented on coins from the second and third centuries, and there is supporting epigraphic evidence as well. (See C. P. Jones, *Culture and Society in Lucian*, 138.)

The work must be dated after 180, the year Marcus Aurelius died, as he is referred to as already dead (48).

My dear Celsus, you probably think it a small and trivial request 1
of yours that I should record in a book and send to you the life of
Alexander, the quack from Abonoteichus, including his daring
schemes and his chicaneries. But in fact, if one were to deal with every
detail carefully, it would be no less a task than to report the deeds of
Alexander, the son of Philip. Our man was as great a villain as the
other was a hero. Still, if you are prepared to read it indulgently and
to supply any deficiencies in my narrative, I will shoulder the task for
you, and try to clean up that Augean stable,* if not completely, at least
to the best of my ability, bringing a few basketfuls from which you can

work out how much was all the untold amount of muck that three thousand cattle could have produced over many years.

2   Actually, I feel ashamed for both of us, you and me—you for wanting an utter scoundrel to be commemorated in memory and writing, and me for exerting myself to record the activities of a man who doesn't deserve to have cultivated people read about him, but to have some huge and crowded amphitheatre watch him being torn apart by apes and foxes. But if anyone reproaches us for this, we shall be able to quote a precedent, namely Arrian,* the pupil of Epictetus. A Roman of great distinction and a devotee of culture all his life, he incurred the same charge, and so his defence can serve for us too. You see, he decided to write the life of Tillorobus the brigand. But we shall be commemorating a much more savage brigand, since his plunderings took place not in woods and mountains but in cities; and he ravaged not just Mysia and Mount Ida, and despoiled not only a few of the more deserted areas of Asia, but you could say he filled the whole Roman Empire with his brigandage.

3   First, I'll sketch out in words for you the best likeness I can make of him, though I'm not very good at descriptions. To give you a picture of his physical appearance, he was tall and good-looking, really god-like, with a fair complexion, a beard which was not very thick, hair partly natural and partly false, but so well matched that most people couldn't tell the difference. His eyes flashed like one possessed, while his voice was very clear and pleasant. In short, with none of these details could you find fault.

4   So much for his outward appearance. But as for his soul and his mind—O Heracles, Averter of Evil, O Zeus, the Protector, O Dioscuri, our Saviours, may it be my fate to encounter any enemy, public or private, but never such a man as that! For in intelligence, sagacity, and shrewdness he was far ahead of everyone; and as for an enquiring mind, a readiness to learn, memory, and a natural capacity for knowledge—every single one of these qualities he had in excess for every occasion. But he used them for the worst purposes, and, equipped with noble instruments, he lost no time in becoming the most accomplished of those who have been notorious for wickedness, surpassing the Cercopes, surpassing Eurybatus or Phrynondas or Aristodemus or Sostratus.* He himself once wrote to his son-in-law Rutilianus,* and (with remarkable modesty) claimed to resemble Pythagoras. But, saving his presence, if Pythagoras, wise and divinely gifted as he was, had been the man's contemporary, I'm quite sure he

would have seemed a child in comparison. And, by the Graces, do not suppose that I mean this as an insult to Pythagoras, or that I am trying to compare them for their achievements. On the contrary, if you brought together all the worst and most slanderous criticisms which have been made of Pythagoras (which I personally cannot believe to be true), they would add up to just a tiny fraction of Alexander's rascality. In short, I ask you to imagine and carefully picture the most complex psychological temperament, consisting of lying, perjury, and malice, a temperament which is unscrupulous, daring, reckless, energetic in forwarding its own schemes, persuasive, plausible, making a pretence of virtue, and with an appearance totally opposite to its real purpose. Indeed, no one who met him for the first time failed to go away with the impression that he was the worthiest and most honest of men, and the most artless and unaffected as well. In addition to all this he had the character of a high achiever and of one who designed nothing petty, but always had his mind set on the highest things.

When he was still a lad and extremely good looking, as you could 5 judge from his appearance later and also learn from those who gave descriptions of him, he sold his favours freely and went with anyone who would pay for his company. Among others he had a lover who was a quack, the type who offer magic spells and marvellous incantations, charms for love affairs, afflictions for your enemies, discoveries of buried treasure, and inheritances to estates. This man saw that he was a talented lad and very well suited to assist him in his dealings, and was just as enamoured of his own villainy as he himself was of the boy's beauty. So he trained him well, and made continual use of him as his assistant, servant, and attendant. He himself, so he claimed, was a public doctor, but, to quote Homer on the wife of Thon, the Egyptian, he knew

> Many a drug compounded for good and many for ill.*

All of this Alexander inherited as his heir. That teacher and lover of his came from Tyana by birth; he had been one of the followers of the famous Apollonius of Tyana* and was familiar with all his pretentiousness. So you see how the man I am describing had spent his time.

But just when Alexander's beard was beginning to fill out, the 6 death of the Tyanean put him into a difficult situation, as he was now also losing his youthful bloom by which he could make a living. He therefore gave up any thoughts of trivial projects, and joined forces with a Byzantine chorus-writer, one of those who enter for public contests. This man—I think he was nicknamed Cocconas*—was a much more disgusting character, and they travelled around, practising witchcraft and quackery, and fleecing the thick-headed, as charlatans usually refer to the public. Well, among these they came across a rich Macedonian woman, who was past her prime but still wanting to be attractive, and they furnished their needs at her expense and accompanied her from Bithynia to Macedonia. She came from Pella, which had once been a prosperous place in the time of the Macedonian kings, but was now unimportant and very depopulated.

7 There they saw huge snakes, which were quite tame and domesticated, so that they were reared by women, slept with children, put up with being trodden on, didn't object to being squeezed, and were suckled just like babies. These creatures abound in the area, which may account for the old story which was widely told of Olympias:* I imagine that one such snake slept in her bed while she was pregnant with Alexander. So they bought the finest one of these reptiles for a

8 few obols, and, as Thucydides says, the war begins here.*

Given two such scoundrels, greatly daring, ready and eager for wickedness, and combining their forces, they easily perceived that human life is at the mercy of the two great tyrannies of hope and fear, and that anyone who could exploit both of them would very quickly get rich. For they saw that both he who fears and he who hopes regard foreknowledge as extremely necessary as well as extremely desirable, and that for this reason Delphi and Clarus* and Branchidae* long ago became rich and famous, because men were always visiting their shrines owing to the aforementioned tyrants, hope and fear, and seeking to learn about the future in advance with sacrifices of hecatombs and offerings of gold ingots. With much twisting and turning between the two of them, they formed a scheme to set up an oracular shrine, hoping, if it succeeded, that they would speedily become rich and prosperous. Thus indeed it turned out, better than their first expectations and beyond their hopes.

9 Next they began to consider, first about the place, secondly how to begin and how to organize the venture. Cocconas considered Chalcedon a suitable and convenient site, being near to Thrace and Bithynia, and not far from Asia and Galatia and all the inland peoples. But Alexander took a different view, preferring his own region, and saying quite rightly that to organize such a business they needed a

host population of the thick-headed and simple-minded. Such were the Paphlagonians, he said, who lived beyond Abonoteichus: most of them were superstitious and simple, and you only have to appear among them followed by someone playing the pipe or tambourine or cymbals, and telling fortunes with a sieve (as they say),* and at once they are all gaping and staring at you as if you were a heavenly being.

They had a bit of a dispute about this, but in the end Alexander got   10 his way; and going to Chalcedon, which nevertheless seemed to them to have some advantages, they buried bronze tablets in the temple of Apollo, the oldest one there, which stated that Asclepius and his father Apollo would very soon be moving to Pontus and settling in Abonoteichus. The opportune discovery of these tablets caused this story to spread easily all around Bithynia and Pontus, and first and foremost to Abonoteichus. Indeed, the people there at once voted to build a temple and lost no time digging the foundations. At that point Cocconas stayed in Chalcedon composing oracles which were ambiguous, doubtful, and misleading; and not long afterwards he died, bitten, I believe, by a viper.

Alexander was sent in first, with his hair now grown long and   11 falling in ringlets, wearing a purple and white tunic, covered by a white cloak, and carrying a scimitar à la Perseus, from whom he traced his descent through his mother. And those wretched Paphlagonians, though they knew that both his parents were humble nonentities, believed the oracle that said:

> Here you can see a descendant of Perseus, dear unto Phoebus:
> Godlike Alexander, who partakes of the blood of the Healer.

So it seems that Podalirius* the Healer was so lustful and mad on women that he came rampaging for Alexander's mother all the way from Tricca to Paphlagonia.

By this time there was another oracle, allegedly a former prophecy by the Sibyl:

> By the shore of the Euxine Sea and close to Sinope
> Shall appear by a Tower, in the time of the Romans, a prophet.
> For his name see the first unit followed by thirty,
> Then five more units, then twenty times three:
> Four elements matching the name of a noble protector.*

So, coming into his country after a long absence and with all this   12 ceremony and parade, Alexander became the centre of attention and

133

admiration, as he pretended to have periodical fits of madness together with foaming of the mouth. He easily contrived this by chewing the root of soapwort, the herb used by dyers; but the sight of the foam filled the people with superstitious awe. They had also long before procured and fitted out a snake's head made of linen: it had a slightly human look to it, and was painted to look completely lifelike. Its mouth opened and closed by means of horse hairs, and the tongue, black and forked like a snake's, would shoot out, also controlled by hairs. They also had the snake from Pella in readiness, being looked after at home, which was due to appear at the right time and act with them in their drama, or rather to play the leading role.

13 When it was time to make a start, he thought up the following device. He went at night to the foundations of the temple which were just being dug, and where water had collected, either issuing from the ground there or falling from the sky, and there he placed a goose's egg, already blown, and now containing a new-born snake. After burying it deep in the mud he went away again. At dawn he ran into the market place, wearing nothing except a gilded loin-cloth, carrying his scimitar, and shaking his hair wildly like the frenzied followers of the Great Mother.* Climbing onto a high altar he addressed the people, and congratulated the city because it was immediately going to receive the god in visible form. His audience—for virtually the whole city had come running up, including women, old men, and children—were astounded, uttered prayers, and prostrated themselves. He uttered some meaningless words, sounding like Hebrew or Phoenician, which dazed the people who didn't know what he was saying, except for his constant mentioning of the names Apollo and

14 Asclepius. Then he raced off to the future temple, and when he got to the excavation and the prearranged source of the oracle, he stepped into the water, sang hymns to Asclepius and Apollo in a very loud voice, and appealed to the god to come bringing good fortune to the city. Then he requested a saucer, and when someone gave him one he neatly dipped it underneath, and drew up together with water and mud the egg in which he had enclosed the god, having plugged the hole with sealing-wax and white lead. Taking it into his hands he announced that he was now holding Asclepius. They stared fixedly to see what might happen, being already astonished at the discovery of the egg in the water. And when he broke it and took the young snake into his hand, and the bystanders saw it moving about and twining round his fingers, they immediately shouted aloud, welcomed the

god, congratulated their city, and proceeded each one to indulge in a surfeit of prayers, begging him for treasures, wealth, health, and all the other blessings. But Alexander rushed back home, carrying with him the new-born Asclepius,

> Twice born when other men are born but once,*

his mother certainly not being Coronis, nor even a crow,* but a goose! All the people followed him, everyone in a frenzy and crazy with hopes.

For some days he stayed at home, hoping, correctly as it turned out, 15 that as soon as the story got around, large numbers of Paphlagonians would come rushing up. When the city was full to bursting with people, all of them already deprived of their minds and their senses, in no way resembling bread-eating men, and differing from cattle only in their shape, he sat himself on a couch in a small chamber, dressed in truly godlike apparel, and clasped to his breast the Asclepius from Pella, which as I said was a very large and fine looking specimen. He coiled it all round his neck, letting the tail hang down, as it was long enough to sweep over his lap and trail part of its length on the ground, and he kept only the head hidden under his arm (the snake submitted to any treatment), showing the linen head beside his own beard, as if it was part of the snake that was clearly visible.

Now, please picture a small room, not brightly lit nor letting in 16 too much daylight, and a motley crowd of humanity, agitated, excited in advance, buoyed up with hopes. When they went in, the thing naturally seemed a miracle to them—that a tiny little snake should in a few days become such a great serpent, and what's more with a human face and so docile. They were immediately pushed towards the exit, and before they could get a close look they were crowded out by the steady stream of those coming in, as another door had been opened in the opposite wall to form an exit. The story goes that this was what the Macedonians did in Babylon when Alexander was ill there: his condition was critical, and the people surrounded the palace hoping to see him and to say goodbye. This exhibition, we are told, the blackguard gave not just once but many times, especially if any rich men arrived as fresh prey.

To tell the truth, my dear Celsus, in these circumstances we can 17 forgive those people of Paphlagonia and Pontus, being stolid and uneducated folk, if they were completely deceived when they touched the snake, for Alexander even let them do this if they wanted: after all it was in semi-darkness that they were seeing its so-called head opening and shutting its mouth. Indeed, it would have taken a Democritus* or Epicurus himself or Metrodorus,* or someone else with a mind proof as adamant against such things, to be sceptical about this device and to guess the truth, and even if he couldn't work out the mechanism, at least to be convinced in advance that though the method of the fraud eluded him, the whole business was a deception which could never happen.

18   Well, bit by bit Bithynia, Galatia, and Thrace came streaming in, as everyone who took the news around probably reported that he had seen the god being born, and later on touched him, when he had in a short time grown very large, and had a human-looking face. Paintings then followed, and images and statues, some of bronze and some of silver, and of course a name was given to the god. He was called Glycon in obedience to a divine command given in verse:

Lo, I am Glycon, grandson to Zeus, and a light unto mortals.

19   When the time came to fulfil the object of all their scheming, that is, to deliver oracles on request and to make prophecies, he took his cue from Amphilochus in Cilicia. After the death and disappearance of his father Amphiaraus* at Thebes, Amphilochus was driven from his country and went to Cilicia; which turned out to be a good move, as he too set up as a prophet among the Cilicians, charging two obols for each prediction. Well, taking his cue from him, Alexander proclaimed to all comers that the god would be delivering oracles on a day he stated in advance. He instructed everyone to put down on paper whatever he wanted and particularly wished to learn, to tie it up, and to seal it with wax or clay or the like. Then he himself took the scrolls, and went into the sanctuary, for by now the temple had been built and the stage was set. His plan was to summon the petitioners in order through the herald and the attendant priest, and having heard the god's reply in each case, to hand back the scroll, sealed as before and with the answer written on it, since the god gave detailed replies to everyone's question.

20   Now the trick was obvious and easily seen through by a man like yourself, and if it isn't presumptuous to say so, like me; but to those drivelling idiots it was an almost incredible prodigy. He worked out various ways of undoing the seals so as to read all the questions and give them appropriate answers. Then he rolled up and resealed the scrolls, and handed them back to the utter astonishment of the

recipients, whose constant reaction was: 'How on earth did he know the questions I gave him so carefully fastened up with seals difficult to counterfeit, unless there really was a god who knows everything?'

'So what ways did he work it out?' you may well ask. Listen, then, 21 so you'll be able to expose such goings-on. His first method, my dear Celsus, was to heat a needle and use it to melt through the wax under the seal so as to remove it; then after reading the question, he warmed up the wax again with the needle, both the wax under the thread and that which held the seal itself, and so easily stuck it together again. Another method was to use what they call collyrium, compounded of Bruttian pitch,* asphalt, powdered crystal, wax, and mastic. Moulding the collyrium from all these ingredients and warming it in a flame, he moistened the seal with saliva and pressed it onto the clay, thereby taking an impression of it. Then, as the clay hardened rapidly, he easily opened and read the contents, after which by applying the wax he produced a seal which was exactly like the original one, just as if he had used a gemstone. And just listen to this third device. He made a paste by mixing gypsum with the glue with which they glue books, and used this to take the impression by applying it while still wet to the seal and removing it when it dried, as it quickly did, becoming harder than horn or even iron. There are several other devices for achieving this, but I need not mention them all in case it seems in bad taste, especially as you yourself have produced sufficient examples, and many more than mine, in your writings against sorcerers, excellent and extremely useful books which successfully instil commonsense in their readers.

He proceeded then to deliver oracles and prophecies, in which 22 he showed much shrewdness in his combination of guesswork and invention. Some of his replies were ambiguous and riddling; others were completely unintelligible: that too was his idea of the oracular technique. Some people he encouraged or discouraged, following his own guess at the right course. To others he recommended medical care and diets, knowing, as I said at the start, many useful cures. His 'cytmids' were his favourite treatment: this was his own name for a pain-killer made of bear's grease. But questions involving expectations and success and property inheritance he put off to another time, with the words 'It will all come to pass when I wish it, and Alexander my prophet asks me and prays on your behalf.'

The fixed charge for each oracle was a drachma and two obols. 23 Don't imagine this was cheap, my friend, or that it gave him a meagre income. He collected up to seventy or eighty thousand a year, as people were so avid they handed in ten or fifteen questions each at a time. He didn't keep what he received for himself or salt it away to become rich; but as by now he had a lot of people around him—helpers, servants, questioners, oracle-writers, oracle-keepers, secretaries, sealers, interpreters—he paid each according to his rank.

24   By this time he was also sending people abroad to spread reports of the oracle among other nations, and to announce that he gave prophecies, found runaway slaves, detected thieves and robbers, showed the way to buried treasure, healed the sick, and sometimes even raised the dead. The result was that crowds came running and jostling from all directions, with sacrifices and offerings—and a double share for the god's prophet and disciple. For this oracle too had become known:

> My orders to you are to honour my servant the prophet:
> I care not so much for possessions, but I care for my prophet.

25   In the end, when many people of good sense came to themselves, as it were from a deep intoxication, and banded together against him, especially the followers of Epicurus; and when throughout the cities they gradually saw through the trickery and contrivances by which the thing was staged; he issued a threatening proclamation against them, stating that Pontus was full of atheists and Christians* who did not scruple to utter the foulest abuse about him. These he said should be driven away by stoning, if the goodwill of the god was to be preserved. He also gave out the following oracle about Epicurus himself. When somebody asked him what Epicurus was doing in Hades, he answered:

> He wears leaden shackles while sitting surrounded by filth.

So are you surprised that the shrine acquired a great reputation, seeing that the questions of those who applied to it were so shrewd and intelligent?

The war he waged with Epicurus was without negotiations or truce, and not surprisingly. Who else would be a more justified object of attack from a quack who loved marvels and hated truth than Epicurus, with his keen perception of the nature of things and his unique knowledge of the truth in them? Alexander regarded the schools of Plato and Chrysippus and Pythagoras as his friends, and there was a deep peace between them. But the 'relentless' Epicurus, for so he called him, was bitterly opposed to him, and rightly so, as he regarded all these activities as childish and ridiculous. So Alexander hated Amastris most of all the cities of Pontus, because he knew that the followers of Lepidus* and those who sympathized with them filled that city, and he would never issue an oracle to an Amastrian. On one occasion when he did venture to give a response to a senator's brother he made a complete fool of himself, as he could neither con-coct a clever reply himself nor find someone who could do a suitable one for him. The man complained of a stomach-ache, and Alexander, intending to prescribe a meal of pig's trotter prepared with mallow, produced the following:

Sprinkle your mallow with cumin in a sacred meal-tub of porkers.

As I said earlier, he frequently exhibited the snake to those who   26
were interested, not the whole of it, but mostly revealing the tail and the rest of its body, but keeping the head invisible under his cloak. But when he wanted to amaze the crowd even more he promised to produce the god actually talking, giving his oracles himself and not through a prophet. He proceeded without difficulty to fasten together cranes' windpipes, and to feed them through the very lifelike head he had constructed. Then he answered the questions through somebody else out of sight, who spoke so that his voice came from that linen Asclepius.

These oracles were called autophones, and they were not issued to everyone without distinction, but only to those who were well dressed, rich, and generous. Thus, the oracle given to Severianus* about the   27
invasion of Armenia was an autophone. Alexander encouraged him to invade with these words:

Your sharp spear shall conquer Armenians and Parthians;
Then you shall reach Rome and the Tiber's fair stream,
Wearing a crown on your brow bright with the rays of the sun.

Afterwards, when that stupid Celt following his advice proceeded to invade with the result that he and his army were cut to pieces by Osroes, Alexander deleted this oracle from his records and replaced it by another:

'Twill do you no good to march to Armenia,
Lest a woman-dressed man shoot grim death from his bow,
And deprive you of life and the light of the sun.

28   This was one of his bright ideas—retrospective oracles to correct those in which he had predicted falsely and missed the mark. Often he promised a full recovery to sick people before their death, and when they died he had another oracle ready in recantation:

> No longer look for assistance in your bitter disease:
> Death stands before you and now there's no way to escape.

29   He knew that the priests in Clarus and Didyma and Mallus* had a high reputation for the same kind of prophecy, and he won their friendship by referring to them many of his visitors, saying:

> Go now to Clarus and there attend to the voice of my father.

Or again:

> Draw near to the shrine of the Branchids and heed their responses.

And yet again:

> Go on to Mallus where are the oracles of Amphilochus.

30   These were his activities within Asia, as far as Ionia, Cilicia, Paphlagonia, and Galatia. But as the fame of his shrine spread to Italy as well and reached the city of Rome, everyone tried to get there before anyone else. Some arrived in person, others sent messengers, especially those who had the highest power and status in the city. First and foremost was Rutilianus, a man of virtue and honour in most respects and put to the test in many Roman offices, but very eccentric in his attitude to the gods and with very odd beliefs about them. He had but to see a stone anointed with oil or decked with a garland, and he would straightway prostrate himself and kiss it, and stand before it for a long time, praying and begging blessings from it.

    Well, when he heard the stories about the oracle, he nearly gave up his official duties and winged his way to Abonoteichus. But he did send deputation after deputation, and these emissaries, being simple-minded servants, were easily hoodwinked and came back reporting not just what they had seen but what they had heard as if they had seen it, and even threw in a bit more for good measure to curry favour with their master. In this way they inflamed the wretched old man and

31 drove him into full-blown madness. Having a great many influential friends, he went around telling them what he had heard from his emissaries and adding further details on his own account. His stories filled and agitated the city, and so disturbed those at court that they

at once made haste to go and hear for themselves anything that concerned them.

Alexander welcomed all who came very cordially, won their good-will by his hospitality and his expensive gifts, and sent them home not just to report the responses to their questions, but to sing the praises of the god and themselves to spread monstrous lies about the shrine.

But the scoundrel also devised a scheme which was pretty astute, 32 and way beyond the average swindler. While opening and reading the scrolls sent to him, if he found anything in the questions dangerous and reckless, he would retain them himself and not return them, in order to keep the senders in his power and virtual slaves, because of their fear in remembering what they had requested. You can understand what sort of questions are likely to be asked by rich and powerful men. So he made a large income from them, as they knew he had them in his nets.

I want to tell you about some of the replies which were given to 33 Rutilianus. He asked about a son he had by a previous marriage, now in the bloom of youth, wishing to know whom he should appoint to direct his studies, and received the reply:

> Pythagoras choose and the noble bard who tells us of warfare.

But a few days later the boy died, and Alexander was in a spot, with no excuse to offer his critics for the obvious putting to shame of the oracle. But the good-hearted Rutilianus himself forestalled him in defending the shrine, saying that the god had predicted this very event, and had therefore told him to choose for the boy not a living tutor, but Pythagoras and Homer, who were long dead and who probably had him even then as a pupil in Hades. So why should we blame Alexander if he chose to occupy himself with such nincompoops?

On another occasion Rutilianus wanted to know whose soul he had 34 inherited, and was told:

> First you were Achilles, and afterwards Menander;
> Then what you seem now; hereafter a sunbeam:
> Eighty years then a hundred are the span of your life.

In fact he died insane when he was 70, without waiting to fulfil the god's promise. This oracle was also one of the autophones.

Once he asked about getting married and he was distinctly told: 35

Take in marriage the daughter of Alexander and Selene.

Long ago he had put out the story that his daughter's mother was Selene, who had been smitten with love for him once when she saw him asleep—a habit of hers, to fall for good-looking men in their sleep!* Without a moment's delay that most sagacious Rutilianus straightaway sent for the girl, celebrated his wedding as a 60-year-old bridegroom, and consummated the match, appeasing his mother-in-law Selene with whole hecatombs, and imagining that he himself had joined the dwellers in heaven.

36   Once he had got Italy in the bag, Alexander's plans became ever more wide-ranging, and he sent oracle-mongers to every part of the Roman Empire, warning the cities to watch out for plagues and conflagrations and earthquakes. He assured them that they could depend on his personal help to prevent any of these happening. He sent round an oracle, one of the autophones, to all the nations during the great plague,* consisting of one line:

Phoebus with hair unshorn averts the dark cloud of the plague.

And you could see the line written over gateways everywhere as a charm against the plague, though in most cases it had the opposite effect. For by some chance it was those houses especially which had the line inscribed on them that were emptied of their inhabitants. Don't imagine that I am suggesting that they perished because of the inscription: it just so happened by chance. Perhaps, too, many people were over-trustful in the verse, didn't take precautions, and lived too carelessly, not cooperating with the oracle in countering the disease, since they had the words to protect them and unshorn Phoebus to ward off the plague with his arrows.

37   Moreover, Alexander set up a great many of his confederates as spies in Rome itself, who reported back to him everyone's opinions, and gave him forewarning of the questions and the particular wishes of the questioners, so that the messengers would find him ready with his answers even before they arrived.

38   These were his tactics to deal with his Italian market; while at home he also devised the following scheme. He organized some mystic rites, involving ceremonies of torch-bearing and initiation, to be performed every year over three successive days. On the first day there was a proclamation, as at Athens, but saying: 'If any atheist or Christian or Epicurean has come to spy on our ceremonies, off with him. But those

who believe in the god may perform the rites, and good fortune be their lot.' Then at the very beginning an expulsion took place, led by himself uttering the words: 'Out with the Epicureans!' There followed the confinement of Leto, the birth of Apollo, his marriage to Coronis, and the birth of Asclepius. The second day saw the epiphany of Glycon and the birth of the god. On the third day came the 39 marriage of Podalirius and Alexander's mother. It was called the Feast of Torches and torches were lit. Finally, there was the passion of Selene and Alexander and the birth of Rutilianus' wife. The torch-bearer and presiding priest was Endymion-Alexander. He lay there for all to see, supposedly asleep, while a very attractive girl called Rutilia came down to him from the ceiling, like Selene from heaven. She was the wife of one of the emperor's procurators, she and Alexander really were in love with each other, and there in public they hugged and kissed with her worthless husband looking on. If there had not been so many torches they might well have gone even further. After an interval he came back wearing his priestly robes and amid total silence, and then intoned in a loud voice, 'Hail, Glycon!', while his retinue of pretended Eumolpidae and Ceryces* from Paphlagonia, wearing brogues and belching garlic, gave the response, 'Hail, Alexander!'

Frequently during the torch-procession and the wild leaping of the 40 initiates his thigh was exposed deliberately and seen to be golden, probably because he was wearing gilded leather which reflected the light of the torches. This once led to a discussion about him between two of our clever dicks, on whether his golden thigh meant he had the soul of Pythagoras or another one like it. When this debate was referred to Alexander himself, King Glycon settled the point with an oracle:

> Sometimes the soul of Pythagoras fades, and again has renewal;
> His gift of prophecy comes from the mind of Zeus as its source.
> The father has sent it to us bringing help to all men good and
>   true;
> Then once more to Zeus it returns, when Zeus with his
>   thunderbolt strikes it.

Though he warned everyone to abstain from having sex with 41 boys as being an unholy practice, this prince of virtue had an artful scheme for his own advantage. He used to order the cities of Pontus and Paphlagonia to send him choirboys for a three-year period, to serve him by singing hymns to the god. They had to examine, choose, and send the noblest born, the most youthful and the handsomest. He then kept them locked up and treated them like bought slaves, sleeping with them and using them offensively in every way. It was his habit too never to welcome and embrace anyone over 18 with a kiss on the lips: he gave his hand to others to be kissed, and kissed only those in the bloom of youth, who were said to be 'within the kiss'.

42   Thus he continued to make a mock of simple-minded people, ruining women promiscuously and sleeping with boys. Indeed, it was generally thought a great compliment and highly desirable if he so much as cast a glance at a man's wife; and if he went further and claimed a kiss, the husband thought that his house would be overwhelmed by a flood of good fortune. Many women even boasted that they had borne children by Alexander, and their husbands confirmed the truth of their claims.

43   I'd like to tell you too of a dialogue between Glycon and a certain Sacerdos of Tieion, whose intelligence you can judge from his questions. I read this exchange inscribed in golden letters in Sacerdos' house at Tius.

'Tell me, lord Glycon,' he asked, 'who are you?'
'I am the new Asclepius,' he replied.
'What do you mean—are you different from the old one?'
'It is not proper for you to be told that.'
'How many years will you stay with us giving oracles?'
'One thousand and three.'
'Then where will you go?'
'To Bactra and the country there; for the barbarians too must have the benefit of my presence among them.'
'Do the other shrines at Didyma and Clarus and Delphi still have your father Apollo delivering oracles, or are the responses now given there false?'
'Do not seek to know that: it is not proper either.'
'Who shall I become after my present life?'
'A camel, then a horse, then a sage and a prophet as good as Alexander.'

Such was the exchange between Glycon and Sacerdos, at the end of which he uttered a metrical oracle, knowing that Sacerdos was a follower of Lepidus:

Put no trust in Lepidus, for a pitiful fate does attend him.

That arose from his deep fear of Epicurus, as I said earlier, seeing him
as a rival sophist whose arguments could expose his own chicanery.

In fact he once caused serious danger to an Epicurean who had the 44
courage to show him up in the presence of a large gathering. This
man came forward and said in a loud voice: 'Look here, Alexander,
you induced some Paphlagonian or other to bring his servants on a
capital charge before the governor of Galatia, accusing them of having
murdered his son, who was studying in Alexandria. But the lad is alive
and has returned large as life, after the servants have been executed,
handed over by you to wild beasts.'

The facts were that the lad had sailed up into Egypt as far as
Clysma, where there was a boat putting out to sea, and he was persuaded to join it and go to India. So, since he didn't turn up when
expected, those poor servants of his assumed that the lad had either
perished when sailing on the Nile or been killed by robbers (there
were many around at the time), and they returned to report his disappearance. Then came the oracle and their sentence—followed by the
appearance of the young man with the story of his travels.

This was the man's account of it; but Alexander, stung by the 45
exposure and unable to endure the truth of this rebuke, ordered the
bystanders to stone him, or they themselves would be put under a
curse and be called Epicureans. The stoning had just begun when
a leading citizen of Pontus called Demostratus, who was on a visit
there, threw his arms around the man and rescued him from death.
But he was very nearly stoned to death, and quite right too! What
need had he to be the only sane man among such lunatics, and be on
the receiving end of Paphlagonian stupidity?

So much for him. When the applicants for oracles were being 46
summoned in order, which took place the day before the responses
were given, if it happened to anyone that when the herald asked 'Is
there a prophecy for this man?', the reply from within was 'Go to the
devil', then nobody would ever welcome that man to his home again
or share fire and water with him; but he had to be driven from country
to country as being profane and godless, and an Epicurean, which was
the worst insult of all.

To be sure, one of Alexander's most grotesque performances was 47
this. He got hold of Epicurus' *Basic Doctrines*,* which, as you know, is
the finest of his books and summarizes the main tenets of the man's

creed, and taking it into the centre of the market square he burnt it on a pile of fig-wood, as if he were burning the man himself. He then threw the ashes into the sea, pronouncing the following oracle as he did so:

Consume with fire, I bid you, the senseless old man's doctrines.

The wretched fellow did not realize what a source of blessings that book is for its readers, and what peace, tranquillity, and freedom it produces in them, releasing them from fears, delusions, and prodigies, from vain hopes and excessive desires; instilling under-standing and truth into them, and really purifying their judgments, not with torch and squills* and that sort of rubbish, but with right reasoning, truth, and frank speaking.

48   But of all this scoundrel's escapades let me tell you of one which was the most daring. Having easy access to the palace and the court through the influence there of Rutilianus, he issued an oracle at the height of the war in Germany, when the late emperor Marcus was now fighting it out with the Marcomanni and the Quadi.* The oracle advised that two lions should be thrown alive into the Danube with a lot of spices and splendid offerings. But you had better hear the oracle itself.

Into the stream of Danube, flowing from Zeus as his source,
I command you to throw a pair of those that attend upon Cybele,
Beasts of the mountains; and all that India nurtures
In flowers and sweet-smelling herbs: then straightway will
    come to you
Victory, great glory, and after them peace that is lovely.

However, when these orders had been carried out, the lions swam across to the enemy's shore and the barbarians killed them with clubs, thinking they were some strange kind of dogs or wolves. And what came 'straightway' was a most appalling disaster to our troops, with something like twenty thousand completely destroyed. Then followed the events at Aquileia, when the city narrowly escaped being captured. Alexander dealt with this outcome of the events by feebly producing the Delphic excuse in the case of the oracle given to Croesus:* that the god had predicted victory, but without indicating whether it was to the Romans or their enemies.

49   By now, as crowds were pouring in, causing congestion in their city through the mass of visitors to the shrine, as well as a shortage of

provisions, he devised what he called 'nocturnal oracles'. He took the scrolls and slept on them, so he claimed, and then gave the replies which he supposedly heard from the god in a dream. Most of them were not clear, but confused and ambiguous, especially when he noticed that a scroll had been sealed with particular care. Without taking any risks with these he would put down any answer that occurred to him at random, thinking that this way of doing it was quite fitting for oracles. And there were interpreters sitting there for the purpose of explaining and unravelling these oracles, for which they took large fees from those who had received them. What is more, this activity was subject to a commission, as the interpreters each had to pay Alexander an Attic talent.

Sometimes, to cause astonishment among the simple-minded, he 50 would give an oracle for someone who had neither asked nor sent a question, and didn't even exist, like the following:

> Seek you the man who is secretly thrashing around
> In bed at your home with Calligeneia your wife?
> 'Tis your slave Protogenes, who was utterly trusted by you.
> You once violated him, and now in return on your wife
> He pays off the score for the outrage he suffered himself.
> But against you a sinister charm by them is devised
> To stop you from hearing or seeing whatever they're doing
>   together.
> This you'll find on the floor, right under your bed and close to
>   the wall,
> By the head: and Calypso your maid knows the secret as well.

What Democritus would not have been worried to hear names and places clearly stated, and then soon expressed his contempt when he understood the device?

On another occasion he replied in prose to someone who was not 51 present and didn't even exist, telling him to go back: 'For the man who sent you was killed today by his neighbour Diocles, assisted by the robbers Magnus, Celer, and Bubalus, who have already been caught and locked up.'

He often gave oracles to barbarians as well, if one of them asked a 52 question in his native language, Syrian or Celtic, since he could easily find foreigners in the city of the same race as the questioners. For that reason a long time elapsed between the offering of the scrolls and the response, to give time for them to be opened safely and at leisure, and for people to be found who could translate them all. An example of this type was the following response to a Scythian:

Morphen eubargoulis eis skian chnechikrage leipsei phaos.*

53   I must tell you also of a few replies given to me. When I asked whether Alexander was bald and sealed the scroll with conspicuous care, the reply came as a 'nocturnal oracle':

Sabardalachou malachaattealos en.

On another occasion I asked the same question in two separate scrolls, using different names; 'Where did Homer come from?' In dealing with the first he was deliberately deceived by my servant, who, when asked why he had come, replied, 'To ask for a cure for a pain in the side.' So the reply came:

I advise you anoint it with cytmis along with the foam of a racehorse.

With the second he was told that the sender was enquiring whether he should go to Italy by sea or by land, and his reply had nothing at all to do with Homer:

Venture not over the sea but travel the highways on foot.

54   Indeed I myself set him many traps like these. For instance, once I asked one question, but wrote on the outside of the scroll, in the usual way, 'So-and-so has eight questions', inventing the name and including eight drachmas and whatever extra amount was required. Trusting in the accompanying fee and in the inscription on the scroll, he sent eight responses to my one question: 'When will Alexander be caught cheating?', which, as they say, had no relation to heaven or earth, but were all of them senseless and unintelligible.

He discovered all this later on, and also that I was dissuading Rutilianus from the marriage and from relying so heavily on his hopes raised by the shrine, and this naturally caused him to hate me and regard me as a bitter enemy. Once when Rutilianus enquired about me, he answered:

Gossip while walking at night does he fancy and unchaste copulation.

So altogether I was naturally his bitterest foe.

55   When he found out that I had come to the city and learnt that I was *the* Lucian—I'd also brought with me two soldiers with pike and spear, lent to me by my friend at that time, the governor of

Cappadocia, to escort me as far as the sea—he straightaway sent for me most courteously and with every mark of friendship. I went along and found a lot of people with him, but by good fortune I took my soldiers with me. He offered me his right hand to kiss, as he did to most people, and I grasped it as if to kiss it, but gave him a hearty bite instead, which very nearly crippled his hand.

Even before that the bystanders had been indignant that I had called him 'Alexander' and not 'Prophet', and now they set upon me for sacrilege, strangling me and beating me. But he controlled himself very nobly and made them desist, promising that he would easily tame me and prove Glycon's power, who could turn the harshest enemies into friends. Then he cleared the place of everyone else, and began to remonstrate with me, saying that he knew perfectly well who I was, and all the advice I was giving Rutilianus. 'What are you up to in treating me like this, when I can do a lot to promote your interests with him?' By now I was glad to accept this offer of friendship, seeing what a dangerous position I had got into; and shortly afterwards I came out having made it up with him, and the onlookers were quite astonished at how easily my feelings had changed.

Later, when I decided to set sail—and I happened to have only 56 Xenophon* with me on my visit, having sent my father and my family ahead to Amastris—he supplied me with many gifts and keepsakes, and promised that he himself would provide a boat and crew to escort me. I thought this a decent and kindly offer, but halfway through the voyage I noticed the skipper in tears and arguing with the sailors, and I thought my future prospects were not hopeful. They had had instructions from Alexander to seize and fling us into the sea, which would have ended his war with me then and there. But the skipper in tears persuaded the crew not to commit any terrible crime against us; and he said to me, 'For sixty years, as you see, I've lived a blameless and devout life, and I wouldn't wish at my age, with a wife and children, to stain my hands with blood.' Then he revealed why he had taken us on board, and the orders Alexander had given. He put us 57 ashore at Aegiali (which is mentioned by noble Homer) and then returned home.

There I found some men from the Bosporus sailing along the coast. They were envoys travelling from King Eupator* to Bithynia to deliver their annual tribute, and when I told them of our predicament I had a kindly reception from them, I was taken aboard, and got safely to Amastris, after so nearly losing my life.

After that I began to arm myself against him, and to use every effort in my desire to get my own back. Even before his plot against me, I loathed him and regarded him as a bitter enemy because of his foul character. So I set out to prosecute him, in which I was joined by many others, especially the followers of Timocrates,* the philosopher from Heraclea. But I was restrained by Avitus, the then governor of Bithynia and Pontus, who practically begged and besought me to lay off, because out of goodwill to Rutilianus he could not punish Alexander, however clearly his guilt was proved. Thus I was checked in my impulse, and had to curb my ill-timed zeal before a judge in that frame of mind.

58   And how about this for another consummate act of impudence by Alexander, to request the emperor to change the name of Abonoteichus and call it Ionopolis, and to mint a new coin, engraved on one side with the image of Glycon and on the other with that of Alexander, wearing the wreath of his grandfather Asclepius and holding the scimitar of his maternal forebear Perseus?

59   Though he had predicted in an oracle about himself that he was destined to live to 150, and then die from being struck by lightning, he suffered a most miserable death before he reached 70. Appropriately for a son of Podalirius,* his leg became gangrenous up to the groin and he was infested with maggots. That was when he was discovered to be bald, as he let the doctors put a lotion on his head to ease the pain, which they couldn't have done without removing his wig.

60   So ended Alexander's dramatic career and this was the final scene in his life of play-acting: you might think it looked like the work of Providence, though in fact it was due to chance. It was appropriate too that there were funeral ceremonies worthy of his life—a contest which was set up regarding the shrine. The most conspicuous of his confederates and quacks appointed Rutilianus to decide which of them should have precedence, take over the shrine, and be crowned with the garland of the priest and prophet. One of them was Paetus, a doctor by profession, and grey-haired, though his behaviour suited neither his profession nor his grey hair. But Rutilianus, who had set up the competition, sent them away ungarlanded, and kept the office of prophet for Alexander after his death.

61   These few details as a sample out of many, my friend, I decided to record, partly as a favour to you, my companion and friend, and one whom of all others I most admire for your wisdom, your passion for

truth, the mildness, reasonableness, and serenity of your character, and your courtesy to everyone you meet; but mainly—and this will gratify you even more—to vindicate Epicurus, a man truly hallowed and saintly by nature, who alone rightly understood noble ideals and passed them on, and who was the liberator of all who became his pupils. And I believe that my work will seem to be of some use to its readers by refuting some things, and confirming others, in the minds of men of good sense.

DEMONAX

THIS account of the Cynic philosopher Demonax is one of Lucian's extended discussions of a contemporary sophist or philosopher (cf. *Nigrinus*, *Peregrinus*), and it is our main source for details of his life. The background of the piece is Athens, just as the *Nigrinus* was set in Rome, and the first part records Demonax's birth, education, and early days in Athens. After this we are given a long list of his sayings to illustrate his reputation for clever repartee, and the piece ends with an account of his closing years, death, and burial. The long series of anecdotes which feature Demonax's witty and cutting retorts exemplify a familiar element of ancient rhetorical training, the *chreia* or clever saying which was the punch-line of a moral anecdote. Such anecdotes were one of the preliminary exercises (*progymnasmata*) forming part of the early training in schools of rhetoric, and there are several extant collections of them. It seemed clear too that lists of their *chreiai* neatly illustrated the character and wit of philosophers, and thus they feature in some philosophers' biographies, as we see in the lives recorded by Diogenes Laertius.

The *Demonax* is a late work of Lucian: references to Herodes Atticus suggest a date in the mid- to late 170s.

1   I suppose our generation was bound not to be totally lacking in noteworthy and memorable men, but to produce someone of extraordinary physical powers, and one with a superbly philosophical mind. I refer to the Boeotian Sostratus,* whom the Greeks called and believed to be Heracles, and particularly to the philosopher Demonax. Both of these I saw and marvelled at, and with one of them, Demonax, I was for a long time a student. I have written about Sostratus elsewhere, describing his bulk and enormous strength; how he lived in the open air on Parnassus, slept rough, ate what the mountain provided, and performed deeds which matched his name—killing robbers, and making roads through unbroken country

2   and bridges over impassable places. Now it is fitting to speak of Demonax for two reasons: so I can do what I can to keep him in the memory of the best men, and so that the most high-minded of our youth, who have an urge to philosophy, won't have to train themselves on ancient models only, but can set themselves a standard from our own time too and emulate the man who is the best philosopher known to me.

He came of a Cypriot family, which was not undistinguished in 3 property and public rank. However, he rose above all this, and thinking himself worthy of the best he aspired to philosophy. This was not indeed from any encouragement by Agathoboulos or his predecessor Demetrius or Epictetus, though he attended all these as a student, as well as Timocrates of Heraclea,* a wise man gifted with particular elegance of speech and thought. But, as I said, it was not the encouragement of these men, but his own individual urge to noble things and his innate love for philosophy from early childhood, which moved him to despise all that men call good and to devote himself totally to liberty and freedom of speech. He lived a life which was throughout upright, wholesome, and blameless, and his judgment and philosophical honesty were an example to all who saw and heard him. Certainly he did not rush into this with unwashed feet,* as they 4 say. He was familiar with the poets and knew most of them by heart; he was a practised speaker; and his knowledge of the schools of philosophy was profound, not just as the proverb says, a finger-tip contact. He had exercised his body and trained it in endurance, and generally speaking he had made it his aim not to have any further wants. The result was that when he found he was no longer self-sufficient, he departed this life voluntarily, leaving behind a high reputation among the best of the Greeks.

He did not limit himself to one philosophic creed, but combined 5 many without giving any indication which of them he favoured. Perhaps he was most akin to Socrates, though in his dress and his undemanding life-style he seemed to be emulating the man of Sinope.* He did not falsify the character of his life in order to attract the wonder and admiration of those he met; his life was like everyone else's, and he was simple and completely unaffected in private society and in public life. He did not adopt the irony of Socrates, but his 6 conversation was full of Attic charm, so that his guests went away neither despising him for being boorish nor repelled by any ill-natured criticism, but were taken out of themselves from joy and were much more well-ordered in their lives and cheerful and hopeful of the future. He was never known to raise his voice or get over-excited or 7 angry, even if he had to rebuke somebody; but while he attacked sins he forgave sinners, thinking that we should follow the example of doctors, who heal sickness but do not get angry with the sick. For he considered that while it is human to go wrong, it is for god or a godlike man to help up the fallen.

8   Leading such a life he needed nothing for himself, but he gave appropriate help to his friends. He reminded those who seemed to be smiled on by fortune that they were priding themselves on blessings which were illusory and brief. To others who were lamenting their poverty, complaining about exile, or finding fault with old age or disease, he offered humorous consolation, pointing out how they failed to see that their troubles would soon be over, and that in a little while all of them would find lasting freedom and forgetfulness of all things good and bad.

9   He was also concerned to reconcile disputing brothers and to establish peace between wives and husbands. He even on occasion gave well-timed addresses to disorderly popular assemblies, and persuaded most of them to give due service to their country.

Such was the nature of his philosophy—gentle, mild, and cheerful.

10   Only the illness or death of a friend distressed him, as he thought friendship the greatest of human blessings. For that reason he was a friend to everyone and there was no human being he did not consider akin to him, though he enjoyed the company of some more than others. He only avoided those whose failings seemed to him beyond hope of a cure. And in all these relationships his actions and his words seemed to be blessed by the Graces and by Aphrodite herself, so that always, to quote the comic poet, 'Persuasion sat on his lips'.*

11   So it was that all the Athenians, from the populace to the magistrates, admired him tremendously and never ceased regarding him as a superior being. Yet at the beginning he caused offence to many of them and incurred no less hatred from the common people than Socrates did for his freedom of speech and his independence. There were men like Anytus and Meletus* who connived against him, repeating the same charges that Socrates once faced, that he had never been seen to make a sacrifice, and he was quite alone in never having been initiated in the Eleusinian Mysteries.* His response was with great courage to put on a garland and a clean cloak and go to the Assembly, where he defended himself elegantly, but also more truculently than accorded with the principles he lived by. To the charge of never having sacrificed to Athena he replied, 'Men of Athens, do not be surprised that I have not previously sacrificed to her, for I did not suppose that she needed any sacrifices from me.' To the other charge, about the mysteries, he replied that the reason he had never joined them in the rite was that if the mysteries were

disreputable he would not remain silent to the uninitiate, but discourage them from the rites; and if they were good he would tell the world about them out of general benevolence. The result was that the Athenians, who already had stones in their hands to throw at him, at once became mollified and well-disposed to him, and from that time showed him honour, respect, and eventually admiration. And yet he had started his speech to them with a fairly bitter preamble: 'Men of Athens, you see me ready garlanded: sacrifice me too, for your former victim* brought you no good omens.'

I want to quote some of his witty and well-aimed quips, and I 12 might as well start with Favorinus* and what he said to him. When someone told Favorinus that Demonax was poking fun at his lectures and particularly at their violently broken rhythms, saying that they were vulgar, effeminate, and quite inappropriate to philosophy, he went to Demonax and asked him, 'Who are you to jeer at my lectures?' Demonax replied, 'A man with ears that are not easily fooled.' The sophist persisted and asked him, 'What equipment did your boyhood education give you to take up philosophy?' 'Balls', replied Demonax.

On another occasion the same man went and asked Demonax 13 which philosophical creed he most supported. He replied, 'Why, who told you I'm a philosopher?', and walked away laughing heartily. Favorinus then asked him what he was laughing at, to which he replied, 'I do find it funny that you think men are philosophers if they have beards, when you don't have one yourself.'

When the sophist from Sidon,* who was popular in Athens, was 14 boasting that he was familiar with the whole range of philosophy— but it's better to quote his actual words: 'If Aristotle summons me to the Lyceum, I shall attend him; if Plato asks me to the Academy, I shall go; if Zeno calls, I shall spend time in the Stoa; if Pythagoras summons, I shall keep silence.'* So Demonax stood up in the middle of the audience and said, 'I say', (addressing him by name), 'Pythagoras summons you.'

When a certain Python, a pretty young fellow, who came from one 15 of the grand families in Macedonia, was quizzing him by putting forward a trick question and asking for a logical solution, he replied, 'I know one thing, my boy, the conclusion requires penetration— like you.' The lad was furious at the double-edged jibe, and said threateningly, 'I'll soon show you what a man is.' Demonax laughed and asked him, 'Oh, you have a man, have you?'

16   When an athlete he had made fun of for being seen in flowery clothes, though he was an Olympic champion, struck him on the head with a stone and drew blood, each of the bystanders was as angry as if he himself had been hit, and they cried out, 'Go to the proconsul!' But Demonax said, 'No gentlemen, not to the proconsul—a doctor instead.'

17   One day when he was going for a walk he found a gold ring on the road. He put up a notice in the agora, asking the owner who had lost it to come and reclaim it by describing its weight and the stone and the engraving on it. Well, a pretty young boy came and claimed he had lost it; but nothing he said fitted its description, so Demonax said, 'Off with you, laddie, and take care of your own ring: this one isn't yours!'

18   A Roman senator at Athens introduced his son to him. He was very good-looking, but effeminate and weakly, and when his father said, 'My son here greets you,' Demonax replied, 'A fine lad: he is worthy of you and takes after his mother.'

19   The Cynic who studied philosophy wearing a bearskin he didn't call by his name Honoratus, but Arcesilaus.*

    When someone asked him for his definition of happiness he replied that only the free man is happy; and when the other rejoined
20 that many people were free, he said, 'But I am thinking of the man who has neither hopes nor fears.' 'But how', said the other, 'can you manage this? Generally speaking, we are all slaves to these.' 'Well, if you think about human affairs, you'll find that they don't justify either hope or fear, since in any case pains and pleasures will come to an end.'

21   When Peregrinus Proteus* criticized him for laughing a lot and making fun of people, saying, 'Demonax, you're not doglike',* he replied, 'Peregrinus, you're not manlike.'

22   And there was the scientist who was talking about the Antipodes: he made him get up, and taking him to a well showed him their reflection in the water and asked him, 'Are these the sort of Antipodes you mean?'

23   There was also a man who claimed to be a magician with such powerful spells that they could induce everyone to give him whatever he wanted. 'Nothing to marvel at there,' said Demonax. 'I'm in the same trade as you: come with me, if you like, to the baker's and you'll see me persuade her to give me a loaf with one spell and a little charm'—hinting that a coin is as effective as a spell.

When the great Herodes* was mourning Polydeuces, who died 24 prematurely, and required a chariot to be made ready for him and horses harnessed to it as if the lad were going for a drive, and a meal to be prepared for him, Demonax went to him and said, 'I bring you a message from Polydeuces.' This pleased Herodes, who thought that Demonax, along with everybody else, was sharing his own emotions, and he asked, 'Well, Demonax, what does Polydeuces want?' 'He is finding fault with you,' was the reply, 'for not joining him immediately.'

He also visited a man who was grieving for his dead son and had 25 shut himself up in a dark place, and told him he was a magician who could raise the boy's ghost for him, if he could just name three people who had never grieved for anyone. When the man hesitated and was at a loss for a long time (for I guess he couldn't name any such), Demonax said, 'So, you silly fellow, do you think that you alone are suffering unbearably, even though you can't see anyone who hasn't his share of sorrow?'

Demonax also made a point of mocking those who use strange and 26 very archaic words in conversation. For example, when a man had been questioned by him and replied in exaggerated Attic, he said to him, 'My friend, I asked you a question now, but you reply as though we lived in Agamemnon's time.'

When one of his companions said, 'Demonax, let's go to the 27 Asclepieion* and pray for my son,' he answered, 'You must imagine that Asclepius is very deaf if he can't hear us praying from here.'

He once saw two philosophers debating a topic quite ignorantly, 28 one asking absurd questions and the other giving irrelevant answers. 'Don't you think, my friends,' he said, 'that one of these fellows is milking a he-goat and the other is holding a sieve for him?'*

When Agathocles the Peripatetic* was priding himself on being 29 the first among logicians and quite unique, Demonax said, 'Come, Agathocles, if you are first you can't be unique, and if unique you can't be first.'

When Cethegus* the consular was travelling through Greece to 30 Asia to serve under his father, he said and did many ridiculous things. One of Demonax's friends noting this remarked that he was a great load of rubbish, to which Demonax replied, 'Goodness me, no—not even a great one.'

He saw Apollonius* the philosopher departing with a crowd of his 31 disciples, obeying a summons to be tutor to the emperor, and remarked, 'Apollonius is setting forth with his Argonauts.'

32   When someone asked him if he thought the soul was immortal, he replied, 'Yes—in the sense that everything else is.'

33   Regarding Herodes he remarked that Plato was right in saying that we have more than one soul; for a man with a single soul would not lay dining places for Regilla* and Polydeuces as if they were still living, and also compose the sort of declamations he did.

34   On one occasion when he had heard the proclamation announcing the Mysteries, he was bold enough to ask the Athenians publicly why they excluded foreigners, especially as the founder of their rites, Eumolpus,* was a foreigner and a Thracian.

35   On another occasion he was about to make a sea voyage in winter, and one of his friends asked him, 'Aren't you afraid that the boat may capsize and you'll be food for the fishes?' His reply was, 'I would be ungrateful if I grudged the fishes eating me, when I've eaten so many of them.'

36   He advised an orator who had delivered an appalling declamation to practise and exercise; and when he replied, 'I am always reciting to myself', Demonax told him, 'Then it's no wonder your speech is like that, if you have a fool for a listener.'

37   Again, he once saw a soothsayer giving prophecies in public for money, and said to him, 'I don't see on what ground you ask for money. If you believe you can alter destiny at all, whatever you charge is too little; but if everything is decreed by god, what is the point of your soothsaying?'

38   When an elderly but powerfully built Roman gave him an exhibition of armed combat against a post, and asked him, 'What do you think of my fighting skills, Demonax?', he replied, 'Excellent—provided you have an opponent made of wood.'

39   And see what shrewd replies he had ready in answer to trick questions. When someone asked him mockingly, 'If I burnt a thousand pounds of wood, Demonax, how many pounds of smoke would that come to?', he replied, 'Weigh the ashes, and all the rest will be smoke.'

40   There was a certain Polybius,* completely uneducated and ill-spoken, who said, 'The emperor has honoured me with Roman citizenship.' To which Demonax responded, 'If only he'd made you a Greek rather than a Roman.'

41   When he saw a grandee priding himself on the width of his purple band, he took hold of the garment, and pointing it out to him whispered in his ear, 'Don't forget, a sheep wore this before you—and stayed a sheep.'

He was taking a bath and hesitating to step into the steaming water, 42
when somebody accused him of cowardice. 'Tell me,' he said, 'was I
expected to endure this for my country's sake?'

When someone asked him, 'What do you think things are like in 43
Hades?', he answered, 'Hang on a bit, and I'll send you a report from
there.'

A ghastly poet, Admetus,* told him he had written a one-line 44
epitaph and had left instructions in his will for it to be inscribed on
his tombstone—I might as well quote it:

'Receive, O Earth, Admetus' shell: to the gods himself has gone.'
Demonax roared with laughter and said, 'It's such a good epitaph,
Admetus, I wish it was already inscribed.'

Somebody noticed marks on his legs of the sort that older people 45
usually get, and asked, 'What's this, Demonax?' He grinned and
replied, 'Charon* bit me.'

Then there was the Spartan he saw beating his slave. 'Stop treating 46
him as your social equal',* he told him.

When a woman called Danae was having a dispute with her brother, 47
he said to her, 'Have the law on him! You are Danae, but not the
daughter of Acrisius.'*

He particularly attacked those who indulge in philosophy not to 48
find the truth but simply to show off. For instance, he saw a Cynic
with his cloak and pouch, but carrying a cudgel (*hyperon*) instead of a
staff, and bawling out that he was a follower of Antisthenes and Crates
and Diogenes. 'Don't lie,' said Demonax, 'you're really a disciple of
Hyperides.'*

When he saw a lot of athletes fighting foul, and against the rules of 49
the games biting instead of boxing and wrestling, he said, 'It's not
surprising that nowadays their supporters call athletes lions.'

Then there was that witty and cutting remark he made to a pro- 50
consul, who followed the practice of those who use pitch-plasters to
depilate their legs and their whole bodies. A certain Cynic had stood
up on a platform and accused him insultingly of effeminacy, at which
he angrily ordered him to be pulled down, and was about to put him
in the stocks or even punish him with exile, when Demonax, who
happened to be present, urged him to pardon the man, as he was just
indulging in the bold outspokenness characteristic of the Cynics. The
proconsul said, 'Well, I'll let him off this time for you, but if he dares
to do such a thing again what punishment will he deserve?' 'Order
him to be depilated,' replied Demonax.

51   He was asked by a man to whom the emperor had entrusted the command of legions and a most important province, how he should best exercise authority. 'Without losing your temper,' said Demonax, 'and with little talking but a lot of listening.'

52   When he was asked if he ate honey-cakes, he replied, 'Do you really think that bees produce their honey for fools?'

53   He saw a statue near the Painted Stoa* with a hand cut off, and remarked that the Athenians had taken a long time to honour Cynegirus with a bronze statue.

54   Note too his remark about Rufinus the Cypriot*—I mean the lame disciple of Aristotle—when he saw him spending much time in the covered walks of the school: 'There's nothing more impudent than a lame Peripatetic.'

55   When Epictetus reproached him and advised him to marry and have children, saying that it was right for a philosopher to leave behind a natural substitute for himself, Demonax demolished him utterly with the reply, 'All right, Epictetus, give me one of your daughters.'

56   Again, his response to Herminus* the Aristotelian is worth recording. Knowing that he was a complete scoundrel, whose crimes were legion, and yet he was always talking of Aristotle and his ten categories, Demonax said, 'Herminus, you really deserve ten categories of punishment.'

57   When the Athenians, through rivalry with the Corinthians, were considering holding a gladiatorial show, he went to them and said, 'Don't vote for this, Athenians, without first pulling down the Altar of Pity.'*

58   When he went to Olympia and the Eleans voted him a bronze statue, he said, 'Don't do this, men of Elea, lest you seem to be reproaching your ancestors for not putting up statues to Socrates or Diogenes.'

59   I once heard him saying to a certain jurist that laws run the risk of being useless, whether they are established for bad men or for good men. For the latter don't need laws, and the former are not made better by them.

60   His favourite line to quote from Homer was:

      The idler and the toiler both come to death alike.*

61   He even praised Thersites,* calling him a Cynic demagogue.

62   When asked which philosopher he approved of he replied, 'They

are all admirable, but personally I honour Socrates, I admire Diogenes, and I love Aristippus.'*

He lived to be nearly a hundred, without illness or pain, troubling 63 nobody and asking no favours, helping his friends, and never making a single enemy. Not only the Athenians but the whole of Greece had such an affection for him, that when he was passing by the magistrates rose up in his honour and everyone fell silent. At the end, when very old he would eat and sleep uninvited in any house he happened to pass, and the occupants would think this some sort of divine visitation, and that a good spirit had entered their house. As he walked past bread-sellers, they would pull him towards them, each wanting him to take her bread, and the one who managed to give him some thought this was her own good fortune. And children too brought him fruit and called him father.

Once when there was some political strife in Athens, he entered the 64 Assembly and just by appearing there he produced total silence. Then seeing that they were now ashamed of themselves he left without saying a word.

When he became aware that he could no longer look after himself, 65 he quoted to his companions the verses spoken by the heralds when closing the games:

> Now ends the contest that gives out the fairest of prizes:
> The time calls you all to delay not your going.*

Then he abstained from food altogether and departed from life as cheerfully as he had always appeared to anyone he met. Shortly before 66 the end someone asked him, 'What are your instructions about your funeral?' 'Don't go to any trouble,' he said, 'the stench will cause me to be buried.' The man went on to say, 'But surely it would be unseemly to expose to the birds and dogs the body of such a distinguished man?' Demonax replied, 'It's not in the least disgusting if even when I'm dead I can be of use to living creatures.' However, the 67 Athenians gave him a splendid public funeral and mourned him for a long time; and as a mark of honour to him they would bow down before and put garlands on the stone seat where he used to rest when he was tired, thinking that even the stone on which he sat was sacred. Absolutely everyone attended the funeral, especially the philosophers. Indeed it was they who carried him on their shoulders to the grave.

These are just a few of the many things I could have mentioned, but they can give my readers a clear idea of the sort of man he was.

LOVERS OF LIES OR THE SCEPTIC

THIS piece shows Lucian indulging in two of his favourite pursuits, an attack on superstition and magic and the telling of stories. The narrator Tychiades tells a friend of his visit to the house of Eucrates, where he finds a group already assembled which includes three philosophers and a doctor. Eucrates and his friends are all believers in the supernatural, and they make a concerted effort to shake Tychiades' robust scepticism towards such beliefs. They try to win him over by a series of seven tales, which form the most attractive part of the piece, and include the famous story now commonly called 'The Sorcerer's Apprentice'. Tychiades remains unmoved and departs, disgusted at their gullibility. This attack on superstitious beliefs includes a familiar Lucianic side-swipe at professional philosophers, since two of the story-tellers are philosophers, Ion a Platonist and Arignotus a Pythagorean, who by implication should have known better.

Some of the stories can be traced to other literary sources. Eucrates' story of his meeting with Hecate has elements from Plato (*Republic* 359d ff.) and Heraclides Ponticus (fr. 93 Wehrli), and his account of his wife's ghost is derived from Herodotus (5. 92). Arignotus' account of laying a ghost recalls Pliny the Younger's similar story (*Epistles* 7. 27). The reverse is true of 'The Sorcerer's Apprentice': it has no known parallels in antiquity, but it later caught the fancy of minds as widely different as those of Goethe and Paul Dukas.

The form of the piece is a familiar Lucianic variant of a dialogue framing an extended narration.

1 TYCHIADES. Can you tell me, Philocles, what on earth induces many people to be so keen on lying that they love to talk utter nonsense themselves, and they pay particular attention to those who do the same?

PHILOCLES. There are many causes, Tychiades, that sometimes compel men to tell lies with an eye to profiting from them.

T. That's not to the purpose, as they say, and I wasn't asking about those who lie for profit. They at least have some excuse; indeed some of them even deserve praise, those who have deceived enemies, or used this as a means to safety in a terrible crisis, as Odysseus often did when trying to save his own life and secure a return for his comrades. No, my good fellow, I'm referring to those who regard sheer pointless lying as far preferable to the truth, enjoying doing it and spending their time thus for no compelling reason. It's these men I want to know about—what they gain by doing this.

P. You really have noticed such people, with this deep-rooted passion   2
for falsehood?

T. Yes indeed, a great many.

P. Well, what other reason can you say they have for not telling the truth than stupidity, since they deliberately make the worst choice instead of the best?

T. That is not relevant either, Philocles, for I could show you lots of people who are in other respects sensible and admirably intelligent, but have somehow been gripped by this evil and become lovers of lying; so that it grieves me that such men, who are the best of fellows in every way, still take delight in deceiving themselves and their associates. You must know those examples of long ago better than I do—Herodotus and Ctesias of Cnidos,* and before them the poets and Homer himself, famous men who employed the written lie, so that not only those who listened to them at the time were deceived, but through successive generations the lie has come down even to us, preserved by the supreme beauty of its phrasing and metre. As for me, I often feel ashamed for them when they describe the castration of Uranus, and the shackling of Prometheus, and the rebellion of the Giants, and the whole grim performance in Hades; and how Zeus turned into a bull or a swan to gratify a passion,* and how some woman was transformed into a bird or a bear;* and also when they describe Pegasuses and Chimaeras and Gorgons and Cyclopes and so on, utterly uncouth and monstrous fictions, fit to beguile the minds of children who are still afraid of Mormo and Lamia.*

And yet, perhaps we can put up with the poets' performances;   3
but when even cities and entire peoples tell lies publicly and in common, is it not ludicrous? The Cretans unblushingly point out the tomb of Zeus, and the Athenians tell you that Erichthonius* sprang from the earth and that the first men were produced from the Attic ground like vegetables. But their story at least is much more respectable than the Thebans' tale of how 'Sown Men' shot up from a serpent's teeth.* But if anyone thinks these ridiculous stories are untrue, and after putting them to the test of common sense considers that only a Coroebus or a Margites* would believe that Triptolemus* drove through the air on winged serpents, or

that Pan came from Arcadia to join the fight at Marathon, or that Oreithyia was snatched away by Boreas,* they regard this man as a blasphemous fool for disbelieving such obvious truths: so widely does falsehood prevail.

4 P. Well, Tychiades, we might pardon the poets and the cities. The poets put into their writings the most alluring charm their stories can produce, which is something they need most of all to win over their listeners; while the Athenians and Thebans and maybe others use these means to make their countries more distinguished. Indeed, if you took away these elements of fable from Greece nothing could prevent the local guides from starving to death, as visitors would not want to listen to the truth even for free. However, those who without such a motive take pleasure in falsehood could reasonably be regarded as totally ridiculous.

5 T. Quite right. Here am I, just come to you from Eucrates the great, and having listened to a heap of incredibly tall stories. To be honest, I made off while they were still talking, as I couldn't stand the way things were getting exaggerated: they were like the Furies, driving me away with their endless accounts of absurd prodigies.

P. And yet Eucrates is a trustworthy fellow, Tychiades, and no one would believe that he, a 60-year-old with a long beard, and what's more, practised in philosophy, would put up with listening to somebody else telling lies in his presence, let alone venturing to do so himself.

T. You don't know the sort of things he was saying, my friend, how he proved them and even took his oath on most of them, producing his children as witnesses; so that as I observed him I had all sorts of different thoughts. At one moment I thought he had lost his composure and gone mad; at another, that he was just a fraud, and all this time I hadn't realized that there was a silly ape under the lion's skin: the tales he told were so ridiculous.

P. In Hestia's name,* Tychiades, what were they? I'd like to know what kind of humbug he was hiding behind that long beard.

6 T. I used to go and see him at other times, Philocles, whenever I had a lot of spare time; and today, as I wanted to meet Leontichus—a good friend of mine, as you know—and his slave told me he had gone off early to visit Eucrates who was ill, I went to his house for two reasons, to find Leontichus and to see Eucrates, as I hadn't known he was ill.

I didn't find Leontichus there (they said he had just left), but lots of others, including Cleodemus the Peripatetic, Deinomachus the Stoic, and Ion—you know, the one who thinks he deserves admiration for his grasp of Plato's theories, as the only man who really understands his thinking and can expound it to the rest of us. You see what sort of men I am telling you about, all-wise, all-virtuous, the leading light of each school, all of them venerable and almost frightening to behold? The doctor Antigonus was there too, summoned, I imagine, because of the illness. Indeed, Eucrates already seemed to be recovering, and his ailment was a long-standing one: rheumatism had again afflicted him in his feet.

He told me to sit beside him on the couch, lowering his voice a little as befits an invalid when he saw me, though as I came in I had heard him shouting and earnestly arguing some point. I was very careful not to touch his feet; and making the usual excuses that I didn't know he was ill and the moment I heard I'd come running, I sat down beside him.

I think the group had already been having a long discussion 7 about his illness, and they were then still at it, each one suggesting his own remedy. At any rate, Cleodemus said, 'Well, if you pick up from the ground in your left hand the tooth of a shrew which has been killed as I have described, wrap it in the skin of a lion which has recently been flayed, and tie it round your legs, the pain stops at once.'

'Not in a lion's skin, as I've heard,' said Deinomachus, 'but that of a young female deer, still unmated; and that makes better sense, for the deer is swift and particularly strong in the legs. The lion is brave, and his fat and his right paw and the straight bristles from his beard are very potent, if you know how to use each of them with the appropriate incantation. But for curing feet he doesn't promise much.'

'I too,' said Cleodemus, 'used to believe that it had to be the skin of a deer, because the deer is swift; but the other day a Libyan, who knows about these things, taught me differently by pointing out that lions are swifter than deer. "Of course," he said, "they pursue and catch them."'

Those present commended the Libyan's words as being correct; 8 but I said, 'Do you really believe that such ailments can be banished by certain incantations, or by external appendages, when the trouble is firmly established internally?' They laughed at my words, and obviously judged me to be extremely stupid, if I didn't understand the clearest facts which nobody in his right mind would deny. But the doctor Antigonus seemed to be pleased with my question; for I suppose he had been ignored for a long time, though he thought he was the one entitled to use his skill to help Eucrates, by urging him to abstain from wine, to be a vegetarian, and generally to reduce his stress level.

But Cleodemus, smiling faintly, said, 'What do you mean, Tychiades? Do you think it incredible that diseases are alleviated by such remedies?'

'Yes, I do,' I replied, 'since I'm not such a drivelling idiot as to believe that external applications, which have no connection with the internal causes of the disease, and are applied, as you say, along with set formulas and wizardry, have any power to produce a cure. That would be impossible, even if you wrapped sixteen whole shrews in the skin of the Nemean lion. Indeed, I have often seen a lion himself limping from pain, with his own skin covering him!'

9   'You are just an amateur,' said Deinomachus, 'and you haven't bothered to learn how such things when applied can benefit diseases. I don't imagine you would accept even the clearest cases, where periodic fevers are banished, snakes are charmed, swollen glands are cured, and everything else that old wives also achieve. But if all that happens, why ever do you not believe that this happens by similar means?'

'That is a false conclusion, Deinomachus,' I replied, 'and, as they say, you are knocking out one nail with another:* for it is not clear that these things you mention happen through such an agency. So, unless you can first prove to me logically that they happen in this way naturally, that the fever or the swelling is afraid of a holy name or an outlandish formula and therefore flees from the gland, I'll still regard what you say as old wives' tales.'

10   'When you talk like that,' said Deinomachus, 'it seems to me you don't even believe in the gods, if you don't think that cures can be achieved through sacred names.'

'Don't say that, my good fellow,' I replied; 'even if the gods exist, that doesn't preclude such practices being false. For myself, I honour the gods, and I note their cures and all the good they do in healing the sick by drugs and medical skill. Indeed, Asclepius* himself and his sons treated the sick by applying soothing drugs, not by fastening lion-skins and shrews onto them.'

'Never mind him,' said Ion, 'and I'll tell you a strange story. 11
When I was still a lad of about 14, someone came and told my
father that Midas the vine-dresser, who was usually a strong and
hard-working servant, had been bitten by a viper and was lying
down, with his leg already festering. While he was tying up the
shoots and twisting them round the poles, the beast crawled up and
bit him on his big toe; then it quickly disappeared down its hole,
while he was left groaning in mortal agony.

'While this news was being reported we saw Midas himself being
carried up on a litter by his fellow-slaves: he was swollen all over
and livid, his skin was clammy, and he was scarcely still breathing.
Of course my father was very upset, but one of his friends who
was there said, "Have no fear: I'll immediately go and fetch a
Babylonian, one of the Chaldeans, as they call them, who will heal
the man." In short, the Babylonian came and restored Midas,
driving the poison from his body with a spell; and he also bound
onto his foot a fragment he broke off from the tombstone of a dead
girl.

'Nothing strange in that perhaps, though Midas himself picked
up the litter he'd been carried on and went away to the farm:
so powerful was the spell and that piece of tombstone. But the 12
Babylonian did other things too which were truly marvellous. Early
next morning he went to the farm, pronounced seven sacred names
from an old book, went round the place three times, purifying it
with sulphur and torches, and summoned forth all the reptiles
that were within its boundaries. They came as though drawn to the
spell, numerous snakes, asps and vipers and horned serpents and
darters, as well as ordinary toads and puff-toads. One old serpent
remained, which because of its age, I suppose, couldn't creep out
and so disregarded the command. The wizard said they weren't
all there, and choosing the youngest of the snakes sent it as a
messenger to the serpent, and presently it too arrived. When they
were all gathered together the Babylonian blew on them, and at
once they were all burned to a cinder by the blast, to our utter
amazement.'

'Tell me, Ion,' I said, 'did that young snake, the messenger, lead 13
the serpent by the hand, as you say he was now very old, or did he
have a stick to support himself?'

'You'll have your joke,' said Cleodemus; 'I myself used to be even
more sceptical than you in such matters, as I thought there was no

rational reason for them to happen; but when I first saw the foreign stranger flying—he said he was a Hyperborean*—after resisting for a long time I was defeated and I believed. For what could you do when you saw him flying through the air in broad daylight, and walking on water, and treading slowly through fire?'

'You did see that?' I said, 'the Hyperborean flying or walking on water?'

'Yes, indeed,' he said, 'wearing brogues in the manner of his countrymen. For why should I go through all the minor powers he displayed, sending passionate feelings upon people, summoning up daemons, restoring mouldy corpses to life, making Hecate herself appear in full view, and pulling down the moon? Still, I will tell you what I saw him do in the house of Glaucias, son of Alexicles.

'Glaucias' father had lately died and he came into the property, and fell in love with Chrysis, the wife of Demeas. He employed me as his tutor in philosophy, and if that affair had not distracted him he would by now have mastered all the Peripatetic teachings, since even when only 18 he was solving problems in logic and had completed a lecture course on physics. But he was desperate about his love-affair and told me all about it; so acting as was natural as his tutor, I brought that Hyperborean wizard to him, for a fee of four minas down payment—I had to pay something in advance for the cost of the sacrifices—and sixteen if he managed to get Chrysis. He waited for the moon to wax, as that is the time that these rites are usually practised, and then he dug a pit in the open area of the house, and about midnight he summoned up to us first of all Alexicles, Glaucias' father, who had died seven months earlier. The old man was annoyed about the love-affair and showed his anger, but at length allowed him to indulge his passion. Then he produced Hecate, bringing Cerberus with her; and he drew down the moon, a many-shaped vision, showing different appearances at different times. For first she seemed to be the shape of a woman; then she became a splendid-looking bull; and after that a puppy. At length the Hyperborean made a little clay Cupid and said, "Go and bring Chrysis." The clay flew off, and in a short while she was standing there, knocking at the door; she came in and embraced Glaucias as if she was madly in love with him, and made love to him until cock-crow. Then the moon flew up the heavens, Hecate sank back into the earth, the other phantoms disappeared, and we sent Chrysis back just about dawn. If you'd seen all that,

Tychiades, you'd no longer have doubted the many advantages there are in spells.'

'You're right,' I said, 'I would have believed if I'd seen it; but as it is, I think I may be forgiven if I'm not as sharp-sighted as you all. But I do know the Chrysis you mention, a sexy lady and available; so I don't see why you needed the clay messenger and the Hyperborean wizard and the moon herself to get her, when for twenty drachmas you could have brought her to the Hyperboreans. The lady has a weakness for that particular spell, and reacts in the opposite way to phantoms: if they hear the rattle of bronze or iron they fly away—or so you say: but if there's a rattle of silver any-where she follows the sound of it. And I'm particularly surprised at the wizard, if he himself could win the love of the richest women and take whole talents off them, and yet was penny-pinching enough to make Glaucias desirable for just four minas.'

'You're being ridiculous,' said Ion, 'to be sceptical about every- 16 thing. For my part I'd like to ask you what you have to say about those who free the possessed of their terrors by openly banishing the daemons by spells. I don't need to elaborate: everyone knows about the Syrian from Palestine,* the expert in this art, and how he takes all those who collapse at the sight of the moon, rolling their eyes and foaming at the mouth, and restores them and sends them away sound of mind, having relieved them of their terrors for a large fee. When he stands by them as they lie there and asks whence the daemons came into their bodies, the sick man is silent, but the daemon replies, in Greek or its native foreign language, saying how and when it came into the man. Then, laying an oath on the daemon, or if it doesn't obey, threatening it, he drives it out. In fact, I actually saw one emerging, black and smoke-coloured.'

'It's not very impressive for you to see such things, Ion,' I said, 'since even the Forms* which your mentor Plato describes are clear to your view, though a pretty faint sight to those of us with weaker eyes.'

'Is it only Ion who has seen such things,' said Eucrates, 'and 17 haven't lots of other people come across spirits, some by night and some by day? Why, I've seen such things not once but almost countless times. At first I was shaken at the encounter, but now of course, having got used to it I don't think I am seeing anything odd, especially after the Arab gave me the iron ring made from crosses and taught me a spell using many names—unless you're going to distrust me too, Tychiades?'

'How could I distrust Eucrates, the son of Deinon,' I replied, 'a learned gentleman who is expressing his views in his own home as he is entitled to do?'

18   'At any rate,' said Eucrates, 'the episode of the statue was seen every night by everyone in the house, children, young men, and old folk, and you can hear about it not just from me but from all our people.'

'What's this about a statue?' I asked.

'Didn't you see as you came in a very fine statue in the courtyard, made by Demetrius* the portrait-sculptor?'

'Do you mean the discus-thrower,' I asked, 'who is bending forward in the act of throwing, looking back at the hand holding the discus, one leg slightly bent, and seemingly about to rise up as he makes his throw?'

'Not that one,' he replied: 'that is one of Myron's* pieces, the discus-thrower, you are talking about. Nor do I mean the one beside it, the man tying a band on his head—a handsome figure, for this is the work of Polyclitus.* Ignore those on the right as you go in, which include the tyrant-slayer fashioned by Critius and Nesiotes.* But if you noticed one near the fountain, a balding, pot-bellied figure, his body partly revealed by his cloak, some hairs in his beard blowing in the wind, and with prominent veins, the very picture of a man, that's the one I'm talking about: it's believed to be Pellichus,* the Corinthian general.'

19   'Yes,' I replied, 'I did see one to the right of the fountain, wearing ribbons and faded wreaths, and gilded leaves on his chest.'

'I myself gilded them,' said Eucrates, 'when he cured me of a tertian fever which was killing me.'

'So, was our noble Pellichus a doctor too?' I asked.

'He is,' said Eucrates, 'and you'd better not mock the man, or he'll soon be after you. I know the power of this statue that you are making fun of. Don't you imagine that he can inflict fevers on those he wants to, as well as banishing them?'

'May the statue be propitious and kindly,' I said, 'since he is so manly. But what else does all your household see him doing?'

'As soon as night falls,' he replied, 'he comes down from the pedestal he stands on and makes a circuit of the house. We all meet him; sometimes he is singing and he has never harmed anyone. You only have to move aside and he passes by without troubling those who saw him. What's more, he often enjoys himself having a bath all night long, so you can hear the water splashing.'

'Well, look here,' I said, 'maybe the statue isn't Pellichus, but Talos* the Cretan, the son of Minos: he was made of bronze and patrolled around Crete. If he were made of wood and not bronze, there would be no reason for him not to be a work by Demetrius but one of Daedalus' handiworks. Anyway, from what you say, he too runs away from his pedestal.'*

'Watch out, Tychiades,' he rejoined, 'that you don't repent of your joke afterwards. I know what happened to the man who filched the obols we offer him on the first of every month.'

'It must have been something pretty awful,' said Ion, 'since it was an act of sacrilege. So how was he punished, Eucrates? I'd like to hear, however sceptical Tychiades here is going to be.'

'Many obols,' he replied, 'were lying at his feet, and some other silver coins were stuck with wax to his thigh, and some leaves of silver, thank-offerings or payment for treatment from those whom he had cured of a fever. We had a rascally Libyan servant, a groom, who attempted to steal everything there, and did so, by waiting for the statue to step down. But as soon as Pellichus returned and realized he had been robbed, see how he caught and punished the Libyan thief. The wretched fellow ran around the courtyard in circles all night long unable to get out, as if caught in a labyrinth, until at day-break he was caught with the stolen goods on him. He was then given a good thrashing; nor did he live long afterwards, but died wretchedly from being flogged every night, he said, so that the weals showed on his body the next day. So, Tychiades, go on mocking Pellichus, and think me as senile as if I was as old as Minos.'

'Well, Eucrates,' I replied, 'as long as bronze is bronze and the work is by Demetrius of Alopece, who made men not gods, I won't ever fear the statue of Pellichus, whom I wouldn't have feared even if he was alive and threatening me.'

At this point Antigonus the doctor said, 'I actually have a bronze Hippocrates, Eucrates, about eighteen inches high. As soon as the candles are put out, he wanders all around the house, making noises, upsetting boxes, mixing up the drugs, knocking over the mortar, especially when we are late with our annual sacrifice to him.'

'Really,' I said, 'does even Hippocrates expect sacrifices and get angry if he doesn't feast punctually on unblemished victims? He ought to be satisfied if anyone sacrificed at his tomb or offered him a libation of milk and honey or put a wreath on his gravestone.'

22   'Well,' said Eucrates, 'you must listen to what I saw five years ago—and I have witnesses to prove it. It happened to be the season of the vintage, and making my way through the farm at midday, I left the grape-gatherers behind and went off alone into the wood while I pondered over something in my thoughts. When I was in the shade, first there was the sound of dogs barking, and I assumed that my son Mnason was as usual hunting with hounds and had come into the undergrowth with his companions. But this proved to be wrong, and shortly afterwards there was an earthquake and simultaneously a noise like thunder, and I saw a fearful-looking woman approaching, about three hundred feet tall. She had a torch in her left hand and a sword in her right thirty feet long; her feet below were snakes, while her upper form resembled the Gorgon, I mean her gaze and the frightfulness of her aspect. Instead of hair she had snakes which fell down like clusters of grapes, curling round her neck and some of them bunching up on her shoulders. Look, my friends,' he said, 'how I shudder even as I talk about it.'

23   And as he spoke Eucrates showed us the hairs on his arm actually standing on end from fright. Ion, Deinomachus, and Cleodemus, were hanging on his words with open-mouthed attention, old men led by the nose, almost worshipping such an unbelievable colossus, a three-hundred-foot woman, a monstrous hobgoblin! Meanwhile, I was reflecting on what sort of men these were, who associate with the young to give them wisdom and are admired by many, but are only different from infants by their white hair and their beards, and in other respects are even more readily taken in by lies than infants.

24   For example, Deinomachus said, 'Tell me, Eucrates, how big were the goddess's dogs?'

'Taller than Indian elephants,' he replied, 'and like them they were black, with rough coats of squalid, dirty hair. Well, when I saw her I stopped, and at the same time I turned the gem which the Arab gave me to the inside of my finger. Hecate stamped on the ground with her snake foot and caused a huge chasm to appear, as deep as Tartarus, and shortly after she jumped into it and disappeared. I took courage and leaned over, hanging on to a nearby tree in case I got dizzy and fell in headlong. Then I could see everything in Hades, the Blazing-Fire River, the lake, Cerberus, and the dead: some of these I recognized, like my father, whom I saw clearly still wearing the same clothes in which we buried him.'

'What were the souls doing, Eucrates?' asked Ion.

'What else,' he replied, 'than spending their time with their friends and relatives, lying on the asphodel grouped in tribes and clans?'

'So,' said Ion, 'let the Epicureans go on contradicting inspired Plato and his teaching about souls.* But did you not see Socrates himself as well and Plato among the dead?'

'I saw Socrates,' he replied, 'though I wasn't even sure of him, but guessed it from his baldness and pot-belly. I didn't recognize Plato, for I suppose one should tell friends the truth.

'Just as I had had a good clear view of everything, the chasm began to close up, and some of the servants who were looking for me, including Pyrrhias here, arrived before it had completely closed. Tell them if I'm telling the truth, Pyrrhias.'

'Yes, indeed you are,' said Pyrrhias, 'and I heard barking too through the chasm, and there was a gleam of fire, which I suppose came from the torch.'

It made me laugh to hear the witness throwing in for good measure the barking and the fire. But Cleodemus said, 'These 25 things you saw are not strange or invisible to others, for I too, when I was ill not long ago, saw something similar. Antigonus here was visiting and looking after me. It was the seventh day and the fever was burning me up at its worst. Everyone had left me alone, shutting the door and waiting outside: for those were your orders, Antigonus, to give me a chance to get some sleep. Well, then it was as I lay awake that a very handsome young man stood beside me, dressed in a white cloak. Raising me up he led me through a chasm to Hades, as I realized straightaway on seeing Tantalus and Tityus and Sisyphus.* I'll spare you all the details; but when I got to the court, where Aeacus, Charon, the Fates and the Furies were all present, a sort of royal figure, Pluto I imagine, sat reading out the names of those about to die because they were now past the term of their lives. The young man took me up to him, but Pluto became angry and said to my guide, "The thread of his life is not yet complete: let him depart, and bring me Demylus the coppersmith, for he is living beyond his appointed span." I hastened back in great delight, and from then on the fever left me, but I told everyone that Demylus was going to die. He was a neighbour of ours and reported to be ill, and shortly afterwards we heard mourners lamenting him.'

26   'What's strange about that?' said Antigonus; 'I know someone who came back to life more than twenty days after he was buried, having looked after him both before his death and after his return to life.'

'And how', I asked, 'did his body not decay in twenty days or just waste away from lack of nourishment, unless your patient was an Epimenides?'*

27   While we were talking about all this, Eucrates' sons came in from the gymnasium, one already a young man and the other about 15 years old. They greeted us and sat down on the couch by their father, while a chair was brought up for me. Eucrates, as though reminded by the sight of his sons, said, 'As I hope for blessings from these boys,' laying his hand on them, 'what I'm going to tell you, Tychiades, is the truth. Everyone knows how much I loved their mother of blessed memory: I made that clear by what I did for her not only when she was alive, but when she died too, as I burned on the pyre with her all the finery and the clothes she delighted in while she lived. On the seventh day after she died I was lying on the couch here, as I am now, consoling myself for my loss by quietly reading Plato's book on the soul.* While I was doing this, Demainete herself came in and sat down beside me, where Eucratides here is now sitting', pointing to his younger son, who immediately shuddered just as a child does, and had already turned pale listening to the story. 'When I saw her,' Eucrates resumed, 'I embraced her with tears and cries of sorrow; but she wouldn't let me cry out, and instead reproached me because, although I had freely offered her everything else, I had not burned one of her gold sandals, which she said had fallen under the chest. That was why we hadn't found it and only burned one of them. While we were still talking a wretched Maltese puppy* under the couch gave a bark, and she vanished at the sound of it. However, the sandal was found under the chest and subsequently burned.

28   'Can one any longer justly doubt these phenomena, Tychiades, when they are clearly seen and happen every day?'

'Goodness me, no,' I replied, 'and those who doubt and are so disrespectful in the face of the truth ought to have their bottoms spanked—with a gold sandal.'

At this point Arignotus the Pythagorean came in, the one with 29 the long hair and a stately look: you know him, he's famous for his wisdom and nicknamed 'holy'. When I saw him I breathed a sigh of relief, thinking that this was a battle-axe come to help me against their lies. The wise man, I said, would put a curb on their monstrous stories; and I thought that Fortune had wheeled him in to me, like the proverbial *deus ex machina*. But when Cleodemus had made room to give him a seat, he began by enquiring about the illness, and when Eucrates told him he was already feeling better, he asked, 'What were you discussing among yourselves? I heard you as I came in, and I thought you were about to direct your discourse towards an uplifting topic.'

'Our only object', said Eucrates, pointing to me, 'is to persuade this man of adamant to believe that spirits and phantoms exist, and that the souls of the dead do go around on earth and appear to those they choose.'

I blushed and bowed my head in respect for Arignotus. 'But look, Eucrates,' he said, 'maybe Tychiades just means that only the souls of those who died violently wander around, for instance if someone hanged himself, or was beheaded, or crucified, or died in some such way; but the souls of those who died naturally do not. If that is his meaning we can't quite dismiss what he says.'

'No, indeed,' said Deinomachus, 'he doesn't believe such things exist at all or can be seen in bodily shape.'

'What do you mean?' said Arignotus, looking at me sharply. 30 'Do you think none of these things happen, though pretty well everyone sees them?'

'You could plead on my behalf,' I replied, 'if I don't believe in them, that I alone don't see them. If I did see them, then obviously I would believe in them, as you all do.'

'Well,' he said, 'if you ever go to Corinth ask for the house of Eubatides, and when it is shown to you by the Cherry Grove, go in and tell the doorman Tibius that you'd like to see the place where Arignotus the Pythagorean dug up the spirit and drove it away, making the house habitable after that.'

'What's that all about, Arignotus?' asked Eucrates. 31

'It was uninhabitable for ages,' he said, 'because of terrifying occurrences. If anyone went to live there he immediately fled in panic, pursued by a fearful and stupefying phantom. So the house was collapsing and the roof was falling in, and absolutely no one was brave enough to go there.

'When I heard this, I took my books—I have a great many Egyptian works on such topics—and went to the house around bedtime, though my host tried to stop me, almost grabbing hold of me, when he heard where I was going—into manifest disaster, as he thought. But I took a lamp and went in alone. I put the light down in the biggest room and began to read, sitting quietly on the floor, when the spirit appeared, thinking that he was approaching an ordinary sort of man and expecting to scare me like the others. He was squalid-looking, with long hair, and blacker than the darkness, and he stood over me and had a go at me, assailing me from all sides to see if he could get the better of me, now in the form of a dog, now of a bull or a lion. But I produced my most horrific spell, speaking it in Egyptian, forced him into a corner of a dark room and charmed him away. Then I noted the spot where he went down and then I went to sleep.

'At dawn, when everyone had given up hope and was expecting to find me dead like the others, I emerged to everyone's surprise, and went to Eubatides to tell him the good news that he could now live in his house, which was free from pollution and horrors. So, taking him with me, and a lot of others who came along attracted by the extraordinary event, I led them to the spot where I had seen the spirit go down, and told them to get forks and spades and dig. When they had done so a body was found buried about six feet deep: it had decomposed, and only the bones were lying in order. We dug it up and buried it, and from then on the house was no longer troubled with phantoms.'

32   After this story by Arignotus, a man of inspired wisdom and venerated by all, there was no longer anyone there who didn't think me guilty of extreme folly in doubting such happenings, especially if Arignotus was relating them.

Still, I wasn't afraid of his long hair or his reputation, and I said, 'What's this, Arignotus? You were truth's only hope, and have you too turned out to be like the others, full of fog and empty delusions? Assuredly, as the old saying has it, our treasure has turned out to be charcoal.'

'Come on,' said Arignotus, 'if you don't believe me or Deino-machus or Cleodemus here or even Eucrates, tell me who you think is more trustworthy in holding the opposite opinion to us in such things.'

'Ah,' I replied; 'that truly astonishing man, Democritus of Abdera,* who was so convinced that nothing like that can exist that he shut himself up in a tomb outside the gates, and wrote and composed endlessly day and night. Some youths, wanting to scare and make fun of him, dressed up as corpses in black robes and masks that looked like skulls, and surrounded him, dancing around with quick leaps in the air. But he showed no fear at their charade and didn't even look up at them, but, without stopping writing, simply said, "Stop playing the fool." So firmly was he convinced that souls no longer exist once they have left their bodies.'

'What you are saying', said Eucrates, 'is that even Democritus was a fool if he really thought that. But I'll tell you something else 33 from personal experience, not hearsay; and perhaps, Tychiades, even you hearing it will be persuaded of the truth of the story. When I was living in Egypt as a young man, where my father had sent me for my education, I was eager to sail up to Koptos, and go from there to the statue of Memnon and hear it make that marvellous sound to greet the rising sun.* Well, I did hear a voice, but not the usual meaningless one that most people hear: Memnon actually opened his mouth and gave me an oracle in seven verses; and if it wasn't adding superfluous detail I would recite the actual lines. But on the voyage up one of our fellow-passengers happened 34 to be a man from Memphis, one of the temple scribes, remarkably learned, and knowledgeable about the whole culture of the Egyptians. He was said to have lived for twenty-three years under-ground in their shrines, learning magic arts from Isis.'

'You're referring to Pancrates,* my own teacher,' said Arignotus, 'a holy man, always close-shaven, intelligent, not fluent in Greek, tall, snub-nosed, with prominent lips and rather thin legs.'

'That's Pancrates himself,' he replied. 'At first I didn't know who he was, but when I saw him performing numerous marvels whenever we came to anchor, especially riding on crocodiles and swimming along with the beasts, as they fawned on him and wagged their tails, I realized that he was a holy man, and gradually through friendly intercourse I found myself becoming his comrade and intimate, so that he shared all his esoteric knowledge with me.

'Eventually he persuaded me to leave behind all my servants in Memphis and to go along with him alone, as we would not lack attendants to serve us, and so we proceeded thereafter. And whenever we came to a lodging-place, he would take the bar of the door or a broom or even the pestle, dress it in clothes, utter a spell and make it walk, looking to everyone else like a man. Then it would go off, draw water, buy food, prepare meals, and in everything serve and wait on us dexterously. Then, when Pancrates was finished with its ministrations, he would once more make the broom a broom or the pestle a pestle by uttering another spell on it.

'I was very eager to learn how to do this from him, but I couldn't, because he kept it to himself, though he was most obliging in everything else. But one day I secretly overheard the spell—it consisted of only three syllables—by standing in a dark corner near to him. Then he went away to the market-square, having given the pestle its orders. So on the next day, while he was doing some business in the square, I took the pestle, dressed it in the usual way, uttered the syllables, and ordered it to bring some water. When it had filled the jar and brought it, I said, "Stop: no more water. Be a pestle once more." But it now refused to obey me, and went on bringing water, until it filled our house with a flood of water. The situation caused me to panic, for I was afraid that Pancrates would return and be angry (which indeed happened), and I seized an axe and chopped the pestle in two. But each half took a jar and brought in water, so that I now had two servants instead of one. Meanwhile, Pancrates arrived back, and sizing up the situation made them wood again, as they were before the spell; then he himself deserted me when I wasn't looking, and vanished, I know not where.'

'So,' said Deinomachus, 'you now know how to turn a pestle into a man?'

'Yes, indeed,' he said, 'but that's only half the problem; for I can't return it to its original shape once it has become a water-carrier, but we'll have the house flooded with water pouring in.'

'Won't you old fellows ever stop talking such moonshine?' I said. 'If not, at least for the sake of these youngsters postpone for another time these incredible and hair-raising stories, or before we know where we are they'll be filled with terrors and outlandish romances. You really ought to be concerned for them, and not let them get used to hearing such stuff, which will stay with them all their lives, worrying them and filling them with all manner of superstition, so that they jump at every noise they hear.'

'I'm glad you reminded me by talking of superstition,' said 38 Eucrates. 'What's your view, Tychiades, of things like that—I mean oracles, prophecies, cries of men possessed by a god or heard coming from sanctuaries, or a girl speaking verses that foretell the future? No doubt you'll be sceptical about such things too? As for me, I won't mention that I have a holy ring with a seal showing the image of Pythian Apollo, and that this Apollo speaks to me, in case you think I am boasting and making an incredible claim. But I would like to tell you all what I heard from Amphilochus in Mallus,* when that hero talked to me when I was fully awake and gave me advice about my affairs, and what I saw myself; and next in order what I saw in Pergamum and heard in Patara.*

'On my way home from Egypt I heard that this shrine in Mallus was very famous and extremely truthful, and gave clear oracles, responding word for word to what you've written on your tablet and given to the interpreter. So I decided it would be a good idea to test the oracle on my way and consult the god about the future—'

Eucrates was still speaking when I realized how the matter was 39 going to end, and that the rigmarole about oracles he was launching on would take some time; so I left him sailing from Egypt to Mallus, not seeing fit to be alone in contradicting them all. I realized too that they were irritated at my presence there to refute their lies. 'Well, I'm off,' I said, 'to look for Leontichus, as I want to have a word with him. As for you, since you aren't satisfied with ordinary human experiences, carry on calling upon the gods themselves to support you in your romancing.' With those words I departed. They were glad to be rid of me, and of course went on stuffing themselves with a feast of lies.

So there you are, Philocles. Having heard all that at Eucrates' house, I'm going around for all the world like those who have drunk sweet must, with a swollen belly and needing an emetic. I'd willingly pay a lot anywhere for a drug to cause forgetfulness of what I heard, to stop the memory of it living with me and causing me harm. Indeed, I think I'm seeing monsters and spirits and Hecates!

P. I too have had the same effect from your story, Tychiades. They do 40 say that not only those bitten by mad dogs go mad and fear water, but if someone who is bitten bites somebody else, his bite has the same effect as the dog, and the other man suffers the same fears. So it seems that you yourself, having been bitten by a host of lies at Eucrates' house, have passed on the bite to me too: you've filled my soul with such a lot of spirits!

T. Well, cheer up, my friend: we have a strong antidote to such things in truth and sound reason applied everywhere; and if we stick to that none of these empty, futile lies will ever disturb us.

HOW TO WRITE HISTORY

THIS treatise of Lucian's has a special interest as it is the most extensive surviving work from antiquity on the theory of historiography. However, it is not a general treatment of the subject as the title might suggest, as Lucian is specifically addressing would-be historians of a particular event, the war in Parthia of 162–6. This was triggered by the invasion of Armenia by the Parthian king, Vologeses III. The co-emperors of Rome at the time were Marcus Aurelius and Lucius Verus: a large Roman army was dispatched under the command of Lucius Verus, and the Parthians were eventually defeated.

Lucian devotes the first part of his essay to stringent and satiric criticism of the host of petty historians who hastily produced histories of this war, and by liberal quotation he exposes their glaring faults (e.g. slavish imitation of their great models, Herodotus and Thucydides). He then turns (33 ff.) to constructive advice on the writing of such a monograph, in which he stresses the essential qualities of mind and the appropriate narrative style of the genuinely successful historian whose work deserves to last.

The work can be dated securely to 166, as Lucian refers (31) to the triumph which was due to take place later that year. The addressee Philo is unknown, but it is a reasonable guess that he too was planning to write an account of the war.

There is a story, my dear Philo, that the people of Abdera, when Lysimachus* was king, were afflicted by a disease which took the following course. First, they all suffered from a fever which was violent and persistent from the beginning; about the seventh day the fever left them, causing some to have a heavy nose-bleed and others to be drenched in a heavy sweat. But it affected their minds in a most ridiculous way: they all got madly excited about tragedy, and created an uproar by declaiming iambics. They generally sang solo songs from Euripides' *Andromeda*, performing Perseus' speech as a song, and the city was full of these seventh-day tragedians, all pale and thin, shouting out

O Love, you rule o'er gods and men,*

and all the rest in a piercing voice, over and over again, until winter and a sharp frost put an end to their gibberish. I think the actor Archelaus was the cause of this behaviour. He was popular at that time, and in the blazing heat of midsummer he had acted the *Andromeda* for them, so that most of them came away from the theatre in a fever, and when they recovered from it they then relapsed into tragedy. The *Andromeda* kept haunting their memory, and Perseus with Medusa still flew around in their minds.

2   To make a comparison, as they say, that affliction of the Abderites has now got a grip on most of the educated world. They don't strike tragic poses—they would be less half-witted if they were possessed by other men's quite respectable iambics. The truth is, ever since the present disturbances began—the war against the barbarians, the serious set-back in Armenia, and the series of victories—every individual is writing history: or rather I should say, we see them all playing at being Thucydides and Herodotus and Xenophon. There does seem to be truth in that saying, 'War is the father of all things',* since at one stroke it has produced so many historians.

3   Well, my friend, as I was noticing and listening to all this, I thought of that story about the man of Sinope.* When Philip was reported to be already approaching,* the Corinthians were all in a turmoil of activity, preparing weaponry, collecting stones, strengthening part of their wall, underpinning a battlement, everyone involved in some useful task. When Diogenes saw this, as he had nothing to do (no one was making use of him), he girded on his old cloak and all on his own he energetically rolled the wine-jar, in which he happened to be living, up and down Craneion.* Asked by one of his friends, 'Why are you doing this, Diogenes?', he replied, 'I'm rolling my wine-jar so that I don't seem to be the only idle man in all this bustle of activity.'

4   So I too, Philo, don't want to be the only voiceless man at such a loquacious time, roaming about like an extra in comedy, open-mouthed but silent; so I thought it expedient to roll my own wine-jar as well as I can. I'm not rash enough to write a history or record men's actual deeds: never fear that I would do that. I know the danger if you roll it over the cliff, especially a badly baked little jar like mine. It only has to hit a small bit of rock and you'll be gathering up its broken pieces.

So, I'll tell you what I've decided, and how I'll manage to take part in the war safely and keeping out of the line of fire. I shall be wise to stay away 'from this billowing spray',* and all the historian's worries. And I shall offer a bit of advice and these few suggestions to historians, so I can share in the construction of their edifice, if not in the inscription on it, by touching the mortar at least with the tip of my finger.

And yet most of them don't think they need any advice for their task, any more than they need a treatise to tell them how to walk or to see or to eat, believing that writing history is perfectly easy and straightforward, and anyone can do it if he can just give expression to what comes into his head. But I am sure you understand, my friend, that history is not something that can be easily organized or assembled without effort. As much as any other work of literature it needs careful thought, if it is to become, in Thucydides' words, 'a possession for ever'.* Now, I'm aware that I shall not convert many of them, and that to some I shall seem an awful nuisance, especially those who have finished their history and by now have given it a public hearing. Furthermore, if they were then praised by the audience, it would be mad to expect such writers to change or rewrite anything which has once been ratified and stored, as it were, in the palace archives. Still, it's not a bad idea to address them as well, so that if another war took place—Celts against Getes or Indians against Bactrians (for no one would dare to attack *us* as we've now beaten everybody)—they may compose better histories by applying this standard, assuming they agree that it is the right one. If not, they'll just have to measure their work by the same yardstick as they do now. The doctor won't be grieving greatly if all the Abderites go on wanting to declaim the *Andromeda*.

The function of advice is twofold, telling you both what to choose and what to avoid. Let us first say what the historian should avoid, and particularly from what faults he must stay free. Then, by what means he can ensure that he does not miss the right path that leads straight ahead: what sort of beginning he must make, how he must order his material, the right proportion for each section, what should be omitted, what dwelt on at length and what passed over summarily, and how to express and fit it all together.

I'll deal with these and similar points later. But now let us talk about the faults that result from slipshod writing. Now, to go through those errors which are common to all types of writing and involve diction, rhythm, thought, and other aspects of poor technique, would take a long time and not be appropriate to this enquiry. For as I said, they are errors common to all writing; but regarding faults in writing history, you will find, if you attend carefully, that they are the sort that I have often found when listening to recitations, especially if you keep your ears open to all those people. But meanwhile, it won't be inappropriate to mention by way of example some of the existing histories which show these faults.

First, let us consider this outstanding failing, that most of them don't worry about recording events, but spend their time praising rulers and generals, applauding their own side to the skies and denigrating the enemy quite unreasonably. They don't understand that the line that separates and marks off history from panegyric is no narrow isthmus, but there is a great wall between them; or to express it in musical terms, the interval is equal to a double octave. For the panegyrist is only concerned with giving all the praise and pleasure he can to the man he is praising, and doesn't much mind even if he has to lie to succeed in his object. History, on the other hand, cannot tolerate introducing a lie, even for a moment, any more than doctors say the windpipe can endure anything swallowed into it.

8   Next, such writers seem to be unaware that the principles and rules of history are different from those of poetry and poems. With the latter freedom is unalloyed and there is one law—the will of the poet. He is inspired and possessed by the Muses, and if he chooses to yoke winged horses to a chariot, or to make some people run over water or even the tops of corn, nobody complains. Not even when their Zeus draws up land and sea together dangling from a single rope, are they afraid it will snap and everything fall and shatter to bits.* If they choose to praise Agamemnon, there's no one to stop him having a head and eyes like Zeus, a chest like Zeus' brother Poseidon, and a belt like Ares: in short, the son of Atreus and Aerope has to be a mixture of all the gods, for neither Zeus nor Poseidon nor Ares alone can fully express his beauty. But if history brings in flattery like that, what else is it but a kind of prose-poetry, without poetry's grandeur of style, but otherwise displaying its love of marvels, without metre and on that account more conspicuously? So it is a great blemish, indeed an overwhelming one, not to know how to distinguish the essential features of history and of poetry, and to introduce the adornments of poetry into history—fable and eulogy and the exaggerations inherent in these. That is like dressing one of your tough, rugged athletes in a purple robe and the other adornments of a courtesan and daubing his face with powder and rouge. Good gracious! How ridiculous you would make him, degrading him with all that ornamentation.

9   I am not saying that praise is not sometimes appropriate in history. But there is a right time for it and it should be practised

in moderation, so as not to irritate future readers. On the whole, you should exercise judgment in this area with an eye to posterity, and I will deal with it a little later.

There are those who think that they can make a fair distinction between two elements in history, the pleasurable and the useful, and on that account introduce eulogy into it because that will give their readers pleasure and enjoyment. But you see how far they have missed the truth? Firstly, they are using a bogus distinction, since history has one function and one aim, to be useful, and that derives from truth alone. Pleasure is an advantage if it is present as an incidental feature, like beauty in an athlete. But if not, there's nothing to prevent Nicostratus,* the son of Isidotus, a high-class performer and a better fighter than his two rivals, from becoming a second Heracles, however ugly he is, while his opponent is the handsome Alcaeus of Miletus, reportedly the lover of Nicostratus. So too, if history stooped to dealing in pleasure as well, it would attract many lovers; but as long as it sticks to dealing fully with what is its own pre-serve—I mean revealing the truth—it won't be much concerned with beauty of style.

Again, it is worth saying that if history includes what is totally 10 fictitious, or praise that is notably hostile to one side, the audience derives no pleasure from it, if you think not of all the vulgar rabble, but of those who will listen judiciously, and indeed those who are looking for faults as well. Nothing will escape their notice: they are more keen-sighted than Argus,* with eyes all over their body: and they test everything that is said like a money-changer, instantly rejecting anything counterfeit, but accepting what is genuine and legal and correctly minted. You must keep your eye on these people when you are writing, paying scant attention to the others, even if they burst themselves applauding you. If you ignore them, and season your history unreasonably with fictions and eulogies and other sorts of flattery, you'll very soon make it look like Heracles in Lydia.* You must have seen him portrayed as a slave to Omphale, dressed in a most extraordinary fashion, while she is wearing his lion's skin and holding his club. She is Heracles, you see, and he is clad in saffron and purple, carding wool and getting slapped with Omphale's sandal. It's a truly shameful sight: his clothes don't fit and fall off him, and a god's masculinity has become shockingly effeminate.

Perhaps the masses will actually praise you for this; but the few you 11 despise will be delighted and laugh their heads off, when they see

how incongruous, ill-proportioned, and loose-textured the work is.
For each section has its own particular beauty, and if you alter that it
becomes ugly and pointless. I don't have to say that eulogies may
please one person, the subject of them, but be irritating to others,
especially if they involve overblown exaggerations of the sort that
most people produce when they are courting the favour of those they
are praising, and going on and on until their fawning is obvious to all.
They show no skill in doing this, and don't conceal the flattery, as they
rush full tilt, piling on all sorts of transparently unbelievable stuff.

12 The result is they don't even achieve what they really want: those they
are courting hate them all the more and rightly reject them as toadies,
especially if they are of a manly temper. For instance, Aristoboulos*
included in his history the fight between Alexander and Porus, and
made a point of reading this passage to Alexander, thinking he would
greatly gratify the king by falsely attributing acts of prowess to him,
and by inventing deeds far surpassing the truth. At the time they
were sailing on the river Hydaspes, and Alexander took the book and
flung it straight into the water, saying, 'That's what you deserve too,
Aristoboulos, for fighting such single-handed combats on my behalf,
and killing elephants with a single spear-cast.' In fact, Alexander was
bound to be annoyed at this, seeing that he had not tolerated the
audacity of the engineer who had undertaken to make Athos into a
statue of the king by reshaping the mountain into his likeness. He saw
at once that the man was a flatterer, and stopped employing him even
on other business as before.*

13   So, where is the pleasure in all this, unless someone is so completely brainless as to enjoy praise which can be instantly shown to be
false? Consider how ugly people, especially women, urge painters to
make them appear as beautiful as possible, thinking that their own
looks will improve if the painter adorns them with a deeper pink and
mixes plenty of white in his colours.

      That's what many historians today are doing, cultivating their own
interest and the benefit they hope to derive from their history. You
could well hate them for being obvious but unskilled flatterers for the
present moment, and for the future bringing their whole trade into
disrepute by their exaggerations. If anyone thinks that pleasure must
at all events be an element in history, there are other forms of an
elegant style by which pleasure can be combined with truth. But most
writers ignore these, and keep bringing on stage things which have no
relevance.

Let me tell you what I heard from some historians the other day in 14
Ionia, and indeed just recently in Achaea, when they were narrating
this very war. And by the Graces, let no one disbelieve what I'm about
to say: I should have sworn it's true if it had been seemly to put an
oath in a written treatise. One of them began at once with the Muses,
calling upon the goddesses to lend him a hand with the work. You see
how apt this opening was, how fitting for a history, how appropriate
for this type of literature! Then, a bit later he compared our general to
Achilles and the Persian king to Thersites,* not realizing that his
Achilles would have been a better man if he had killed Hector rather
than Thersites, and if it was a valiant man who was fleeing ahead

and a far greater man pursuing.*

Next he added some praise of himself, how worthy he was to recount
such glorious exploits. Coming towards the end, he praised his native
Miletus as well, adding that he was improving on Homer, who never
mentioned his native country. Then, finishing his introduction,
he promised clearly and explicitly to extol our side, and to do all he
could personally to vanquish the foreigners. Then he began his
account by giving the causes of the war like this: 'That abominable
villain Vologeses began the war for the following reason.'

So much for him. Another was a keen imitator of Thucydides, 15
so that he slavishly copied his model, and like Thucydides began
with his own name—the most charming of all openings, fragrant with
Attic thyme. Consider it: 'Crepereius Calpurnianus of Pompeiopolis*
wrote the history of the war between the Parthians and the Romans,
starting at its very beginning.' After such a beginning, need I carry
on?—the kind of speech he reported in Armenia, introducing the
Corcyrean orator in person to give it; the sort of plague he inflicted
on the people of Nisibis who refused to join the Romans, which
he copied entirely from Thucydides, only omitting references to the
Pelasgians and the Long Walls, where those who had then caught the
plague were living. For the rest, he also made it 'originate in Ethiopia'
and 'move down into Egypt and much of the territory of the king of
Persia', where it happily stayed.* Well, I left him still burying the
unfortunate Athenians at Nisibis, and went away knowing exactly
what he was going to say after I'd gone. Again, you see this is
now pretty well the fashion, to imagine that you are reproducing
Thucydides' style if, with some minor changes, you copy his phrase-
ology. And, I nearly forgot to say that this same historian has

described many kinds of arms and engines of war by their Roman names, as also the words for ditch and bridge and so on. You can just imagine the noble character of his history, and how fitting it is for Thucydides to have these Italian words mixed up with Attic ones, like a conspicuous addition of purple adornment, and a perfect harmony!

16   Another one has put together a bare record of events, and written it down in a completely flat and prosaic style, as if a soldier had composed it as a diary, or maybe a carpenter or camp sutler. However, this amateur was at least less pretentious: it was at once clear what he was up to, and he has done the preliminary work for another more elegant and talented historian to take over. My only criticism was that his book-titles are more bombastic than suits the likely fate of his writings: 'History of the Parthian War, by Callimorphus, doctor for the sixth regiment of lancers', followed by the number of each book. And my goodness, wasn't his preface terribly frigid, which argued thus: that it was appropriate for a doctor to write history, since Asclepius was the son of Apollo, and Apollo was leader of the Muses and chieftain over all culture. I also disliked his practice of beginning to write in Ionic,* and then for some unknown reason suddenly switching to the vernacular, continuing to write the Ionic forms of 'medicine', 'attempt', 'how many', and 'diseases', but otherwise words in ordinary everyday use and generally the sort you hear at street corners.

17   If I have to mention a philosopher, his name must be concealed, but I'll tell you about his opinion and what he wrote recently in Corinth, which exceeded all expectation. At the very beginning, in the first sentence of his preface, he fired a series of questions at his readers in his eagerness to put forward an over-clever argument: that only a philosopher should write history. Shortly after that came another syllogism, then another. In short, his preface revealed every type of syllogistic questioning; the flattery was nauseating, the eulogies vulgar and quite ribald, and they too were not free of syllogistic conclusions. I really did think it vulgar, and not at all worthy of a philosopher with a long grey beard, to assert in his preface that it would be a real privilege for our commander that even philosophers now think it worth their while to record his exploits. That sort of remark it would be more seemly for us, if anyone, to think of, rather than for him to say it. Again, it wouldn't be right not to mention

18 the historian who began thus: 'I am going to speak of Romans and Persians', and shortly afterwards, 'The Persians were doomed to

suffer disaster'; and again, 'It was Osroes, whom the Greeks call
Oxyrhoes',* and many other examples like that. Do you understand?
He resembled Crepereius, though he was a slavish imitator of
Herodotus, as the other was of Thucydides.

Another, famous for his forceful style, also resembled Thucydides 19
or even went one better, describing all cities, mountains, plains, and
rivers to clarify and reinforce his narrative, or so he thought. May the
god who averts evil turn this style of his against our enemies, so frigid
was it, colder than Caspian snow and Celtic ice! For instance, he
took nearly a whole book to describe the emperor's shield, with the
Gorgon on its boss, and her eyes of blue and white and black, and her
girdle like a rainbow, and her curls formed of coiling and clustering
snakes. As for Vologeses'* trousers, or the bit on his horse, Heavens!
what thousands of words were devoted to each, and to Osroes' hair as
he swam the Tigris, and the cave where he took refuge, which was
completely overshadowed by a tangle of ivy and myrtle and bay. Do
observe how essential these details are to history: without them we
wouldn't know anything of what happened there.

They take refuge in this sort of description of landscape and caves, 20
because they are weak in the essential points or ignorant about what
should be said. And when they happen on a lot of major events they
are like a newly enriched servant, who has just become heir to his
master, and doesn't know how to dress or how to eat his dinner
decently. Instead, he wades in greedily, when perhaps poultry and
pork and hares are set before him, and stuffs himself with soups or
salt fish until he bursts from eating. Well, this writer I just mentioned
described quite unbelievable wounds and outlandish deaths: how
someone was wounded in the big toe and died immediately; and how
Priscus the general only had to give a loud shout and twenty-seven of
the enemy fell dead. Furthermore, when giving the number of those
killed, his false report even went against the generals' dispatches.
By his account, there were 70,236 of the enemy killed at Europus,
compared with two Romans killed and nine wounded. I don't think
anyone in his right mind would accept that.

I should also mention another point, which is not a trivial one. 21
Because this man is a committed Atticist and has purified his speech
even to the tiniest details, he thought it right to change the Roman
names and alter them to Greek forms; saying, for example, Kronios
for Saturninus, Phrontis for Fronto, Titanios for Titianus, and other
much sillier forms. Furthermore, this same writer, when dealing with

the death of Severianus,* declared that all the others had been
deceived in thinking he was killed by the sword, as he had died from
voluntary fasting, believing this to be the most painless form of death.
The writer did not know that his sufferings lasted in all three days,
I believe, while most people who abstain from food can survive for
up to a week—unless you imagine that Osroes stood around waiting
for Severianus to die of starvation, and therefore didn't attack for a
week.

22   And what is one to make of those, my dear Philo, who use poetical
words in their histories, like 'Round whirled the crane and mightily
fell the wall with a crash', and again in another section of this estim-
able history, 'Thus was Edessa girdled with the clatter of arms, and
naught was there but clanging and din'; and 'Long pondered the
general how best to assail the wall'. Then in the middle of all this, he
crammed in a heap of words that are cheap, trivial, and beggarly: 'The
commander sent a message to the lord'; and 'The soldiers bought the
needful'; and 'They'd had a wash before they concerned themselves
with them'; and so on. Such a performance is like a tragic actor
wearing the high boot of tragedy on one foot and a sandal on the
other.

23   And then you'll see others writing prefaces which are brilliant,
stately, and inordinately long, leading you to expect to hear a really
marvellous narrative to follow. But the main body of their history is
such a petty and paltry production, it seems like a small child—
perhaps you've seen a Cupid at play, wearing a huge mask of Heracles
or a Titan. Anyway, the audience's comment comes at once: 'The
mountain was in labour.'*

This is not in my view the right technique: there should be uni-
formity throughout, with evenness of tone and harmony between the
rest of the body and the head, so that you don't get a golden helmet
coupled with an utterly ridiculous breastplate cobbled together out of
rags or rotten leather, and a shield of wickerwork and greaves covered
in pigskin. You can see lots of writers like that, who stick the head
of the Colossus of Rhodes on a dwarf's body; and others again who
produce headless bodies, books without a preface that launch straight
into the narrative of events. These claim Xenophon as a colleague,
because he starts with the words 'Darius and Parysatis had two sons',*
and other old authors, not realizing that some passages are effectively
prefaces, though most people don't notice it. We shall deal with this
elsewhere.

Still, we can put up with all this, so far as it concerns faults of style 24
and organization of topics; but when it comes to getting localities
wrong, not just by parasangs but even by whole days' journeys, can
you see any distinguished model for that? For instance, one writer was
so careless in assembling his facts, never having met a Syrian or, as
they say, listened to barber-shop gossip, that in talking about Europus
he said, 'Europus is situated in Mesopotamia, two days' journey from
the Euphrates: it was a colony of Edessa.'* Nor did he stop there: in
the same book this distinguished writer lifted my own native city
Samosata, acropolis, walls and all, and placed it in Mesopotamia,
with both rivers flowing round it, passing close on each side and
all but lapping the wall. What a ridiculous idea, Philo, that I should
have to defend myself to you from the charge of being a Parthian or
Mesopotamian, where this admirable historian has settled me!

And, my goodness, that was a really credible story the same writer 25
told about Severianus, swearing that he'd heard it from one of the
survivors of the actual event. He said Severianus did not wish to die
by the sword, nor drink poison, nor hang himself, but he devised a
dramatic way of dying, which was both strange and daring. He
chanced to have some very large goblets of the finest crystal, and
when he had decided that death was inevitable, he broke the largest
cup and used one of the fragments to cut his throat with the glass.
Could he really not have found a dagger or spear to give himself
a manly and heroic death? Then, as Thucydides had reported a 26
funeral oration for the first to die in that celebrated war,* he thought
he too ought to say something over Severianus. For they all vie with
Thucydides, though he had no responsibility whatever for the
troubles in Armenia. So, having buried Severianus in fine style, he
has a centurion, one Afranius Silo, climb onto the tomb as a rival to
Pericles. This man declaimed over him in such a strange and overblown way, that, by the Graces, I couldn't stop crying with laughter,
especially when Afranius the orator at the end of his speech burst into
tears, and with passionate groans reminded us of all those lavish
dinners and toasts. Then he capped it all by acting like Ajax:* he drew
his sword, and with the absolute nobility befitting an Afranius he
killed himself on the tomb in view of everyone—and by the god of
war he deserved to die long before for making a speech like that. The
writer went on to say that all the onlookers were astonished and
praised Afranius to the skies. As for me, I condemned him overall for
all but telling us about the soups and the shell-fish, and crying over

the memory of the cakes; but most of all I blamed him for dying before he had first slaughtered the historian who had stage-managed the show.

27   I could recount many other writers like these, my friend, but I'll mention just a few, and then proceed to my other design of suggesting how one could write history better. There are some who omit or just deal cursorily with major and memorable events, and, lacking professionalism, good taste, and the knowledge of what should be mentioned and what passed over, spend ages on detailed and laborious descriptions of the most trivial things. It's as if someone didn't observe or praise or describe for those who do not know it all the supreme beauty of the Zeus at Olympia,* but admired the careful workmanship and the fine finish of his footstool, and the well-proportioned base, and concentrated hard on all these details.

28   For example, I heard one of them race through the battle at Europus in under seven complete lines; but he took twenty or even more measures of the water-clock in a boring and irrelevant narrative about a Moorish horseman, named Mausacas. This man was wandering over the mountains, suffering from thirst, when he came across some Syrian peasants laying out their lunch. At first they were afraid of him, but learning that he was a friend they welcomed him to their meal; for it happened that one of them had travelled abroad to Mauretania, as he had a brother on military service in that country. There followed long stories and narratives; how he had been hunting in Mauretania, and how he had seen a lot of elephants grazing together, and how he had nearly been eaten by a lion, and the size of the fish he bought in Caesarea. And this impressive historian ignored the massacres and charges and enforced truces and garrisons and counter-garrisons at Europus, and well into the evening he stood watching Malchion the Syrian buying huge wrasses cheap in Caesarea. If night hadn't come on he might have been sharing his dinner of cooked wrasse. If all this had not been carefully included in the history, we should never have known some important things, and the loss would have been unbearable to the Romans if Mausacas the Moor hadn't found a drink when he was thirsty, but returned to the camp without his supper. But here I am now leaving out other much more essential items: how a music-girl arrived from the nearby village; how they exchanged gifts, the Moor giving Malchion a spear, and Malchion giving Mausacas a buckle; and all the many such crowning achievements of the battle at Europus! So, all in all, you

could reasonably say that such writers don't look at the rose itself, but take careful note of the thorns that appear by its root.

Another writer, Philo, is also utterly ridiculous. He had never set 29 foot out of Corinth or even gone to Cenchreae, and never seen Syria or Armenia; yet he started off with these words, as I recall: 'The ears are more untrustworthy than the eyes,* so I am writing what I have seen, not what I have heard.' And he had seen everything so clearly that, referring to the serpents of the Parthians (an ensign they use for a body of troops: I think a serpent leads a thousand men), he said they were alive and enormous, and born in Persia a short distance beyond Iberia; that they are tied to long poles and lifted up high to frighten the enemy from a distance, as the Parthians approach, but during the actual encounter at close quarters they are set free and let loose upon the foe; that they had actually swallowed many of our men in this way, and coiling themselves around others had choked and crushed them. He said he himself had been present and seen all this—though he had made his observations from the safety of a tall tree. He was wise not to approach the beasts, or we wouldn't now have such a marvellous historian, who casually performed great and glorious feats in this war. For he encountered many dangers and was wounded at Sura—no doubt while taking a stroll from Craneion to Lerna.* All this he read to an audience of Corinthians, who knew perfectly well that he had never even seen a wall-painting of a battle. Indeed, he didn't even know what armour and siege-engines looked like, or the terms 'battle-array' or 'muster-rolls'. A fat lot it mattered to him if he called an army in column an extended front, and confused movements 'in line' and 'in column'.

One superb historian compressed all the events that took place 30 from start to finish in Armenia, Syria, Mesopotamia, by the Tigris, in Media, into under five hundred lines; and having done this claims he has written a history. Yet his title is almost longer than the book: 'An account of the recent achievements of the Romans in Armenia, Mesopotamia and Media, by Antiochianus, victor in the games of Apollo'—I suppose he'd once won the boys' long-distance race.

There's one I've heard of who even included the future in his 31 account: the capture of Vologeses, the killing of Osroes—how he would be thrown to the lion, and to crown it all the triumph we long for so much—so oracular was he as he rushed to finish his work. In fact, he has even founded a city in Mesopotamia of enormous size and outstanding beauty. He is still pondering and deliberating whether to name it Nicaea, after the victory,* or Harmony or Peaceful. There's no decision yet, and we lack a name for that beautiful city, which is full of so much waffle and historical drivel. He has now promised to write about the future of India, and the circumnavigation of the outer sea: and this is not only a promise, as the preface to his 'History of India' is already written, and the third legion with the Celts and a small division of Moors under Cassius have all crossed the river Indus. What they will achieve, or how they are going to withstand the charge of the elephants, our distinguished historian will soon tell us by letter from Muziris or the Oxydraci.*

32   Such a heap of rubbish do they talk through their lack of culture, not seeing what is worth seeing, and not able, if they did see it, to describe it suitably. Instead, they contrive and invent whatever comes to an ill-timed tongue, as they say;* and they pride themselves on the number of their books, and especially on their titles. These too are utterly silly: 'So-and-so's Parthian Victories in so many books'; and again, 'First and Second Parthis' (like 'Atthis',* you see). Another one wrote rather more elegantly (I've read it), 'The Parthonicica of Demetrius of Sagalassus'. I am not just mocking and making fun of such excellent histories, but I have a practical purpose. Whoever can avoid these and similar faults has made a big advance towards correct historical writing, or rather he needs to acquire only a little more, if it is a valid argument that if you remove one of two opposites you necessarily establish the other.

33   Well then, someone may say, the ground has been carefully cleared and all the thorns and brambles chopped out, and all the rubbish carried away, and all the rough areas made smooth: so you must now build something yourself, to show that you are good not only at knocking down other people's constructions, but at devising something clever yourself, such that nobody, not even Momus,* would criticize.

34   My own view, then, is that the best historian comes naturally endowed with these two supreme qualities, an insight into statecraft and powers of expression. The former cannot be taught and is a gift of nature; powers of expression should be acquired by constant practice, unremitting toil, and imitation of the ancients. So these need no rules and no advice from me: my treatise does not claim to make people intelligent and sharp who are not naturally so. It would be worth a lot—everything indeed—if it could convert and refashion

things to such a degree, or produce gold from lead or silver from tin, or create a Titormus from a Conon or a Milo from a Leotrophides.*

So, where is there a place for rules and advice? Not to create 35 qualities, but to show the appropriate use of them. Thus, for example, Iccus, Herodicus, Theon, and other trainers would not promise you to take Perdiccas—if it was he and not Antiochus, son of Seleucus,* who fell in love with his stepmother, and wasted away because of this—and make him into an Olympic victor and a match for Theagenes the Thasian or Polydamas of Scotussa.* But if they were given raw material naturally adapted for athletic exercises, they would greatly improve him by their training. So let me too not suffer any ill-will due to my claim to have discovered a technique for dealing with such an important and difficult activity. I do not claim to be able to take just anyone and produce an historian, but to show one who is naturally intelligent and well practised in using language some straight paths (if indeed they seem to be such) by which he can more quickly and easily achieve his goal. After all, you wouldn't say that an 36 intelligent man does not need training and instruction in things he doesn't know: otherwise, he would strum the lyre and play on the pipe and grasp everything without learning it. In fact, he couldn't practise any of these without learning; but with someone to show him, he can very easily learn and practise them well by himself.

So, let us now have a student like this, not dim in intelligence 37 and self-expression, but sharp-sighted and capable of dealing with practical matters if entrusted with them; one with the mind of a soldier as well as of a citizen, and an acquaintance with generalship; and yes indeed, one who has at some time been in a camp, and seen soldiers training or in battle-array, and has some knowledge of arms and siege-engines, and knows the meaning of the terms 'in line' and 'in column', and how infantry and cavalry are deployed, and the origin and meaning of 'lead out' and 'drive round': in a word, not an armchair expert or one who has to rely on what he is told.

But the most important thing by far is that he should be a free 38 spirit, fear nobody, and expect nothing: otherwise, he will be like corrupt jurymen, who sell judgments to win favour or gratify enmity. It should not matter to him that Philip's eye was put out by Aster of Amphipolis,* the archer at Olynthus: he is to be portrayed just as he was. Nor should he worry that Alexander will be angry if he describes clearly how Cleitus was brutally murdered at the banquet.* Nor will Cleon,* with all his influence in the Assembly and his power over the speaker's platform, scare him off saying he was a dangerous madman; nor indeed the whole of Athens stop him narrating the disaster in Sicily,* the capture of Demosthenes, the death of Nicias, how parched the soldiers were, and the sort of water they drank, and how many of them were slaughtered as they drank. For he will be quite right to think that no sensible person will blame him for recording actions which are unlucky or stupid: after all, he was not responsible for them, but simply reported them. So if they are defeated at sea, he isn't the one who sinks them, and if they are put to flight, he isn't the one pursuing them—unless he forgot to put in a seasonable prayer on their behalf. Indeed, if by omitting or reversing the facts he could have put them right, it would have been very easy for Thucydides with one fragile pen to overturn the cross-wall at Epipolae and sink Hermocrates' trireme, to transfix that abominable Gylippus as he was blockading the roads with walls and ditches, and finally to throw the Syracusans into the quarries, while the Athenians sailed round Sicily and Italy as Alcibiades had originally hoped. But my belief is that when actions are finished and done with, not even Clotho the Spinner can unspin them nor Atropos the Unchanging* change them back.

39 The single task of the historian is to tell of things as they happened. But he cannot do this as long as, being Artaxerxes' doctor,* he is afraid of him, or is hoping for a purple cloak, a gold collar, and a Nisaean horse as a reward for praising him in his work. Xenophon, an impartial historian, won't do that, nor will Thucydides. On the other hand, even if he personally hates certain people, he will regard himself as much more constrained by the public interest, and put truth above enmity. So too, if he has a friend involved, he won't spare him if he is doing wrong. As I said, this is the peculiar characteristic of history: if you are going to write history you must sacrifice to truth alone, ignoring everything else. In short, your one clear rule and yardstick is to keep your eye not on your present audience, but on those who will come to your work in the future.

40 Whoever courts the present will rightly be considered a flatterer: history has rejected such people right from the very beginning, no less than athletic training has rejected personal adornment. For instance, Alexander is quoted as saying, 'When I'm dead I should like to come back to life for a while, Onesicritus,* in order to find out how men will then be reading these events. If they now praise and welcome them, don't be surprised: they are all thinking that this is no mean bait to win my favour.' It's true that Homer generally treated Achilles

in a fictional fashion; but nowadays some people tend to believe him, adducing as the one important proof of his truthfulness the fact that Achilles was not alive when he wrote about him: they cannot see any motive for his telling lies.

Well, my historian should be like that: fearless, incorruptible, frank, 41 a friend of free speech and the truth, determined, as the comic poet* puts it, to call figs figs and a tub a tub, indulging neither hatred nor friendship, sparing nobody, not showing pity or shame or diffidence, an unbiased judge, kindly to everyone up to the point of not allowing one side more than it deserves, a stranger without a state in his writings, independent, serving no king, not taking into account what any man will think, but simply saying what happened.

Thucydides did very well in establishing this rule, and he dis- 42 tinguished virtue from vice in the writing of history when he saw Herodotus so much admired that his books were named after the Muses. For he says he is writing a possession for ever, rather than a prize-composition for the present occasion, and that he does not favour fabulous elements, but is leaving for posterity a true account of what happened. He also mentions the question of usefulness, and what any sensible person would assume to be the purpose of history, that if ever again people are faced with a similar situation, taking due notice of the records of past events they can, he says, deal competently with the present.*

So, please let the historian come equipped with that cast of mind. 43 With regard to his language and power of expression, he should not set about his work with a mind sharpened to achieve that biting vigour, which has endless periods and intricate logic and all the other trappings of forceful rhetoric. Rather he should settle for a more tranquil effect; his thinking should be coherent and shrewd; and his diction clear and practical, so as to display his subject-matter as vividly as possible.

For just as we have established freedom of speech and truth as the 44 aims for the historian's mind, so the single first aim for his language is to clarify and explain the subject-matter as lucidly as he can, using words which are neither esoteric and out of the way, nor the vulgar language of the market-place, but such as ordinary people understand and the educated approve. In addition, the work may be decorated with figures that won't give offence and above all seem unforced, or he'll be turning out language that resembles highly spiced sauces.

45   His mind should also have a share in and a feel for the poetic, inasmuch as that too offers an element which is elevated and sublime, especially when he is involved with battle-lines and land and sea fights. For then he will need a poetic wind to waft his boat along and help to keep it riding the crest of the waves. Yet his diction should keep its feet on the ground, rising to match as far as possible the beauty and grandeur of his topics, but without becoming more exotic or high-flown than suits the occasion. For then it runs the risk of getting wildly excited and caught up in the frenzy of poetry; so that at those times most of all he should obey the curb and exercise self-control, knowing that getting on your high horse is not a trivial fault even in literature. So, it is better that while his mind is on horseback his language should run along beside him, holding on to the saddle-cloth so as not to fall behind.

46   Furthermore, he should practise temperance and moderation when arranging words, not separating and detaching them too much, which produces harshness, or (as many do) virtually linking them together through rhythm. The latter is to be censured, the former is disagreeable to the audience.

47   Regarding the actual details of events, he should not just collect them haphazardly, but only after careful, painstaking, and repeated enquiry. Ideally, he should have witnessed them himself; but failing that, he should rely on the least biased informants and those least likely to suppress or add anything to the facts through favour or ill-will. At this stage, he must show a capacity to arrive at and put
48   together the more credible account of things. And when he has collected all or most of the facts, he should first organize them in note form, and produce a text which is still unadorned and not completely articulated. After that he must put them into order, and add beauty, and embellish them by means of diction, figures, and rhythm.

49   In a word, he must then be like Zeus in Homer, looking now at the land of the horse-rearing Thracians, now at that of the Mysians.* He too must similarly take his own individual look now at the actions of the Romans, and explain how they seemed to him from on high, and now at those of the Persians, then at both sides if they start fighting. In a pitched battle itself he should not look at one single area or any individual cavalryman or infantryman—unless it is a Brasidas leaping forward, or a Demosthenes beating back his attack;* but first of all at the generals, having also listened to their exhortations (if any), and the method, plan, and intention of their deployments. When the battle

starts, he should keep an overall view and weigh the events as in a balance, and join in both the pursuit and the rout. He must handle all 50 this with moderation, showing an easy detachment without being extravagant, vulgar, or naive. Let him pause at some points, and move from here to there if necessary; then up sticks and back again if events there call him. He should always be moving quickly, following the order of events so far as possible; he must fly from Armenia to Media, and from there in one swoop to Iberia; and then to Italy, so as not to miss any crisis.

Most important, he must apply his mind like a mirror which is 51 clear, gleaming, and sharply focused, he must display the facts in accordance with the form of them he receives, and with no trace of distortion, false colours, or alteration. Historians do not write on the same terms as orators: what they have to say is in front of them and will be said, because it has already happened, their task being to organize and formulate it. So what is required is not what to say but how to say it. In short, we must think of comparing the historian with Pheidias or Praxiteles or Alcamenes or some other sculptor. They certainly did not create their own gold or ivory or whatever other material, but had it ready to hand, supplied by the Eleans or the Athenians or the Argives; their job was to give it form, sawing and polishing the ivory, and glueing, shaping, and gilding it, and they showed their skill in the proper treatment of their material.

Well, the task of the historian is something like that: to arrange events artistically and to exert all his powers to make them vivid. And when one of his audience, after having heard him, thinks that he can visualize what is being described and praises him, then indeed the work of this Pheidias of history has been perfectly crafted, and has won the praise it deserves.

Now, when he has assembled all his materials he will sometimes 52 begin even without a preface, if his theme does not strictly require any preliminary treatment in a preface. But even then he will use a virtual preface to explain his subject.

When he does have a preface, he will start with two points only, not 53 three like the orators. Omitting the request for goodwill, he will give his hearers what will hold their attention and offer them instruction; they will attend to him if he shows that he is going to discuss topics that are important or vital or personal or useful. And he will make what follows instructive and clear if he sets out the causes in advance and summarizes the main episodes. The best historians have prefaces 54 of this type: Herodotus writing 'so that events will not be forgotten in the passage of time',* the great and marvellous account of victorious Greeks and defeated barbarians; and Thucydides, believing that his war would be great and more important and worth recording than any previous ones—and indeed it produced tremendous sufferings.

55   After the preface, long or short as suits the subject matter, the transition to the narrative should be easy and unforced. For the whole body of the history is in effect a long narrative. So it should be adorned with virtues suitable to narrative, moving along smoothly, steadily, and consistently, without bulges or gaps. Then it should have a surface clarity which is achieved by diction, as I said, and by the inter-connection of events. He will make every section separate and complete, and when he has worked out the first he will bring in the second, linked and attached to it like a chain, avoiding interruptions and a long series of adjacent narratives. The first and second themes must always not just lie side by side, but overlap with shared material at the edges.

56   Rapidity is always helpful, especially if there is no lack of material, and this should arise from the subject matter rather than from words or phrases: I mean, by passing rapidly over trivial and less important things, but dealing adequately with major issues. Indeed, many details should even be left out. When you are giving your friends a dinner and everything is prepared, you don't in the midst of all your pastries, poultry, shell-fish, wild boar, hares, and tunny, also offer them salt-fish and pea-soup just because it's available too: you'll ignore the cheaper stuff.

57   There is particular need of moderation in descriptions of mountains, fortifications, and rivers, so that you don't seem to be giving a vulgar display of your facility with words, and neglecting the history in favour of your own interests. You can touch on them briefly when you need to and for the sake of clarity, but then move on, avoiding the seductions of the subject, and all such self-indulgence. This you can see in Homer's practice, in his lofty-minded way: though a poet he passes rapidly by Tantalus, Ixion, Tityus* and the others. But if Parthenius or Euphorion or Callimachus* were telling the story, you can imagine how many words he would have taken to bring the water to Tantalus' lips; how many to set Ixion spinning round! Certainly Thucydides wastes few words on this sort of passage: observe how quickly he moves on from describing a siege-engine, or explaining an essential and useful method of attacking a city, or the plan of

Epipolae, or the harbour of Syracuse. On the other hand, when he seems to be tedious in his account of the plague, you must think of the facts and you'll realize how rapid he actually is, and how the plethora of details holds him back as he tries to escape.

If someone must be brought in to make a speech, it is most impor- 58 tant that his language suits his character and his subject, and these also should be made as clear as possible. However, on these occasions you are allowed to act the orator and display your oratorical powers.

Praise and blame should be carefully considered and circumspect, 59 free from calumny, supported by evidence, delivered quickly and not ill-timed, as those concerned are not in court, and you will face the same charge as Theopompus,* who uttered quarrelsome accusations against most people, making such a practice of it that he appeared to be a prosecutor rather than historian.

Again, if a myth happens to arise, you must record it but not 60 believe it totally: set it out for your audience to make their own conjectures about it. You yourself should run no risks by leaning to one side or the other.

On the whole, I ask you to remember this—and I shall keep on 61 repeating it: don't only write with an eye to the present, hoping that the present generation will praise and honour you. You should aim at eternity, writing for posterity and claiming payment for your book from them; so that it can be said of you: 'He was a free man, totally frank in his speech, untouched by flattery or servility, showing truth-fulness in everything.' Any sensible man would rate that above all present hopes, seeing how short-lived they are.

You know about the achievement of that architect from Cnidos?* 62 He built the tower in Pharos, the largest and most splendid of all works, so that it might send a beacon-light to sailors far over the sea, and stop them being driven on to Paraetonia, a very dangerous spot, they say, from which there is no escape once you hit the reefs. Well, when he had finished the building, he wrote his own name on the stonework inside, plastered it over with gypsum, and having thus concealed it wrote over it the name of the reigning king. He knew (which indeed happened) that after a very short time the letters would fall off with the plaster, revealing 'Sostratus of Cnidos, son of Dexiphanes, to the saviour gods, on behalf of those who sail.' In this way not even he was looking to the immediate present or his own brief lifetime, but forward to our time and to eternity, as long as the tower stands and his skill survives.

63   Well, that is the spirit in which history should be written: with truthfulness and a regard for future hopes, rather than with flattery aimed at getting pleasure out of present praise. Here is your rule and standard for writing impartial history. If any will make use of it, that is all to the good, and my work has served its purpose. If not, I've rolled my wine-jar in Craneion.

A TRUE HISTORY

This is probably Lucian's best known work, and it is his most extended exercise in parody. We see his gift for parody also in *Lovers of Lies*, and in *A True History* there is the same malicious wit in poking fun at his victims. At that period there was clearly a vogue for travel tales which were full of wildly fabulous and fantastic elements: these are Lucian's chief targets, and he singles out by name the travel writer Iambulus for criticism. But he also attacks the historians Ctesias and incidentally Herodotus for telling lies in their works. By contrast, he overtly admits that there are fantastic lies in his own travel tale, but claims at least to tell the truth in saying that his narrative is false. The ninth-century scholar Photius correctly saw the nature of Lucian's work, but his suggestion that Antonius Diogenes' *Wonders beyond Thule* was an important source of *A True History* is difficult to assess, partly because of the uncertainty about Diogenes' dates.

Some of Lucian's familiar literary and philosophical preoccupations recur here: there are, for example, sardonic references to Plato and Pythagoras (2. 17, 21, 24), and at greater length he gives us evidence (2. 20) of contemporary interest in Homer and Homeric scholarship.

Book I

Those who are interested in athletics and the care of their bodies are 1
concerned not just with keeping themselves in good condition and well exercised, but with timely relaxation: indeed, they regard this as the most important part of training. In the same way, I think it does students of literature good, after hard and serious reading, to relax their minds and invigorate them further for future efforts. It would 2 be suitable recreation for them to occupy themselves with the kind of reading which not only affords simple diversion derived from elegance and wit, but also supplies some intellectual food for thought—just the qualities I think they will find in this work of mine. For they will be attracted not only by the exotic subject-matter and the charm of the enterprise, and by the fact that I have told all manner of lies persuasively and plausibly, but because all the details in my narrative are an amusing and covert allusion to certain poets, historians, and philosophers of old, who have written a lot of miraculous and fabulous stuff. I would give their names if they weren't bound to be obvious to you as you read. For example, there is Ctesias,* son 3 of Ctesiochus, of Cnidos, who wrote about India and details of the

Indians which he had neither seen himself nor heard from any truthful witness. Iambulus* also wrote a lot about the marvels to be found in the countries of the great sea: he concocted a lie which is obvious to everyone, yet his subject matter is not unattractive. Many others with the same idea have written ostensibly about their journeys and visits abroad, giving accounts of huge creatures and brutal men and strange ways of living. Their leader and teacher in such tomfoolery is Homer's Odysseus, who tells Alcinous* and his court all about captive winds and one-eyed men and cannibals and savages; creatures, too, with many heads, and how his comrades were transformed by drugs. All this was the fantastic stuff with which he beguiled the simple-

4 minded Phaeacians. Well, when I read all these writers I didn't blame them greatly for their lying, as I'd already seen that this was habitual even to those professing philosophy. But what did surprise me was that they thought they could report untruths and get away with it. So, as I too was vain enough to want to leave something to posterity, and didn't want to be the only one denied the right to flights of fancy, and since I had nothing truthful to report (not having experienced anything worth recording), I turned to lying. But I am much more honest in this than the others: at least in one respect I shall be truthful, in admitting that I am lying. Thus I think that by freely admitting that nothing I say is true, I can avoid being accused of it by other people. So, I am writing about things I neither saw nor experienced nor heard about from others, which moreover don't exist, and in any case could not exist. My readers must therefore entirely disbelieve them.

5   I started out once from the Pillars of Heracles, and with a favourable wind I set sail for the Western Ocean. The purpose and the occasion for my journey was intellectual curiosity, eagerness for new experiences, and a wish to learn what was the end of the ocean and who lived beyond it. With this end in view, I put on board a large supply of provisions and a sufficient stock of water, drafted fifty like-minded companions of my own age, procured a hefty supply of arms, hired the best skipper I could for a large fee, and fitted out my

6 boat—she was a small craft—for a long and taxing voyage. Well, we sailed gently before the wind for a day and a night without getting very far out to sea, and having land still in view; but at dawn on the second day the wind strengthened, the waves increased, darkness descended, and we could no longer even furl our sails. So we gave up and abandoned ourselves to the wind, and were driven before the

storm for seventy-nine days. On the eightieth day the sun suddenly appeared, and we saw not far away a high, thickly wooded island, with only moderate breakers sounding around it, as by now the force of the gale was abating.

Having landed and gone ashore, we lay on the ground for a long time to recover from our long ordeal. Then at last we got up, and chose thirty of our group to stay and guard the ship and twenty to go inland with me and explore the island. We had gone about six 7 hundred yards from the sea, passing through a wood, when we saw a bronze slab, inscribed with Greek letters, faint and worn away, which stated: 'Heracles and Dionysus came as far as here.' And there were also two footprints on the rock near by, one of them a hundred feet long, the other shorter: I suppose the smaller one was that of Dionysus and the other that of Heracles. We saluted them respectfully and went on, but we hadn't got far when we arrived at a river flowing with wine, which was extremely like Chian. It was wide and full, so that in some places it was even navigable. This made us much more inclined to believe the inscription on the slab, as we could see evidence of Dionysus' visit. I decided to find out the source of the river and went up beside its stream. I didn't find one single source, but a lot of large vines full of clusters, each having by its root a spring of clear wine, and from these the river took its rise. We could also see lots of fish in it, very like wine in colour and taste. Indeed, when we had caught and eaten some of them we got tipsy, and when we cut them open we actually found them full of lees. However, we later had the idea of mixing them with other fish, which came from water, and so diluting our alcoholic intake.

Then, having passed over the river where it could be forded, we 8 found a most extraordinary kind of grapevine. In each one the trunk itself that came out of the ground was thick and well-grown, but the upper part was a woman, perfectly formed from the waist up: just like the paintings we've seen of Daphne changing into a tree when Apollo is about to catch her.* Out of their finger-tips grew branches covered in grapes. Even the hair on their heads was formed of tendrils and leaves and grape-clusters. As we approached they greeted us warmly, some speaking Lydian and some Indian, but most of them Greek. They even kissed our lips, and each one who was kissed immediately became reeling drunk. But they didn't let us pick their fruit, but cried out in pain if we tried to pull it off. Some even wanted to make love to us, and when two of my companions had intercourse with them, they couldn't detach themselves, but were gripped firmly by their genitals, which took root with the woman's so that they grew together. And now branches had grown from their fingers, and they were so 9 covered in tendrils that they too were almost ready to bear fruit. We abandoned them and rushed back to the boat, and having got there we told the men we'd left behind all that had happened, including our companions' love-making with the vines. Then we took some jars and filled them with water as well as with wine from the river, and made our camp there on the beach close by. At dawn we set sail with the help of a moderate breeze.

Around noon when we were now out of sight of the island, a whirlwind suddenly appeared, and spinning the boat around lifted it up to a height of about forty miles and didn't let it down again onto the sea; but while it was hanging up there a wind struck the sails, 10 and filling the canvas drove us forward. For seven days and nights we travelled through the air, and on the eighth day we saw in it an extensive land, seemingly an island, circular and shining bright with a great light. We put in to it, and dropping anchor we disembarked, and exploring it we found the place was inhabited and cultivated. From there we could see nothing by day, but after nightfall a lot of other islands began to appear near by, some quite large and some smaller, and of a fiery colour. There was also another land below us, with cities and rivers on it, and seas and forests and mountains. We assumed that this was our own world.

11 We decided to venture even further inland, but then we encountered what were known locally as Vulture-Cavalry, and they captured us. These are men riding on large vultures and using the birds as horses. The vultures are large and generally have three heads. You can get some idea of their size if I tell you that each of their feathers is longer and thicker than the mast of a large merchantman. These Vulture-Cavalry have orders to fly around the country, and to bring any stranger they find before the king; so naturally they collared us and took us to him. He inspected us, and making a guess from our clothes said, 'So, strangers, you are Greeks?' We admitted we were, and he said, 'Well, how did you get here, having so much air to cross over?' We told him everything, and then he began and told us his story: that he too was a human being, named Endymion,* and once while he was sleeping he had been snatched away from our land, and arriving there had been made king of that country. He told us that the land there was what to us below appears as the moon. But he urged us

206

not to worry or feel we were in any danger, for all our needs would be taken care of. 'And', he went on, 'if I am successful in the war I am now waging against the inhabitants of the sun, you shall spend your lives as happily as you like with me.' We asked who were his enemies and the reason for the dispute, and he replied: 'Phaethon, the king of the sun's inhabitants—for it is inhabited, just like the moon—has been making war against us for a long time. It began like this. I once collected all the poorest people in my kingdom, wishing to establish a colony on the Morning Star, since it was empty of inhabitants. Phaethon was envious of this and prevented the colonization, confronting us halfway through the journey with his Ant-Cavalry. We were defeated on that occasion, as we couldn't match their equipment, and retreated; but now I want to resume the contest and set up the colony. So, if you wish, join forces with me, and I will supply you each with one of the royal vultures, and the rest of your equipment. We shall set out tomorrow.' 'Agreed,' I said, 'since that is your plan.'

So we stayed and had dinner with him, and at dawn we got up and were allotted our stations: for the scouts reported that the enemy were near. Our army numbered a hundred thousand, not counting porters, engineers, and the infantry and foreign allies. Of this number eighty thousand were Vulture-Cavalry and twenty thousand were mounted on Cabbage-Wingers. This is a massive bird, which is covered all over thickly with cabbage instead of feathers and has wings much resembling lettuce-leaves. Stationed next to these were the Millet-Shooters and the Garlic-Fighters. Allies also came to Endymion from the Great Bear: thirty thousand Flea-Archers and fifty thousand Wind-Runners. The Flea-Archers ride on huge fleas (hence the name), and each flea is as big as twelve elephants. The Wind-Runners are infantry, but they are borne through the air without wings. Their method of flight is that they girdle up their long tunics to form folds that fill with wind like sails, and so they are carried along like boats. Generally they serve as light-armed troops in warfare. There was a report too that seventy thousand Sparrow-Acorns and five thousand Crane-Cavalry were to come from the stars over Cappadocia; but as they never arrived I didn't see them, so I've not ventured to describe their appearance, as amazing and incredible things were said about them.

This was the force that Endymion led. They all had the same equipment: helmets made of beans, their beans being big and tough; all their scale-armour of lupins (the lupin-husks being stitched together to make the armour, and the husk of lupin in their country is as unbreakable as horn); and their shields and swords of Greek design. When it was time, they were deployed as follows: on the right wing were the Vulture-Cavalry and the king, with the crack troops around him (including ourselves); on the left, the Grass-Wingers; in the centre, the allies, in whatever formation they chose. The infantry numbered around sixty million, stationed as follows. Spiders in that region are numerous and very large—each of them much bigger than the Cyclades islands. These were ordered by Endymion to cover with a web the air between the moon and the Morning Star. As soon as they had done this and created a plain, he deployed the infantry on it, under the leadership of Batlet, son of Fairweather, and two others.

16   Turning to the enemy, on the left were the Ant-Cavalry, and among them Phaethon. These are huge creatures with wings, resembling our ants except in size, as the largest was two hundred feet long. Not only the riders on the ants fought, but the ants themselves too, making particular use of their feelers. There were said to be about fifty thousand of these. On their right were stationed the Sky-Gnats, also numbering around fifty thousand, all of these being archers riding huge gnats. Next to them came the Sky-Dancers, light-armed infantry, but good warriors for all that; for they catapulted enormous radishes at long range, and anyone so struck collapsed immediately and died of a foul-smelling wound. Apparently they smear their missiles with mallow poison. Next to them were stationed ten thousand Stalk-Mushrooms, heavy-armed troops used for close fighting. Their name arises from the fact that they used mushrooms for shields and asparagus stalks for spears. Beside them stood the Dog-Acorns, sent to him by the inhabitants of the Dog Star: these were five thousand dog-faced men, who fight mounted on winged acorns. We were told that Phaethon too had late-arriving allies, slingers whom he had sent for from the Milky Way, and the Cloud-Centaurs. The latter did arrive just when the battle was decided—if only they hadn't; but the slingers never turned up at all, which it is said made Phaethon furious with them afterwards, so that he ravaged their country with fire.

17   Such was the armament Phaethon brought with him. The battle began as soon as the standards were raised and the donkeys on both sides had brayed (donkeys being their trumpeters), and the fight went on. The left wing of the Heliots immediately fled, without even waiting for the charge of the Vulture-Cavalry, and we chased and slaughtered them. But their right wing was too much for our left, and

the Sky-Gnats advanced in pursuit right up to our infantry. But when these too came to the rescue, they turned and fled, especially when they saw that their left wing had been beaten. The defeat was decisive, many being killed and many taken alive; and so much blood was spilt on the clouds that they seemed as if they were dyed red, as they look to us when the sun is setting. A lot of blood also dripped onto the earth, so that I surmised that something like this must have happened up there long ago, which made Homer suppose that Zeus had caused a rain of blood because of the death of Sarpedon.*

We returned from the pursuit and set up two trophies, one on the spider-webs celebrating the infantry battle, and the other on the clouds for the air battle. We were just in the middle of this when the scouts reported that the Cloud-Centaurs, who should have come before the battle to help Phaethon, were approaching. And there they were indeed advancing on us, an extraordinary sight, creatures compounded of men and winged horses. The men were as large as the Colossus of Rhodes measured from the waist up, and the horses as big as a large merchantman. However, I have not recorded their number, in case no one believes it, it was so enormous. They were led by the Archer from the Zodiac. When they realized that their friends had been defeated, they sent a message to Phaethon to return to the attack, and then putting themselves into formation they fell on the disorganized Selenites, who had abandoned battle-order and scattered in pursuit and to plunder. They routed them all, pursued the king himself to the city, and killed most of his birds. They then tore up his trophies and overran the whole spider-web plain, and they captured me and two of my companions. By now Phaethon too had arrived, and other trophies were being set up in turn by the enemy.

Well, that same day we were taken away to the sun, with our hands tied behind us with lengths of spider-web. The enemy decided not to besiege the city, but as they made their way back they built a wall across the intervening air, to stop the sun's rays reaching the moon. It was a double wall and formed of cloud, so that a real eclipse of the moon resulted, and it was covered totally in continual darkness. Endymion was distressed by all this, and sent to beg them to pull down the wall and not to let them live their lives in darkness. He promised to pay tribute, and joining them as allies not to make war on them again, saying he was willing to offer hostages as pledges for all this. Phaethon called two assemblies: in the first their anger remained

18

19

implacable; but in the second they changed their minds, and peace was agreed on these terms:

20 On the following conditions the Heliots and their allies have made a truce with the Selenites and their allies:

That the Heliots destroy the dividing wall and do not attack the moon again, and that they return their prisoners, each for an agreed sum.

That the Selenites allow the stars to be self-governing, and do not bear arms against the Heliots.

That each comes to the aid of the other if it is attacked.

That each year the king of the Selenites pay as tribute to the king of the Heliots ten thousand jars of dew, and give ten thousand of his people as hostages.

That the colony on the Morning Star be established jointly, and anyone who wishes may join it.

That the truce be inscribed on a block of electrum and set up in mid-air on the boundaries of their territories.

Sworn to by Pyronides, Therites, and Phlogios for the Heliots; and Nyctor, Menios, and Polylampes for the Selenites.

21 These were the terms of the peace; the wall was at once pulled down, and they handed over us prisoners. When we arrived at the moon, our companions and Endymion himself met us and gave us a tearful welcome. He was anxious that I should stay with him and join in the colony, and as there are no women there, he promised me his own son in marriage. But I refused firmly, and asked him to send me back down to the sea. When he saw that he couldn't persuade me, he sent us back after entertaining us for seven days.

22 But in the course of my stay on the moon I noticed some strange and remarkable things, of which I want to tell you. Firstly, they are not born of women but of men: they marry men, and they don't even have a word for woman. Up to the age of 25 each acts as a wife, and after that as a husband. They carry their babies not in the belly but in the calf of the leg. After conception, the calf starts swelling, and when the time comes they cut it open and deliver the baby dead. They then bring it to life by holding it up to the wind with its mouth open. My guess is that we Greeks have got our word 'belly of the leg'* from there, since among them the calf acts as a belly. And I'll tell you something else even stranger. There is a race of people among them called Tree-men, who are born as follows. They cut a man's right testicle and plant it in the ground. From this grows a very large tree,

made of flesh and shaped like a phallus, with branches and leaves, and fruit in the form of acorns a cubit long. When these are ripe they pick them and shell out the men. These are given artificial genitals, some of ivory, others (in the case of poor people) of wood, and these serve them in having intercourse with their mates.

When a man grows old, he doesn't die but evaporates like smoke. 23 They all have the same food. Having lit a fire they roast frogs on the coals: they have a lot of frogs flying around in the air; and while they are roasting, they sit around as if at a table, greedily inhaling the rising steam, and so feast themselves. This is their food, and their drink is air, which is squeezed into a cup and condenses like dew. They pass neither urine nor stool, not even having orifices where we have them. And youths offer themselves to their lovers not using the rump, but behind the knee, above the calf, where there is an opening.

They think a man is handsome if he is bald and hairless, and they loathe long-haired people. It is quite the reverse on the comets, where long-haired men are admired:* some visitors to the moon told us about them. Furthermore, they grow beards just above their knees; and they don't have toe-nails, and in fact have only one toe. Each man has a large cabbage growing over his bottom like a tail: it is always green, and doesn't break if he falls over backwards. Their nose mucus 24 is a very pungent sort of honey; and when they work hard or take exercise they sweat all over with milk, such that they can make cheese from it by adding a few drops of the honey. They make oil from onions, which is very rich and fragrant, like myrrh. They also have a lot of water-bearing vines, on which the grape-clusters are like hail-stones; and my theory is that our hailstorms are caused by the clusters bursting when these vines are roughly shaken by a wind. They use their belly as a pocket for putting useful things into, as it can be opened and shut again. They don't seem to have bowels there: the belly is just lined all over inside with thick hair, so that their children can shelter there when it is cold.

Rich people among them have clothes of pliable glass, while the 25 poor wear woven bronze; for the country there is rich in bronze, which they prepare like wool by soaking it in water. But when it comes to their eyes, I hesitate to tell you about them, in case you think I'm lying because my account is so incredible. Still, I will tell you this as well. They have removable eyes, and when they wish to they take them out and keep them safe until they want to see, when they put them back in so they can see. Many of them lose their own and borrow others' eyes to see with; and rich people keep a large supply of them. Their ears are formed of plane tree leaves, except for the acorn-men,

26 who are unique in having wooden ones. And here's another strange thing I saw in the royal palace. A large mirror is placed over a well, which isn't very deep, and if you go down into the well you can hear everything that is said amongst us on earth; and if you look into the mirror you can see all the cities and all the countries, as if you were actually standing in each. I too was then able to see my own family and the whole of my country; but I can't tell you for certain whether they saw me too. If anyone doesn't believe all this, he'll know I'm telling the truth should he ever get there himself.

27 Well, anyway, we bade the king and his friends a fond farewell, embarked and set off. Endymion also gave me some gifts: two tunics of glass and five of bronze, and a suit of armour made of lupin—all of which I left behind in the whale. He also sent a thousand of the

28 Vulture-Cavalry to escort us for about sixty miles. On our journey we passed by many other countries, and landed on the Morning Star while it was still being colonized, where we disembarked to replenish our water. Putting out again, we headed for the Zodiac, keeping the sun on our left and staying close to the shore. We didn't land there, though my companions were very keen to do so, as the wind was against us. But we saw that the land was flourishing and fertile and well watered, and full of many good things. When they spotted us the Cloud-Centaurs, who were serving with Phaethon, flew on to the ship; but learning that we were allies under treaty they went away.

29 The Vulture-Cavalry had already left us.

Sailing for the following night and day, we arrived around evening at Lamp City, which was already on our downward journey. This city lies in the air between the Pleiades and the Hyades, but much lower than the Zodiac. We landed, but couldn't find any men, only a lot of lamps rushing around, and busy in the square and around the harbour. Some were small and poor-looking, but a few, who were large and powerful, shone very bright and clear. They all have their own separate houses and lamp stands, and they have names like men, and we could hear them speaking. They didn't harm us, but offered us entertainment as their guests. However, we were afraid, and none of us dared to eat anything or fall asleep. They have a public building in the middle of the city, where their chief magistrate sits throughout the night and summons each of them by name; and anyone who does not answer is condemned to death for deserting his post—death meaning to be extinguished. We attended the hearings and saw what happened, and we heard the lamps defending themselves and explaining why they were delayed. There I recognized our own lamp, and I spoke to him and asked him for news from home, and he told me how everything was there.

We stayed there that night, and on the following day we set sail, being now close to the clouds. There we also saw Cloudcuckoo-city* and marvelled at it; but the wind didn't allow us to land there. The king there was said to be Crow, son of Blackbird; and I was put in mind of Aristophanes, a wise and truthful poet whose works are quite unreasonably distrusted. Two days later we could clearly see the ocean, but no land anywhere except the territories in the air, and these were starting to look exceedingly bright and fiery. On the fourth day about midday, the wind gradually fell and subsided, and we landed on the sea. As soon as we touched the water we felt wonder- 30 fully pleased and happy, and enjoyed ourselves as fully as we could, jumping overboard for a swim, as the weather was fine and the sea smooth.

But it seems that a turn for the better often means the start of worse troubles. We'd been sailing for just two days in good weather, and the third dawn was breaking, when towards the east we suddenly saw a large number of sea-monsters and whales. One of them in particular, the largest of all, was about one hundred and seventy miles long. He came up on us with gaping mouth, lashing up the sea to a surge of foam far in advance of him, and showing teeth much larger than human phalluses, all of them sharp as stakes and white as ivory. We embraced and bade one another a last farewell, and waited. In no time he was on us, and with one gulp swallowed us down, ship and all. However, he didn't manage to crush us first with his teeth, as the ship slipped through the gaps into his interior. When we were 31 within him, there was darkness at first and we couldn't see anything, but presently he opened his mouth and we saw a great hollow cavern, flat everywhere and high, and big enough to hold a populous city. Inside it there were small fish lying around, as well as many other dismembered creatures, and the sails and anchors of boats, and human bones and merchandise. In the middle there was land and hills on it, which I suppose was the deposit formed from the mud he had swallowed. Indeed, a forest of all sorts of trees had grown on it, and vegetables had sprouted, and everything seemed to be carefully cultivated. The circuit of the area was about twenty-seven miles. We could also observe sea-birds, gulls, and kingfishers, nesting on the trees.

32   Then indeed we wept for a long time; but after a while we made our companions stir themselves, and we shored up our boat, and ourselves rubbed sticks together to make a fire and made a meal with what was available. We had a plentiful supply of all kinds of fish, and there was still the water from the Morning Star. On rising the next morning, whenever the whale opened his mouth we could sometimes see mountains, sometimes only the sky, and often islands; from which we realized that he was rushing quickly in all directions over the sea. When at last we got used to our surroundings, I took seven of my companions and went into the wood, wanting to have a general scout around. I hadn't yet gone a thousand yards when I came upon a temple of Poseidon, as the inscription revealed, and not far away a lot of graves with tombstones on them, near to a spring of clear water. We also heard a dog barking, there was some smoke in the distance, and we guessed that there was a farm-building as well.

33   So we went on eagerly and came across an old man and a youth working very hard in a garden, which they were irrigating with water from the spring. We stood there with mingled delight and fear; and they too, no doubt with the same feelings, stood there silently. After a while the old man said, 'Who are you, strangers? Are you sea-gods, or just unfortunate men like us? For we are men and bred on the land, but now we have become creatures of the sea and we swim around along with this beast that contains us. We don't even know for certain what is happening to us: we guess we must be dead, but trust we are still alive.' I replied to him: 'We too are men, good sir, newly arrived as we were lately swallowed up, ship and all. We have just now set out, wishing to find out the state of things in the forest; for it seemed very big and dense. But it seems that some god has brought us to see you, and to learn that we aren't the only ones trapped in this beast. But do tell us what's happened to you—who you are and how you came here.' But he said he wouldn't either tell or ask us anything until he had entertained us as best he could; and he took us to the house, which was an ample building, equipped with beds and other furnishings. He served us vegetables and fruit and fish, and poured wine for us as well; and when we had had sufficient he asked us for our story. I told him everything from beginning to end—the storm, the island, the journey through the air, the battle, and everything else up to our descent into the whale.

He was utterly amazed, and then in turn he told us his own 34
adventures in these words: 'Well, strangers, I am a Cypriot by birth.
I set out from my country on a trading trip with my son, whom you
see, and many servants as well, and I sailed for Italy with a mixed
cargo on a large ship, which you probably noticed wrecked in the
whale's mouth. As far as Sicily we had an untroubled voyage; but
there we were caught in a violent gale and carried out to the ocean for
three days, where we encountered the whale and were swallowed up
crew and all: the others were killed, and only the two of us survived.
We buried our companions, built a temple to Poseidon, and now live
this life, growing vegetables and living on fish and fruit. It's a large
forest, as you see, and besides it is full of grape-vines which yield a
very sweet wine. And you may have noticed the spring of lovely cold
water. We make our bed from leaves, have plentiful fires, hunt the
birds that fly in here, and catch fresh fish by going out to the gills of
the beast, where we also have a bath when we want to. There is also
a lake not far off, about two and a half miles round, with all kinds of
fish in it, where we swim and sail in a little boat I built. It is now
twenty-seven years since we were swallowed up. We can perhaps put 35
up with everything else, but our neighbours living around us are
extremely surly and unpleasant, being a fierce and unsociable lot.'
'Really?' I said, 'there are other people in the whale?' 'Yes, lots,' he
replied, 'and they are unwelcoming and uncouth in appearance. In the
western or tail-end of the forest live the Saltfish tribe, with their eel's
eyes and crayfish faces: they are quarrelsome, bold, and flesh-eating.
On one side, by the right-hand wall, are the Sea-Satyrs, who are
like men in their upper halves and lizards in their lower: but they are
less wicked than the others. On the left are the Crabclaws and the
Tunnyheads, who have a friendly alliance with each other. In the
interior dwell the Crabs and the Solefeet, a warlike race and very
fast runners. The eastern area, near the whale's mouth, is mainly
uninhabited, being washed over by the sea. But I live here, paying the
Solefeet an annual rent of five hundred oysters. Well, that is the 36
nature of the land, and you must consider how we are going to fight
all these tribes and how we can survive.' 'How many are there
altogether?' I asked. 'More than a thousand,' he said. 'And what
weapons do they have?' 'Only fish-bones,' he replied. 'Then the best
plan,' I said, 'would be to meet them in battle, since they are unarmed
and we are armed. If we win, we shall live here in peace for the rest of
our lives.'

This was agreed, and we went back to the boat to make our preparations. The pretext for the war was to be non-payment of the tribute, and the appointed date had now arrived. So, when they sent and demanded it, he gave the messengers a disdainful reply and sent them packing. Then first of all the Solefeet and the Crabs, furious with Scintharus—that was his name—arrived with a tremendous

37 uproar. But we expected the attack and were waiting for them fully armed, having posted an ambush of twenty-five men. The ambush had been ordered to fall on the enemy when they saw them go past, and they did so. Falling on them from behind they cut them down, while we ourselves, being twenty-five in number (Scintharus and his son having joined our force), encountered them head on, and risked the engagement with strength and spirit. At length we routed them and chased them right to their lairs. One hundred and seventy of the enemy were killed; on our side only one, the helmsman, who was

38 pierced through the back with a mullet's rib. During that day and night we camped on the battlefield, and set up a trophy made of the dried spine of a dolphin. On the next day the others arrived, having heard what had happened. The Saltfish were on the right wing, led by Pelamys, with the Tunnyheads on the left and the Crabclaws in the middle. The Sea-Satyrs did not engage, as they weren't willing to join either side. We advanced to meet them, and closed with them shouting loudly by the temple of Poseidon, so that the whale echoed like a cave. We routed them, as they were lightly armed, and chased them into the forest, and thereafter we were masters of the country.

39 Shortly afterwards they sent heralds, wishing to collect their dead and treat for peace, but we weren't prepared to come to terms. In fact, on the next day we set out against them and completely wiped them out, all except the Sea-Satyrs, who, when they saw what was happening, rushed away through the gills and threw themselves into the sea. Then we wandered over the country, now free of our enemies, and lived there untroubled from then on. For the most part we occupied ourselves in exercising, in hunting, in cultivating vines, and in gathering fruit from the trees; and, in short, we were like people who live in luxury and are free to roam around in a large prison they cannot escape from.

40 Such was our way of life for a year and eight months; but on day five of the ninth month, around the second mouth-opening (for the whale did this once every hour, so we could tell the time by his openings), around the second opening, as I said, loud shouts and

uproar could suddenly be heard, and what sounded like boatswains' calls and the beating of oars. Full of excitement we crept right up to the mouth of the beast, and standing inside his teeth we saw the most astonishing sight I've ever beheld: enormous men, a hundred yards tall, sailing on enormous islands as though on triremes. I know no one will believe what I'm going to report, but I'll say it anyway. The islands were long but not very high, about fourteen miles in circuit; and on each of them were sailing about a hundred and twenty of those men. Some of these were sitting in a row along each side of the island, rowing with oars made of enormous cypress trees, not even stripped of their branches and leaves. On the stern, so to speak, stood the helmsman on a high hill, gripping a bronze tiller a thousand yards long. On the prow were about forty warriors fully armed, like men in all respects except for their hair, which was blazing flames, so they had no need of helmets. Instead of sails, the wind struck the forest—there was a dense one on each island—filled it like a sail, and so carried the island wherever the helmsman wished. They had a boatswain appointed to keep time for the oarsmen, as they moved on swiftly, like warships.

At first we could see only two or three, but later about six hundred 41 appeared, which took up their positions for action and began a sea-fight. Many dashed together prow to prow, and many were rammed and sank. Some grappled one another, fought fiercely, and weren't easily separated; for the men stationed on the prow showed the utmost zeal in boarding and slaughtering, and gave no quarter. Instead of grappling-irons they threw huge octopuses, linked together with lines, which caught on to the wood and so firmly gripped the island. They struck and inflicted wounds using oysters as big as waggons and hundred-foot sponges. One side was led by Flashing- 42 centaur, and the other by Seadrinker, and the fight apparently arose from an act of plunder: Seadrinker was alleged to have driven off many herds of dolphins belonging to Flashingcentaur. We gathered this from hearing them accusing one another and calling the names of their kings. At length Flashingcentaur's side won, and sank about a hundred and fifty of their enemy's islands, capturing three others with their crews. The rest backed water and fled. They pursued them for a while, but as evening came on they turned back to the wrecks, taking possession of most of the enemy's, and recovering their own: for not less than eighty of their islands had sunk. They also set up a trophy of the island-fight by staking one of the enemy's islands on to the head of the whale. They spent that night by the beast, fastening cables to him and riding at anchor close by: for they had large strong anchors, made of glass. The following day they made a sacrifice on the whale, buried their friends on it, and sailed away rejoicing and singing what seemed to be victory-hymns. That is the story of the island-fight.

A TRUE HISTORY

Book II

After this I could no longer bear life in the whale; I was oppressed by the long continuance there, and I began to look for a way out of it. First we decided to dig our way through the right side and so escape, and we made a start on cutting through it. But when we had got about a thousand yards without achieving anything, we abandoned the tunnel and decided to set the forest on fire, as that would cause the whale to die and thus make our escape easy. So, we started by setting fire to the tail end. For seven days and nights he seemed insensible to the blaze, but on the eighth and ninth we realized that he was suffering: he yawned more listlessly, and whenever he did so he shut his mouth again quickly. By the tenth and eleventh days he was dying and smelling foul. On the twelfth we realized just in time that if his teeth weren't propped open when he yawned, so as not to close again, we would be in danger of being shut up in the corpse and perishing too. So we wedged his mouth open with some large beams, and got our boat near by, storing on it all the water we could and other supplies. Scintharus was to be our helmsman.

Next day the whale finally died, and dragging the boat up we brought it through the gaps, lashed it to the teeth, and gently lowered it onto the sea. Then we climbed onto the whale's back, sacrificed to Poseidon there by the trophy, and camped for three days as there was no wind. On the fourth day we set sail, whereupon we encountered and grounded on many of the corpses from the sea-fight, and we were flabbergasted when we measured the bodies. For a few days we sailed with a mild breeze, but then a strong northerly blew up and it got very cold. This caused the whole sea to freeze, not just on the surface but to a depth of three hundred fathoms, so that we could jump off and run around on the ice. As the wind persisted and we couldn't bear it, we contrived the following—the idea was Scintharus'. We dug a very big cave in the water and stayed in it for thirty days, keeping up a fire, and eating fish which we found by digging them up. When our supplies gave out we emerged, pulled up the boat, which had stuck fast, spread the sail, and were carried along, gliding over the ice as smoothly and easily as if we were sailing. On the fifth day it got warm, the ice dissolved and all was water again.

3   So we sailed for about thirty-four miles, until we put in to a small deserted island, where we took on water, as we had now run out, and shot two wild bulls, and then sailed on. These bulls have horns not on their heads, but under their eyes, as Momus* suggested. After a short while we came to a sea of milk, instead of water, and a white island appeared in it, full of vines. The island was composed of a huge cheese, as we learned later by eating it, and it was about three miles in circuit. And the vines were covered in grapes, but when we squeezed and drank them, it wasn't wine but milk. In the middle of the island a temple had been built to the Nereid Galatea,* as the inscription revealed. So for as long as we stayed there the earth provided us with meat and bread, and our drink was the milk from the grapes. The ruler of this region was said to be Tyro, daughter of Salmoneus, who received this honour from Poseidon after her death.

4   We stayed on the island for five days, and left on the sixth, carried by a breeze over a gentle swell. By the eighth day we were no longer sailing in milk, but in blue salt water, and we could see a host of men running over the sea. They were like us in every respect of shape and size except in their feet, which were made of cork, which I suppose accounted for their name Corkfeet. We were astonished to see them not sinking, but travelling about confidently on the top of the waves. Some of them approached us and greeted us in Greek, saying that they were making for their native Corkland. For a while they journeyed with us, running alongside, and then they turned off and continued their journey, wishing us a good trip.

After a while a lot of islands appeared, close on the left being Corkland, where the men were going, a city built on a huge round cork. Further off and more to the right were five very large and tall islands with fires blazing up extensively from them. Straight ahead

5   was a flat low-lying one, not less than fifty-seven miles off. When we got near it, a marvellously sweet and fragrant breeze blew around us, like the one the historian Herodotus tells us breathes from Arabia the blessed. The sweetness we experienced was like the scent from roses and narcissi and hyacinths and lilies and violets, yes and myrrh and bay and vine-flowers. Enjoying the fragrance and hoping for a successful outcome of our wearisome troubles, we gradually approached the island. There we saw many large harbours all around it, sheltered from the waves, and clear rivers flowing gently into the sea; and meadows too and woods and tuneful birds, some singing on the shores, and many of them in the branches. The air which bathed

the place was pure and fresh, and sweetly blowing breezes stirred the woods gently, so that the swaying branches gave out a constant delightful whistling, like flutes in a lonely place. We could also hear a continuous mingled sound, not clamorous, but like the sort you hear at a party, when some are playing the pipe, others praising the pipers, and others beating time to pipe or lyre. Charmed by all this we put in, 6 moored our boat and disembarked, leaving Scintharus and two companions on board. Making our way through a flowering meadow we met guards on patrol, who bound us with rose-garlands (this being their strongest fetter), and took us to their chief. On the way we learnt from them that this was called the Isle of the Blest, and its ruler was the Cretan Rhadamanthus.* When we were brought to him we found ourselves standing fourth in a queue awaiting judgment. The first 7 case to be heard was Ajax, son of Telamon,* to decide whether it was right for him to associate with the heroes or not: the charge against him was that he had killed himself in a fit of madness. In the end, after much evidence had been heard, Rhadamanthus decreed that for the time being he should be put under the care of Hippocrates, the doctor from Cos, for a dose of hellebore,* and after he was sane again he could join the convivial table. The second judgment dealt with a love-affair, 8 Theseus and Menelaus disputing over Helen to decide which of them should have her to live with. Rhadamanthus decided she should be with Menelaus, since he had endured so much toil and danger for the sake of his marriage. Moreover, Theseus had other wives—the Amazon and the daughters of Minos.* The third case concerned 9 the question of precedence between Alexander, son of Philip, and Hannibal the Carthaginian; and Alexander was judged to be ahead of Hannibal, so his chair was placed next to Cyrus the elder of Persia. We were presented as the fourth case. He asked us what we meant by 10 stepping on holy ground while still alive, and we told him the whole of our story. He had us removed for quite a while, so he could consider and consult his colleagues about us. There were many of these colleagues, including the Athenian Aristides the Just.* When he had arrived at his verdict, the sentence was that we should stand trial after death for our meddlesomeness and roaming around; but for the present we could stay for a fixed period on the island and share in the lives of the heroes, after which we had to leave. They fixed the term of our stay at not more than seven months.

At that point our garlands fell off of their own accord, and we were 11 freed and taken into the city and to the hall of the Blessed. The city itself is made entirely of gold, and there is an emerald wall surrounding it. There are seven gates, all made of single cinnamon-trunks. The foundations of the city and the ground area within the walls are ivory. Then there are temples of all the gods built of beryl, which contain huge monolithic altars of amethyst on which they offer sacrifices. Around the city flows a river of the finest myrrh, a hundred royal cubits wide and five deep, so you can easily swim in it. They have large bathhouses of glass, heated by burning cinnamon; but instead of

12 water in the tubs there is hot dew. Their clothes consist of fine purple spider's webs. They themselves don't have bodies, but are without flesh and intangible: all you see is a semblance of shape; yet though disembodied they are substantial and they move and think and speak. In short, it seems as though their naked souls go around clad in a likeness of a body. Indeed, if you didn't touch them you couldn't prove that what you saw wasn't a body: they are like upright shadows, though not black. No one grows old, but stays the same age he was when he arrived there. Furthermore, there is no night there, nor is day very bright; but the country is covered with a light which is like the greyness towards dawn before the sun has risen. Again, they know only one season of the year; for they have an eternal spring, and the

13 only wind that blows there is the west wind. The country is blooming with all sorts of flowers and cultivated plants, which also give them shade. Their vines give them twelve vintages, yielding a harvest every month; while they said their pomegranates, apples, and other fruit-trees produced thirteen times annually, as they bear twice in one month which is called Minoan.* Instead of wheat the corn-stalks produce ready-baked loaves at their tips, which look like mushrooms. Around the city there are three hundred and sixty-five springs of water, as many again of honey, five hundred of myrrh, though these are smaller, seven rivers of milk and eight of wine.

14 Their dining area is prepared outside the city in the so-called Elysian Plain, which is a lovely meadow, surrounded by dense trees of all sorts to give shade to the diners. Their couches are made of flowers, and winds wait on them and serve them, except for pouring the wine. They don't need this service, as there are tall glass trees around the table made of the clearest crystal, and their fruit consists of cups of all shapes and sizes. So when anyone comes to the table he picks one or two of the cups and puts them beside him: they are immediately filled with wine, and so they have their drink. Instead of garlands, nightingales and other song-birds pick flowers with their

beaks from the neighbouring meadows and drop them like snow on the party, as they fly overhead singing. Moreover, perfume is supplied by thick clouds, which draw up myrrh from the springs and the river, and hanging over the table produce a light rain like dew under gentle pressure from the winds.

While eating they indulge themselves with music and songs, 15 especially singing the epics of Homer. He too is there in person, sharing the feast and reclining in the place above Odysseus. They have choruses of boys and girls, who are conducted and accompanied by Eunomus of Locris, Arion of Lesbos, Anacreon, and Stesichorus*— I did actually see the last named there, as he had by now made his peace with Helen. When these have finished singing, another chorus appears, consisting of swans and swallows and nightingales, and while they are singing the whole wood accompanies them led by the winds. But the biggest contribution to their good cheer is provided by two 16 springs near the table, one of laughter and one of delight. At the start of the festivities they all drink from both of these, and proceed to enjoy themselves with constant laughter.

But I want to tell you what famous men I saw there, who included 17 all the demigods and the men who fought at Troy, except Ajax of Locris:* he alone, they said, was being punished in the place of the ungodly. The foreigners included both Cyruses and the Scythian Anacharsis, the Thracian Zamolxis and the Italian Numa. Then there were Lycurgus of Sparta, Phocion and Tellos of Athens, and the sages except for Periander. I also saw Socrates, son of Sophroniscus, arguing with Nestor and Palamedes, and surrounded by Hyacinthus the Spartan, Narcissus of Thespiae, and Hylas* and other handsome lads. He seemed to me to be in love with Hyacinthus: at any rate he spent most of his time refuting him. The story went that Rhadamanthus was annoyed with Socrates, and had often threatened to banish him from the island if he kept on talking rubbish, and didn't give up his argumentative irony and enjoy himself. Plato alone was missing: allegedly he was living in his imaginary city under the constitution and the laws he drew up himself.* Aristippus and Epicurus* were the 18 most popular there as pleasant and charming drinking-companions. Aesop the Phrygian* was there too, and they treat him as their jester. And even Diogenes of Sinope had altered in character so much that he had married the courtesan Lais,* and he often got up and danced and misbehaved himself when he was drunk. None of the Stoics was there: they were said to be still climbing the steep hill of virtue.*

Chrysippus, so we heard, is forbidden to set foot on the island until he has taken a fourth dose of hellebore.* They said the Academicians wanted to come, but they were still hesitating and thinking about it, because they couldn't even decide whether such an island actually existed. Anyway, I imagine they were afraid to be judged by Rhadamanthus, as they themselves had abolished standards of judgment. Though it was said that many of them had set out to follow those who were coming, but through slowness they couldn't keep up, and so fell behind and turned back halfway.

19   These were the most noteworthy of the company. They honour Achilles in particular, and next to him Theseus. Their attitude to sexual pleasure and intercourse is such that they make love openly and in full view of everyone, male and female, and think there is nothing to be ashamed of in this. Socrates alone used to swear that his association with young people was quite innocent, but everyone judged him guilty of perjury. Indeed, Hyacinthus and Narcissus often gave the game away, but he went on denying the charge. They all have their women in common, and no one is jealous of his neighbour: in this respect they are the most Platonic of the Platonists. And boys offer themselves without argument to anyone who wants them.

20   Two or three days had scarcely passed before I went up to the poet Homer, both of us being at leisure, and asked him lots of questions: in particular where he came from, telling him that this was still a topic of the keenest interest at home.* He replied that he was perfectly aware that some people thought he came from Chios, others thought Smyrna and many thought Colophon. In fact, he said, he was from Babylon, and among the people there he was called not Homer, but Tigranes. Later, when he was a hostage among the Greeks, he had changed his name.* I went on to ask him if he had written the lines the grammarians had rejected, and he said they were all his own. So that made me accuse the grammarians Zenodotus and Aristarchus* of arrant pedantry. Since he had satisfied me on these questions, I asked him next why he had begun the poem with the wrath of Achilles, to which he said there was no deliberate purpose, and it had just come to him like that. Again, I was anxious to know whether he had written the *Odyssey* before the *Iliad*, as many claim, and he said he had not. I realized at once that he was not blind, which is also said about him: he was obviously using his eyes, so there was no need to ask. Often at other times I would do this if I saw him at leisure: I would go up and ask him something, and he willingly answered

every question, especially after the lawsuit, which he won. A libel suit had been brought against him by Thersites* for ridiculing him in the poem, and Homer had won the case, with Odysseus acting as his lawyer.

During this period Pythagoras of Samos also arrived. He had had 21 seven transformations and lived in seven bodies and had now ended the cycles of his soul. His right side was entirely of gold.* He was judged fit to join their community, but the question remained whether he should be called Pythagoras or Euphorbus. Empedocles also arrived, burnt all over and his body thoroughly roasted,* but he was not admitted though he pleaded very strongly.

In the course of time their games took place, the Festival of the 22 Dead. They were presided over by Achilles for the fifth time, and Theseus for the seventh. It would be tedious to tell you all that happened, but I'll mention the most interesting things. The wrestling was won by Caranus,* a descendant of Heracles, who beat Odysseus for the victory wreath. The boxing was a draw in a match between Areius the Egyptian, who is buried in Corinth, and Epeius.* In the combined boxing and wrestling they gave no prizes. I can't remember who won the footrace. In poetry Homer was in fact much the best performer, but Hesiod won the prize.* Every prize was a crown woven with peacock feathers.

The contests were scarcely over, when there was news that those 23 who were being punished in the place of the ungodly had broken their bonds, overpowered their guards, and were making for the island. They were led by Phalaris of Acragas, Busiris of Egypt, Diomedes of Thrace, and Sciron and Pityocamptes.* On hearing this Rhadamanthus drew up the heroes on the beach, under the command of Theseus, Achilles, and Ajax, son of Telamon, who by now had recovered his senses. They clashed in battle and the heroes won. Achilles was chiefly responsible for the victory, but Socrates on the right wing also distinguished himself—rather more than when he fought at Delium as a living man. He stood his ground with unchanged expression when attacked by four of the enemy; and for this he was later given a special mead of honour, a lovely large park in the suburbs, where he used to invite his friends to debate with him. He named the place the Academy of the Dead. The defeated side 24 were seized and bound and sent away for still more severe punishment. Homer wrote an account of this battle too, and when I was leaving he gave me the book to take back to our people at home; but I lost it afterwards along with everything else. This was the opening of the poem:

Sing to me now of the battle, O Muse, which was fought by the shades of the heroes*

Well, they then boiled beans, as they usually do when they have won a battle, and had a feast and a long holiday to celebrate the victory. Pythagoras alone did not take part in it: he sat apart without eating, because he loathed beans.*

25 And so six months passed, and around the middle of the seventh a serious disturbance occurred. Cinyras, Scintharus' son, a tall, good-looking fellow, had long been in love with Helen, and it was quite obvious that she too was absolutely smitten with the lad. So, they often used to exchange glances at meals and toast one another, and they would get up together and wander about the wood on their own. And so it happened that Cinyras was driven by passion and despair to plan to carry Helen off—with her full agreement—and depart to one of the outlying islands, either Corkland or Cheese Island. They had long since recruited three of my boldest companions as accomplices, but Cinyras did not tell his father, as he knew he would try to stop him. Having decided on their plan they carried it out. When it got dark (I wasn't around, as I happened to have fallen asleep at dinner), unnoticed by the others they took Helen with them

26 and set sail with all haste. About midnight Menelaus woke up, and realizing that his wife was not in bed, he raised the alarm, and taking his brother with him went to King Rhadamanthus. As day was breaking the look-outs reported that the ship was visible far out to sea; so Rhadamanthus put fifty of the heroes on board a ship made of a single trunk of asphodel with orders to pursue it. By rowing energetically they caught them up about noon, just as they were approaching the milky part of the ocean near to Cheese Island—so nearly did they escape. They secured the boat with a cable of roses and sailed back. Helen wept and hid her face in shame. Rhadamanthus first asked Cinyras and his associates if they had any other accomplices, and when they said no, he had them bound by their genitals and sent off to

27 the place of the ungodly, after first being whipped with mallow. It was also voted that we should be dismissed from the island before our time was up, being allowed to remain for one more day.

Then indeed I began to weep and wail at the thought of leaving such blessings and renewing my wanderings. But they consoled me by saying that in a few years I would come back to them, and they could already show me my future chair and couch next to the most distinguished company. And I went to Rhadamanthus and begged him earnestly to tell me about my future, and to indicate the course of my voyage. He said I would come to my native land after many wanderings and dangers, but he wouldn't tell me the time assigned for my return. However, he pointed to the islands near by—there were five clearly visible and a sixth further off—and told me that the five nearer ones were the islands of the ungodly. 'You can see', he said, 'a lot of smoke rising from them; the sixth one over there is the City of Dreams. Beyond that is Calypso's island,* but you can't see it yet. After you have sailed past these, you will come to the great continent opposite to the one where your people live. Then, after many adventures and travelling through different nations and living among hostile men, you will come at last to the other continent.'

Saying this, he picked up a mallow-root from the ground and gave 28 it to me, telling me to pray to it at times of extreme peril. And he urged me if ever I reached this country not to stir the fire with a sword,* nor to eat lupins, nor to make love to a youth over 18: if I remembered these things I could hope to come back to the island.

So I then prepared for the voyage, and when the time came I shared a feast with them. Next day I went to the poet Homer and asked him to compose me an epigram in two lines, and when he had done this I carved it on a block of beryl which I set up near the harbour. It ran as follows:

> Dear to the blessed gods did Lucian here survey
> All things, and then returning homeward made his way.*

That day too I remained, and on the following put to sea with an 29 escort of heroes. It was then that Odysseus came to me unknown to Penelope, and gave me a letter to take to Calypso on the island of Ogygia. Rhadamanthus sent the pilot Nauplius with me, so that if we put in at the islands, no one would seize us, as he could explain that we were sailing on other business.

When we had progressed beyond the sweet-smelling air, we were suddenly greeted by a foul odour, as of asphalt and brimstone and pitch all burning together, and vile and intolerable fumes as of roasting human flesh. The air was thick and murky, and a pitchy dew dripped out of it; and we could hear the crack of whips and the wailing of many people. We did not put in to the other islands, but 30 the one we landed on was surrounded by sheer cliffs; the ground was hard, rugged and stony; and there were no trees nor water. Still, we managed to crawl up the cliffs, and went along a path full of brambles and sharp stakes, the whole being hideous to look at. Then we came to the enclosure and the place of punishment, and the first thing that astonished us was the nature of the spot. The ground itself was bristling with swords and sharp stakes, and three rivers flowed around it, one of mud, the second of blood, and the innermost one of fire. This last was very wide and impassable; it ran like water and had billows like the sea, and it was full of fish, some resembling torches, and others, which were smaller, like live coals: they were called lampfish.

31   There was one narrow path leading in by all the rivers, and the warder on duty was Timon of Athens.* But we managed to get past, and with Nauplius as our guide we saw many kings being punished, and many ordinary people too, some of whom we recognized. We saw Cinyras hanging by his genitals over a slow fire. The guides told us about the lives of each one and the crimes for which they were being punished, and the severest penalties awaited those who had written falsehoods—these included Ctesias of Cnidos and Herodotus and many others. Seeing them I had good hopes for the future, for I have
32   never knowingly told a lie. Well, I quickly turned back to the ship, for I couldn't bear the sight of this, and bidding farewell to Nauplius I sailed away.

In a short while the Island of Dreams appeared close to us, though it was dim and hard to make out. It was itself somewhat like a dream, for as we drew near it withdrew and receded and seemed to move further and further off. But at last we got to it, and sailing into the harbour called Sleep, we landed in the late afternoon near the ivory gates, where the sanctuary of the Cock is; and we proceeded into the city, where we saw many dreams of various sorts. But I want to tell you first about the city, since nobody else has described it, and the
33   only one even to mention it, Homer, hasn't given full details.* It is surrounded on all sides by a wood, the trees consisting of tall poppies and mandrakes, in which dwell large numbers of bats, the only flying creature in the island. Near by a river flows which they call Sleepwalker, and there are two springs by the gates, called Unwaking and Nightlong. The city wall is high and multi-coloured, very like a rainbow to look at, and it has four gates in it, not two as Homer says. Two of these look towards the Plain of Stupor, one made of iron and

the other earthenware: it is through these they say that terrifying, murderous, and cruel dreams go forth. The other two face the harbour and the sea, one of which is of horn, and the other, by which we came in, of ivory. On the right as you enter the city is the temple of Night; for the gods they worship are mainly Night and the Cock, and he has a sanctuary near the harbour. On the left is the palace of Sleep. He is their ruler, and he has appointed two viceroys or lieutenants, Nightmare, son of Meaningless, and Richsounding, son of Fantasy. In the middle of the market square is a spring, called Heavyhead, and near by are two temples, one of Falsehood and one of Truth. There also is their innermost shrine and oracle, presided over by the prophet Antiphon,* who interprets the dreams, being appointed to this office by Sleep. The dreams themselves had no fixed nature or appearance: 34 some being tall, good-looking, and well-shaped, others short and ugly; and some seemed made of gold, and others humble and shabby. Among them too there were some with wings, some monstrous, and others equipped as if for a pageant, dressed up as kings and gods, and so on. Many of these we even recognized, having seen them long ago among us: indeed, they came up to us and greeted us like old friends, and taking charge of us they put us to sleep, and entertained us very lavishly and kindly. It was a splendid reception, including a promise to make us kings and viceroys. Some even took us off to our homelands to show us our friends, returning the same day. We 35 stayed there for thirty days and thirty nights, enjoying our long sleep enormously. Then suddenly a great clap of thunder woke us, and we jumped up, laid in supplies, and sailed off.

On the third day after that we arrived at the island of Ogygia and disembarked. But I previously opened the letter and read the contents, which ran as follows: 'Odysseus greets Calypso. I want you to know that as soon as I had built the raft and sailed away from you I was shipwrecked, but with the help of Leucothea I just managed to get safely to the land of the Phaeaceans. They gave me an escort home, where I found a lot of men courting my wife and living it up in our home. I slew them all, but was myself later killed by Telegonus my son by Circe; and now I am in the Island of the Blessed, bitterly regretting having given up my life with you and your offer of immortality. So if I get the opportunity, I shall run away and come to you.' Apart from this the letter asked her to look after us. I went up a 36 short way from the sea and found the cave, just as Homer described it,* and Calypso herself, spinning wool. She took the letter and read it, and first wept bitterly, but then she invited us in hospitably and gave us a lavish meal. She asked us about Odysseus and Penelope, what she looked like, and whether she had good sense, as Odysseus long ago boasted of her. We gave her the sort of answers we thought would cheer her up.

37   Then we went back to the ship and slept near to it on the shore. At dawn we put out as the wind was rising, we were driven by a storm for two days, and on the third we fell in with the Pumpkin-pirates. These are fierce men from the islands near by, who prey on passing sailors. Their boats are large pumpkins, sixty cubits long: they take a dried pumpkin, hollow it out and remove the pith, and then sail in it, using reeds for masts and a pumpkin-leaf for a sail. They attacked and fought us with two crews, and wounded many of us by shooting pumpkin-seeds at us. For some time the battle was even, then around midday we saw the Nut-sailors coming up behind the Pumpkin-pirates. They were hostile to each other, as became clear; for when the Pumpkin-pirates saw them coming, they forgot about us and turned

38   round to engage with them. Meanwhile, we hoisted sail and made off, leaving them fighting; and it was obvious that the Nut-sailors would win, as there were more of them—they had five crews—and they were fighting from stronger boats. Their ships were empty half-nutshells, each fifteen fathoms long.

When we were out of sight of them, we dressed our wounded, and after that we generally kept under arms, constantly expecting to

39   be attacked, and not without reason. The sun hadn't set when we were assailed from a deserted island by about twenty men riding on enormous dolphins, and these were pirates too. The dolphins carried them safely, leaping up and neighing like horses. As they approached us they separated into two groups, shooting at us from both sides with dried cuttlefish and crabs' eyes. But we returned fire with spears and arrows, which they couldn't withstand, and most of them were wounded and fled back to the island.

40   About midnight there was a calm, and we unexpectedly ran on to a huge halcyon's nest: it was actually almost seven miles in circuit. The bird was floating on it, warming her eggs, herself not much smaller than the nest; and indeed as she flew up she almost sank the ship with the gust from her wings. Anyway, she flew off with a mournful cry. We landed as day was breaking, and noticed that the nest was like a very large raft made of huge trees. In it were five hundred eggs, each larger than a jar of Chian wine, and we could

already see chicks inside, and hear them chirping. We cut open one of the eggs with axes and took out the unfledged chick: it was bigger than twenty vultures.

We left the nest and sailed on for about twenty-three miles, when 41 some truly remarkable portents occurred to us. Our stern-post goose figure suddenly flapped its wings and gave a cackle, our helmsman Scintharus, bald up to now, grew a shock of hair, and, most incredible of all, the ship's mast put forth buds and branches and bore fruit at its top—figs and black grapes, not yet ripe. Seeing this we naturally felt very agitated, and the strangeness of the phenomenon made us offer a prayer to the gods. Before we had gone sixty miles further 42 on our course we saw a large, dense forest of pines and cypresses. We supposed it was land, but it was actually a bottomless sea, planted over with rootless trees, though the trees still stood up straight and motionless, as though floating. As we drew near and grasped the whole picture, it was difficult to decide what to do: we couldn't sail between the trees, they were so closely massed together nor did it seem feasible to turn back. I climbed the tallest tree to see what things were like on the other side, and I could see that the forest extended for five or six miles or a bit more, and that another ocean lay beyond it. So we decided to lift the boat on to the tree-tops, which were dense, and see if we could carry it over to the sea on the other side. This we managed to do. We attached a strong cable to it, and climbing the trees dragged it up with a great effort, set it on the branches, and spreading our sails we sailed along as if on the sea, propelled by the force of the wind. At that point I thought of that line of the poet Antimachus, who says somewhere:

And as they thus their woodland voyage pursued.*

However, we managed to force our way through the wood and got 43 to the water. There in the same way we lowered the boat again, and sailed on through clear, pure water until we came to a great chasm caused by the parting of the water, like the cracks we often see in the earth caused by earthquakes. We furled our sails, but the boat was slow to halt, and was very nearly swept into the chasm. Peering over we saw a gulf about a hundred and fifteen miles deep—a truly frightful and incredible sight: the water stood there as if split in two! But as we stared around, we saw not very far away to the right a bridge constructed of water, which linked the surfaces of the two seas, flowing from one to the other. So we rowed hard and ran hastily to that point, and by a great effort made the crossing, though we never thought we'd do it.

44   After that we came to a smooth sea, and a smallish island, easy of access and inhabited; but the men who dwelt there were savages, the Bullheads, with horns that make them like portrayals we see of the Minotaur. We disembarked and went inland to look for food and water, if we could, as we had run out. We found water close by, but nothing else was to be seen, though we could hear a loud bellowing not far away. We thought it was a herd of cattle, and going forward a short way we came upon these men. When they saw us, they chased us and captured three of my companions, while the rest of us fled back to the sea. But then we all armed ourselves—for we couldn't let our friends go unavenged—and fell on the Bullheads while they were sharing out the flesh of their victims. We routed them all and pursued them, killing about fifty and capturing two, and then returned again with our prisoners. Still, we didn't find any food, so the others urged killing the captives; but I disagreed and kept them under close guard, until an embassy came from the Bullheads, asking for their return on payment of a ransom. We could understand them by the signs they made, and the way they pleaded by plaintive bellowing. The ransom consisted of several cheeses, dried fish, onions, and four deer: these had three feet each, two behind and one in front formed of two grown together. For this payment we gave back the prisoners, and after staying there one more day we set sail.

45   By now we were beginning to see fish, there were birds flying around, and other signs were appearing that we were near to land. In a short time we saw men too, who were engaged in a strange form of sailing, seeing that they were both the boatmen and the boats. I'll tell you how this worked. They lie on their backs on the water, and erecting their organs—which are very large—they spread sails on them, holding the sheets in their hands, and as soon as the wind strikes them away they sail. Others followed them, sitting on corks, and harnessing a pair of dolphins, which they drove with reins, so as they moved along they pulled the corks with them. These did us no harm, nor did they try to avoid us, but drove along unconcerned and peacefully, wondering at the style of our boat and examining it carefully from every side.

46   In the evening we arrived at a smallish island, inhabited by women (as we thought) who spoke Greek. They came up to us and welcomed us warmly, all of them young and pretty and dressed much like

courtesans with long robes that swept the ground. The island was called Mischief Island and its city Wantontown. Each of the women took one of us home to be her guest; but I had forebodings and stayed behind for a while, and when I looked around more carefully I saw a lot of human bones and skulls lying about. I decided against raising an outcry to summon my friends and arm ourselves; but I got out my mallow and prayed fervently to it that I might escape the danger threatening me. A little later, when my hostess was looking after me, I noticed that she didn't have a woman's legs but the hooves of an ass. So, drawing my sword I seized and bound her and demanded that she tell me everything. She replied, although reluctantly, that they were women of the sea, called Asslegs, and they made a meal of visiting strangers. 'When we have got them drunk,' she said, 'we go to bed with them and attack them while they are sleeping.' After hearing this I left her tied up there, and going on to a roof-top I gave a loud shout to summon my companions. When they had assembled I told them everything, showed them the bones, and took them in to my prisoner. But she at once turned to water and vanished. I plunged my sword into the water to see what happened, and it turned to blood.

We hastened back to the ship and sailed off; and when day began to dawn, we saw land and assumed it was that which lay opposite to our own world. We greeted it with homage and offered up prayers, and then began to ponder our future. Some of us thought we should just land, and then turn round and go back again; others proposed leaving the boat there and going inland to see who lived there. But while we were deliberating this, a violent storm struck us and dashed the boat to pieces on the beach; and we had great difficulty swimming out, snatching up our arms and anything else we could.

Well, that's what happened to me up to the point that I reached the other continent, first at sea, then during the voyage among the islands and in the air, and after that in the whale, and, when we escaped from it, among the heroes and the dreams, and finally among the Bullheads and the Asslegs. What happened in that continent I'll tell you in the following books.*

DIALOGUES OF THE COURTESANS

THE *Dialogues of the Courtesans* form one of the four sets of usually short comic dialogues by Lucian (the others being *The Gods*, *The Sea-Gods*, and *The Dead*), and the whole group are his most obvious exercise in literary adaptation and pastiche. In particular, the names, the situations, and the themes of the *Courtesans* take us into the world of Greek New Comedy and the mime, the same sort of imaginative reproducing in literature of a lively level of society which we find in the authors of the Greek fictional letters, especially Alciphron and Aristaenetus. Lucian's courtesans are much like those portrayed in other writers, cunning, blunt, and money-grubbing, but also loyal, loving, and quick to defend the honour of their trade. The satirist is at his humorous best in some of these usually unmalicious portrayals of a familiar aspect of Greek society. The following selection is about half the whole set.

Readers will notice the large number of female names in *-ion*: these are neuter diminutives in Greek which were conventional as names for courtesans.

I
Glycerion and Thais

1 G. Thais, you know the Acarnanian soldier, who long ago used to keep Abrotonon and then fell for me, the well-dressed fellow in the military cloak—or have you forgotten him?

T. No, Glycerion, I do know him: he had a drink with us at the harvest festival last year. Why do you ask? You seemed to have something to say about him.

G. That wretch Gorgona, my seeming friend, has got hold of him and is dragging him away from me.

T. So he's made Gorgona his mistress and he won't be coming to see you any more?

G. That's right, Thais, and I find the whole thing very galling.

T. It was a dirty trick, Glycerion, but not surprising—normal behaviour among us courtesans. So you mustn't be too upset or take it out on Gorgona: after all, Abrotonon didn't take it out on

2 you over him, even though you were friends. But I do marvel at what this soldier fellow sees in her, unless he's totally blind and hadn't seen that her hair is going thin and receding a good way from her forehead; her lips are livid; she has a scraggy neck with

the veins sticking out on it; and that long nose! Her one redeeming feature is that she's tall and carries herself well, and she has a very winning smile.

G. Why, Thais, you don't imagine that the Acarnanian has been smitten by her beauty? Don't you know that her mother Chrysarion is a witch who is skilled in Thessalian spells and can summon down the moon?* And they say she even flies around at night. It's she who's driven the fellow mad by giving him one of her potions to drink, and now they're reaping a good harvest from him.

T. Well, you'll find another man to harvest, Glycerion: let this one go.

2

Myrtion, Pamphilus, and Doris

M. So, Pamphilus, you're getting married to the daughter of Philo, ₁ the shipowner—they even say you're already married. So much for all your oaths and your tears—vanished in a moment; and have you forgotten your Myrtion, especially now, Pamphilus, when I'm eight months pregnant? And all I've gained from your love is that you've given me a huge belly, which means a child to be looked after shortly, and that's not good news for a courtesan. For I won't be exposing the child, especially if it's a boy. I'll call him Pamphilus, and keep him as a consolation for my love, and some day he'll reproach you for deserting his poor mother. And it's no beauty you're marrying. I saw her recently at the Thesmophoria* with her mother, though I didn't realize at the time that because of her I wouldn't be seeing Pamphilus again. You'd better examine her too, while there's time, especially her face and her eyes. You mustn't be too put out by her rather greenish eyes or the fact that they squint inwards. But actually, you've seen your bride's father, Philo, and you know his face, so there's no need to look at his daughter.

P. Myrtion, do I have to go on listening to this rubbish you're talking ₂ about girls and shipowner marriages? Do I know any bride, snub-nosed or good-looking? Or that Philo of Alopece—I suppose you mean him—even had a marriageable daughter? He's not even a friend of my father: I remember my father suing him for debt the other day. He owed him a talent, I believe, and refused to pay up; so my father took him to the Admiralty Court* and with difficulty got him to pay it, and not even the whole sum, as my father claimed. But even if I had decided to marry, would I have passed over the daughter of Demeas, who was made general last year—and she is a cousin on my mother's side—to marry Philo's daughter? Where on earth did you hear all this? What empty rivalry have you jealously invented for yourself, Myrtion?

3 M. So you're not getting married, Pamphilus?

P. Are you mad, Myrtion, or just hung-over? Though we didn't get too drunk yesterday.

M. It was Doris here who got me so worked up. I sent her to buy some wool for the baby, and to pray for me to Artemis, who watches over childbirth; and she said she'd met Lesbia—but you'd better tell him yourself what you heard, Doris, unless you made it all up.

D. May I come to a bad end, madam, if I lied. When I got near to the town-hall I met Lesbia, who grinned cheerfully and said, 'Your lover Pamphilus is marrying Philo's daughter.' If I didn't believe her, I was to peep into your street and observe all the garlands and pipe-players and the bustle and the wedding hymn being sung.

P. Well, did you have a peep, Doris?

D. Indeed I did, and I saw it all, as she said.

4 P. I see what led to the misunderstanding. They weren't all lies that Lesbia told you, Doris, and what you told Myrtion was true. But there was no reason at all for your panic, as the wedding wasn't happening in our house. Still, I do now remember my mother saying when I got back from seeing you yesterday, 'Pamphilus, your young friend Charmides, son of our neighbour Aristaenetus, is doing the sensible thing and getting married at last: how long are you going to keep a mistress?' Not paying much attention to her I fell asleep; then it was very early when I left the house, so I didn't notice any of the things that Doris saw later on. If you don't believe me, Doris, go back and look carefully, not just at the street, but to see which door has the garlands. You'll find it's our neighbours' house.

M. You've saved my life, Pamphilus. I would have hanged myself if that's what had happened.

P. It couldn't have happened: I'd never be so mad as to forget Myrtion, especially now she's carrying my child.

4

Melitta and Bacchis

1 M. Bacchis, you know all those Thessalian women,* who are said to utter incantations and can make a woman loved, even if she is deeply hated before: a blessing on you if you could get hold of one

of them and bring her to me. I'd willingly give up all these dresses and gold, if only I could see Charinus coming back to me and hating Simiche as he now hates me.

B. What do you mean? Aren't you two still living together, Melitta, or has Charinus deserted you and gone off to Simiche—you for whom he endured all that anger from his parents, by refusing to marry that rich girl who they said was bringing a dowry of five talents? You yourself told me that.

M. It's all over, Bacchis, and for five days I haven't even laid eyes on him, while he and Simiche have been carousing with his mate Pammenes.

B. That's awful for you, Melitta. But what caused you to split up? It 2 must have been serious.

M. I can't tell you all the details. But the other day, when he came back from the Piraeus* (I think his father had sent him down there to collect a debt), he didn't look at me as he came in, or give me a hug when I ran up to him as usual, but he pushed me away as I tried to embrace him, saying, 'Off you go to Hermotimus the shipowner, or read what's written on the walls in the Ceramicus,* where your names are inscribed together on a stone.' 'What Hermotimus?' I said; 'who's he? And what stone are you talking about?' He didn't reply or have anything to eat, and went to sleep, turning his back to me in bed. You can imagine all the ploys I devised to deal with this, hugging him, pulling him over to me, and kissing him while he kept his face averted. He didn't relent one little bit, and only said, 'If you don't stop bothering me, I'm off, even though it's midnight.'

B. But did you know Hermotimus? 3

M. May you see me even more wretched than I am now, Bacchis, if I know any shipowner called Hermotimus. However, next morning he was up and gone at cock-crow, and I recalled what he'd said about the name being written on some wall in the Ceramicus. So I sent Acis to have a look, and all she could find was this, written near the Dipylon Gate,* on the right as you enter it: 'Melitta loves Hermotimus', and again a bit lower down, 'The shipowner Hermotimus loves Melitta.'

B. Oh, those interfering youths! I see it now: somebody knowing how jealous Charinus is and wanting to vex him, wrote it there, and he believed it immediately. If I see him I'll talk to him: he's still just a child and inexperienced.

M. Where could you see him, when he is spending his time shut up with Simiche? His parents keep looking for him at my house. But, as I said, Bacchis, if we could just find an old woman: if she were here she would be my salvation.

4 B. Well, my love, there's a terribly useful sorceress, Syrian by race, still hale and hearty, who once brought Phanias back to me, when for four whole months he had been angry with me for no reason at all, just like Charinus. I'd given up hope, but through her incantations he was reconciled to me.

M. Can you remember what the old woman charged?

B. She doesn't want a large fee, Melitta—a drachma and a loaf of bread; but in addition you have to leave out seven obols, sulphur, and a torch, along with salt. These she takes up, and she also has to have a bowl of wine mixed, to drink herself. She also needs to have something belonging to the man himself, like clothing or boots or a few hairs, or something of that sort.

M. I have his boots.

5 B. She hangs them on a peg and fumigates them with sulphur, sprinkling salt on the fire and pronouncing both your names. Then she produces a magic wheel* from under her clothes and spins it round, while she glibly reels off an incantation full of fearful and outlandish names. That was her procedure on that occasion, and not long afterwards Phanias, despite the rebukes of his friends and the ceaseless pleading of his mistress Phoebis, came back to me, being mainly induced by the spell. And what's more, the Syrian taught me this spell to make him hate Phoebis: to watch for any footprints she left, and to wipe them out by putting my right foot on her left footprint and my left on her right, saying, 'I have stepped on you and I have got the better of you.' And I did as I was told.

M. Quick, quick, Bacchis! Bring the Syrian woman here at once. And you, Acis, prepare the loaf and the sulphur and everything else we need for the spell.

6

Crobyle and Corinna

1 CROB. So, Corinna, you now know it's by no means as awful as you thought for a girl to become a woman. You've been with a good-looking lad and you've earned your first mina, which I'll use shortly to buy you a necklace.

COR. Yes, please, Mummy; and it must have bright red beads like Philaenis' one.

CROB. Of course. But I must tell you what else you have to do and how to conduct yourself with men. For we have no other means of livelihood, daughter, and you well know what a wretched life we've had during these two years since your blessed father died. When he was alive we were amply provided for; for he was a smith with a great reputation in the Piraeus, and you can hear everyone swearing that there'll never be another smith to match Philinus. When he died, first I sold his tongs and anvil and hammer for two minas, which kept us going for seven months. Since then I've scarcely provided us with enough food, either by weaving or by spinning thread for the weft or the warp. But I have fed you, daughter, and waited in hope.

COR. Do you mean the mina?   2

CROB. No, but I calculated that when you'd attained your present age, you could easily support me and keep yourself in clothes, and you'd be rich and have purple dresses and maids.

COR. But how? What do you mean, mother?

CROB. By consorting with young men, and drinking and sleeping with them for money.

COR. Like Daphnis' daughter, Lyra?

CROB. Exactly.

COR. But she's a courtesan.

CROB. What's wrong with that? You'll also be rich like her, and have lots of lovers. Why are you crying, Corinna? Don't you see what a lot of courtesans there are, how sought after they are, and how much money they make? Dear lady Adrasteia,* I know indeed that Daphnis' girl wore rags until she grew up; but you can see what a figure she makes in public now, with her gold, her bright dresses, and her four maids.

COR. But how did Lyra get all that?   3

CROB. First of all, she's neat and attractive in her dress, she has a cheerful look for all the men, she's not so ready to laugh loudly as you are, but she has a sweet and winning smile. Then, she manages things skilfully when they are together, and doesn't cheat anyone, whether client or escort; and she doesn't throw herself at men. If she goes out to dinner for a fee, she doesn't get drunk: that looks ridiculous, and men hate women like that; nor does she stuff herself vulgarly, but picks up her food with her finger-tips, taking quiet mouthfuls and not filling both cheeks; and she drinks with restraint, and pausing frequently, not gulping it down.

COR. Even if she's feeling thirsty, mother?

CROB. Especially then, Corinna. And she doesn't talk too much or make fun of any of the guests, and she only has eyes for her client. This is why the men all like her. Then, when it's bed-time, she wouldn't do anything wanton or unseemly: she seeks only to attract the man to make him her lover. That's what they all praise in her. If you can really learn all this, we too shall be well off. For in everything else you're way ahead of her – but no more of that, dear Adrasteia: I only pray for long life for you.

4 COR. Tell me, mother, are all the clients like Eucritus, whom I slept with last night?

CROB. Not all: some are better; some are mature men; others not in the least good-looking.

COR. Have I got to sleep with those too?

CROB. Most certainly, my daughter: they pay more, while the good-looking ones want to pay just by being good-looking. You've always got to think of the higher fee, if you want all the women to be soon pointing to you and saying, 'Do you see how tremendously rich Crobyle's daughter Corinna is, and how very fortunate she has made her mother?' What do you say? Will you do it? I know you will, and you'll easily surpass all the other girls. Now go and have a bath, in case your lad Eucritus comes again today: he promised he would.

7
Musarion and her Mother

1 MOTHER. If we find such another lover as Chaereas, Musarion, we'll have to sacrifice a white goat to the earthly Aphrodite, and a heifer to the heavenly Aphrodite of the Gardens,* and offer a garland to Demeter, the Giver of Riches, and we shall be altogether blessed and very fortunate! You can see how much we are getting from the lad at the moment: he's never yet given you even an obol, or a dress, or a pair of shoes, or any perfume; only never-ending excuses and promises and distant hopes. He's always saying, 'If only my father . . .* and I were in possession of my inheritance, it would all be yours.' And you say he has sworn to make you his lawful wedded wife.

MUS. Yes, mother, he swore it by the two goddesses* and by Athena.

MOTHER. And of course you believe him. That's why, when he couldn't pay his contribution to the party recently, you gave him your ring without my knowledge—which he then sold, and drank the proceeds—and your two Ionian necklaces, weighing two darics each, which Praxias, the Chian shipowner, had made in Ephesus and brought back for you. Of course Chaereas had to pay his stint to his dinner companions. I say nothing of your fine linen and your dresses: he really has been a godsend and a blessing fallen among us!

MUS. But he is handsome and beardless, and he says tearfully that 2 he loves me, and he's the son of Dinomache and Laches, the Areopagite,* and he says he'll marry me, and we have great hopes of him if only the old man drops off.

MOTHER. Well then, Musarion, if we need some shoes and the shoemaker wants his two drachmas, we'll tell him, 'We don't have any money, but take a few of our hopes.' And we'll tell the barley-merchant the same thing; and if we are asked for the rent we'll say, 'You'll have to wait until Laches of Colyttus dies: I'll pay you after the wedding.' Aren't you ashamed to be the only courtesan without an earring or a nice wrap?

MUS. So what, mother? Are they happier or prettier than me? 3

MOTHER. No, but they have more sense and they know how to play the courtesan; and they don't trust pretty speeches and young men whose promises are only on their lips. But you are loyal and constant to your man, and won't let anyone approach you but Chaereas. Indeed, the other day when the Acharnian farmer came offering two minas—and he too was beardless, and he'd got the money for the wine he had sold for his father—you sent him packing, and slept with your Adonis, Chaereas.

MUS. So what? Was I supposed to desert Chaereas and take that rustic, who smelt of goat? As the saying goes, I find Chaereas smooth and soft, but the Acharnian a bit of a pig.*

MOTHER. All right, then: he's boorish and smells awful. But you wouldn't have Antiphon, Menecrates' son, either, though he was offering a mina. Wasn't he a good-looking city type, and the same age as Chaereas?

MUS. But Chaereas threatened to cut both our throats if he ever 4 caught me with him.

MOTHER. Don't lots of others make the same threat? Will you on that account do without lovers and live chastely, as if you weren't a courtesan but a priestess of Demeter? Well, enough of that. Today it's the Harvest Festival: what has he given you for the occasion?

MUS. He hasn't anything to give, mummy.

MOTHER. Has he alone not found a way to trick his father, or put up a slave to deceive him, or appealed to his mother, and threatened to sail away to the wars if he's not given something? No, he just sits around, sponging on us, offering nothing himself and not allowing you to accept offers from others. Do you think you'll always be 18, Musarion, or that Chaereas will feel the same for you when he's rich himself and his mother finds a rich match for him? Do you suppose he'll still remember his tears and his kisses and his oaths when he's looking at a dowry of maybe five talents?

MUS. He will remember, and the proof is that he's not yet married, and he's refused to do so, in spite of all the bullying and coercion.

MOTHER. I only hope he's not lying, but I'll remind you of all this when he does marry.

10
Chelidonion and Drosis

1 C. Is young Clinias no longer coming to you, Drosis? I haven't seen him at your place for a long while.

D. No longer, Chelidonion: his tutor has prevented him visiting me any more.

C. Who is he? You don't mean Diotimus, the trainer? He's a friend of mine.

D. No, it's that villainous scoundrel of a philosopher, Aristaenetus.

C. You mean the sullen fellow, with shaggy hair and a thick beard, who's generally walking with his lads in the Painted Hall?*

D. That's the charlatan I mean. I hope I see him dying horribly, with the public executioner dragging him along by his beard.

2 C. What made him persuade Clinias to do that?

D. I've no idea, Chelidonion. But though he'd never slept away from me from when he started going with women—and I was his first woman—for the past three days he hasn't been near our street. This upset me, as somehow I felt a bit involved with him, so I sent Nebris to look out for him while he was in the market square or the Painted Hall. She said she saw him walking around with Aristaenetus, and nodded to him from a distance; but he blushed, fixed his gaze on the ground, and didn't look towards her again. Then they walked together to the Academy.* She followed him as far as the

Dipylon Gate, but he never even turned round, and so she returned with nothing definite to report. You can imagine what a state I've been in since then, as I can't even guess what's come over the lad. 'Surely I haven't upset him in any way,' I kept saying. 'Or does he hate me because he has fallen for another woman? Has his father forbidden him to come?' Many such ideas I turned over in my wretchedness; but late in the afternoon Dromo came to me with this letter from him. Take it and read it, Chelidonion: no doubt you can read.

C. Let's have a look. The writing isn't very clear: it's such a scrawl 3 that the writer must have been in great haste. He says, 'The gods are my witnesses how much I loved you, Drosis.'

D. Woe is me! He didn't even start with a greeting.

C. 'And now I am leaving you not because I hate you but because I'm forced to. My father has entrusted me to Aristaenetus to study philosophy with him; and he, having learnt all about us, rebuked me very seriously, saying that it was shameful for the son of Architeles and Erasiclia to be consorting with a courtesan, as it was much better to prefer virtue to pleasure.'

D. Curses on the old humbug for teaching the lad such a lesson!

C. 'So I have to obey him, as he follows me closely and keeps a strict eye on me. Indeed, I'm not even allowed to look at anyone but him. If I live a life of moderation, and do everything he tells me, he promises me I'll be completely happy and I'll become virtuous through training in hardships. It's been difficult stealing away to write to you. I hope you'll be happy, and do not forget Clinias.'

D. What do you think of the letter, Chelidonion? 4

C. The rest of it could have been written by a Scythian,* but the bit about not forgetting Clinias offers some hope.

D. That's my view too; and anyway I'm dying from love. But Dromo said that Aristaenetus is the type who likes boys, and only makes an excuse of teaching them in order to make the best looking youths his lovers; and that privately he makes propositions to Clinias, promising to make him like a god. What's more, he reads with him amorous treatises of the old philosophers written to their pupils, and is completely taken up with the lad. Dromo threatened to denounce him to Clinias' father as well.

C. Dromo deserved a jolly good meal for that, Drosis.

D. I gave him one, but even without that he's on my side: he too is consumed with love—for Nebris.

c. Cheer up: all will be well. I think I'll write up on the wall in the Ceramicus, where Architeles usually goes for a walk, 'Aristaenetus is seducing Clinias,' so we can help Dromo to run him down.*

d. How can you manage that without being seen?

c. When it's dark, Drosis: I'll find a piece of charcoal.

d. Splendid! Oh Chelidonion, if only we can join forces against that charlatan Aristaenetus!

14

Dorio and Myrtale

1 d. Now you shut the door against me, Myrtale, now I'm impoverished because of you, though when I was bringing you all those presents I was your beloved, your man, your master, your everything. But now I'm drained completely dry, and you've found that Bithynian merchant to be your lover, I'm shut out and stand weeping before the door;* while he enjoys your love at night and spends the whole night alone with you, and you say he's made you pregnant.

m. That really makes me choke, Dorio, when you talk about all the things you've given me and how you're impoverished because of me. Now, just begin at the beginning and count up all the things you've brought me.

2 d. Good idea, Myrtale: let's work it out. First of all, shoes from Sicyon worth two drachmas. Put down two drachmas.

m. But you slept two nights with me.

d. And when I came back from Syria, a jar of Phoenician perfume, and, by Poseidon, that was also two drachmas.

m. But when you were setting sail I gave you that little thigh-length coat to wear while you were rowing. Epiurus, the prow-officer, left it here by mistake when he spent a night with me.

d. Epiurus recognized it the other day in Samos and took it back, though, by the gods, we fought hard over it. Then I brought you onions from Cyprus, and five tunny and four perches when we came back from the Bosporus. What else? A basket full of eight dry ship's loaves, and a jar of figs from Caria; and on another occasion some gilded sandals from Patara, you ungrateful thing! And once I remember bringing you a large cheese from Gythium.

m. Altogether that's about five drachmas, Dorio.

3 d. Oh Myrtale, it was all that a serving seaman could afford. Even now when I'm in charge of the starboard side you despise me; but

didn't I recently at the feast of Aphrodite place a silver drachma at the feet of the goddess on your behalf? Then I also gave your mother two drachmas for some shoes, and often I've slipped Lyde here a couple of obols, sometimes four. Add all this up and it comes to the whole of a sailor's wealth.

M. You mean the onions and the tunny fish, Dorio?

D. Yes: that was all I had to give. I wouldn't be rowing in a boat if I were rich. I've never yet brought my own mother even a head of garlic. I'd love to know what presents the Bithynian has given you.

M. Have a look first at this dress. He bought it, and the bigger of my necklaces.

D. He did? I knew you'd had it a long time.

M. No: the one you're thinking of was much thinner and didn't have emeralds. Then there are these earrings and this rug, and the other day he gave me two minas, and paid our rent for us—a bit better than sandals from Patara and cheese from Gythium and the other trash.

D. But do tell me what sort of a lover he is. He's surely over 50, his hair is receding, and his complexion is like a crayfish. And have you looked at his teeth? And, by Castor and Pollux, what accomplishments he has, especially when he sings, and wants to appear refined, like the proverbial donkey playing the lyre to himself.* Well, good luck to you: you're a well-matched pair, and I hope your child takes after his father. As for me, I'll find some Delphis or Cymbalion who will suit me, or the girl next door to you who plays the pipe, or somebody anyway. We don't all have rugs and necklaces and two-mina fees to give you.

M. Won't she be lucky, whoever has you for a lover, Dorio! You'll be bringing her onions from Cyprus, and cheese whenever you come back from Gythium!

EXPLANATORY NOTES

4 *Homer. When he wants to praise the greatest hero*: *Iliad* 17. 570–2: Athena puts strength and courage into Menelaus.

flying in a mass looking for milk: *Iliad* 2. 469–71; 16. 641–3.

Athena . . . a woman caring for her sleeping child: *Iliad* 4. 130–1.

5 *Hermotimus of Clazomenae*: this story is found elsewhere in Apollonius, *History of Marvels* 3, Pliny, *NH* 7. 174, and Plutarch, *De Genio Socratis* 592c (see the Loeb note here).

a girl called Muia: Muia is the Greek for fly, and the story recalls the similar legend that Tithonus was turned into a grasshopper.

There also lived . . . poetess: this presumably refers to Corinna of Tanagra, a lyric poetess said to be contemporary with Pindar, who was apparently also called Muia (*Suda* s. v. Korinna).

'Twas Muia bit him to the heart: from an unknown play: Kock, *Com. Adesp.* 475.

6 *Strange . . . spear*: from another unknown play: Nauck, *Trag. Adesp.* 295.

Muia the Pythagorean: she is not at all familiar to us, but we are told that Pythagoras had a daughter called Muia (Porphyry, *Life of Pythagoras* 4); and also that Milo of Croton had a wife called Muia who was a Pythagorean philosopher (Iamblichus, *Life of Pythagoras* 267). Possibly they were the same person.

the child of Hermes and Aphrodite . . . twofold beauty: Ovid tells the story (*Met.* 4. 285–388) that the youth Hermaphroditus united with the nymph Salmacis to form one bisexual body.

I am making an elephant out of a fly: the equivalent to our proverb 'to make a mountain out of a mole-hill'. For its diminutive size and its weakness the fly commonly featured in proverbial expressions in Greek and Latin literature. See M. Davies and J. Kathirithamby, *Greek Insects* (Oxford 1986), 155.

8 *Well begun is half done*: Lucian has the proverb also at *Hermotimus* 3, and Horace gives a Latin version at *Epistles* 1. 2. 40.

In my sleep . . . night divine: from *Iliad* 2. 56–7, where Agamemnon is addressing a council of elders.

9 *Pheidias . . . Polyclitus . . . Myron . . . Praxiteles*: four of the most celebrated Greek sculptors. Pheidias, Polyclitus, and Myron belong to the fifth and Praxiteles to the fourth century BC. Pheidias' Zeus was a colossal seated figure which he made for the temple of Zeus at Olympia. Polyclitus' most famous work was his statue of Hera created for the Heraeum at Argos.

living a hare's life: a proverbial expression which is found also in Demosthenes' most famous speech, *De Corona* 263.

10 *Demosthenes . . . Aeschines*: Demosthenes and Aeschines were the two most famous Athenian orators, active at the time when Athens was confronting the increasing menace of Philip of Macedon in the 340s BC onwards.

Socrates himself was nurtured by Sculpture here: Socrates' father Sophroniscus was said to have been a sculptor.

11 *Niobe*: a mythical character who boasted that she had more children than Leto. Consequently Leto's two children, Apollo and Artemis, killed all those of Niobe, who after prolonged weeping was turned into stone. The story was very popular, e.g. Ovid, *Met.* 6. 146 ff.

sowing something over the earth like Triptolemus: Triptolemus of Eleusis was the first to be taught by Ceres the farming skills of ploughing and sowing seed: see Ovid, *Fasti* 4. 559–60.

three nights to conceive, like Heracles: Heracles was conceived during a night which Zeus spent with his mother Alcmena, and which he tripled in length for his visit to her. The story forms the theme of Plautus' play *Amphitruo*.

when Xenophon described his dream: Xenophon, *Anabasis* 3. 1. 11. The dream about his father's burning house was interpreted by Xenophon as either a consolation or a warning: a consolation because in the midst of his difficulties it could represent a shining light from Zeus, or a warning that there was no escape for him.

CHARON

13 *like that Thessalian youth*: Protesilaus, the first Greek to be killed at Troy. His wife obtained leave for him to visit her from Hades for a few hours.

upper Zeus: 'upper' in contrast with the 'lower Zeus', i.e. Pluto.

as he treated Hephaestus: Hephaestus tells how he was thus treated by Zeus at *Iliad* 1. 590–4.

14 *Cyllenian*: a common title for Hermes, from Mount Cyllene in Arcadia, where he was born.

the toll-collector Aeacus . . . even an obol: Aeacus was one of the judges of the dead. An obol was a small Greek coin put into a dead person's mouth as a fee to the ferryman Charon.

Homer tells us that the sons of Aloeus: Otus and Ephialtes: the story is told in *Odyssey* 11. 305–20.

15 *Then upon Ossa Pelion with quivering leaves*: *Odyssey* 11. 315–16.

16 *See . . . distinguish a man from a god*: *Iliad* 5. 127–8, where Athene is addressing Diomedes.

Lynceus: one of the Argonauts and famous for his extraordinarily keen sight: Apollonius, *Argonautica* 1. 153–5.

17 *Poseidon gathering the clouds . . . that sort of thing*: this is a recognizable echo of the passage where Poseidon stirs up a storm in *Odyssey* 5. 291 ff.

Who is that . . . head and broad shoulders?: adapted from *Iliad* 3. 226–7 (as is the 'Homeric' question in section 9 below) where Priam asks Helen to identify Ajax.

Milo: an athlete of legendary strength, who won many victories in wrestling at the Olympian and Pythian games. Cicero also records this anecdote about the bull in *De Senectute* 33.

Cyrus: the founder of the Achaemenid Persian Empire, which he ruled from 559 to 529 BC. He was killed fighting against the Scythian Massagetae (see section 13 below).

Croesus: the last king of Lydia (c.560–546 BC), who was overthrown when his capital Sardis was captured by Cyrus in 546. Solon was a great Athenian poet and lawgiver (chief archon 594–593 BC). Lucian has derived the conversation between these two about the most fortunate of men (but not the discussion about ingots) from Herodotus (1. 30–3). However, in Herodotus' version Tellos comes first.

18 For Croesus' lavish sacrifices and gifts to Apollo see Herodotus 1. 50 ff.

20 *Clotho*: 'the Spinner': one of the three personified Fates (Clotho, Lachesis, and Atropos), whose function was to spin the thread of everyone's life.

the Massagetae: see note to p. 17.

Apis: the sacred bull worshipped by the Egyptians. The story is again in Herodotus (3. 27–38).

In a sea-girt isle: he claims to be some king: an adapted conflation of two Homeric lines, *Odyssey* 1. 50 and 16. 67.

Polycrates: he ruled Samos for about ten years until c.522 BC. Herodotus 3. 120–5 gives an account of his end.

23 *bubbles . . . life of man*: 'Man is a bubble' was proverbial: see Otto, *Sprichwörter*, s.v. *bulla*. Our passage caught the eye of Jeremy Taylor, who quoted it approvingly in his *Holy Dying* (1651).

he compares the race of men to leaves: Glaucus makes the comparison when talking to Diomedes, *Iliad* 6. 146–9.

Lethe: 'forgetfulness': a plain in the underworld. The river which was its boundary (not itself called Lethe, though this is commonly stated) caused the souls who drank of its water to forget their earthly life: see Virgil, *Aeneid* 6. 713–15.

24 *They are equally dead . . . in the asphodel mead*: Lucian writes a patchwork of phrases from many Homeric lines: *Iliad* 1. 130, 4. 512, 9. 319, 320, *Odyssey* 10. 521, 11. 539.

25 *'holy' and 'wide-streeted' . . . 'well-built'*: Charon quotes three commonly used epithets in Homer: often these terms are not particularly significant, but rather evidence of the formulaic elements in the Homeric poems.

Othryadas, inscribing the trophy with his own blood: the fight took place in 546 BC over the possession of the plain of Thyreatis, and Othryadas was the single Spartan to survive for a while: see Herodotus 1. 82; [Plutarch], *Parallela* 306b.

TIMON

26 *O Zeus . . . terrifying bolt*: the Greek phrases here recall Euripides, *Phoenissae* 182–3.

27 *Salmoneus*: a mythical king of Elis who tried to mimic Zeus by simulating lightning and thunder, and was killed by a real thunderbolt: Virgil, *Aeneid* 6. 585 ff.

Deucalion's: in this Greek version of the story of Noah, Deucalion and his wife Pyrrha were forewarned that Zeus would be sending a flood over the earth in anger at the sins of men. They built an ark in which they floated until the waters subsided, and they landed on Lycoreus, the highest summit of Parnassus.

Cronus: the father of Zeus, who in time dethroned him and took his place.

Phaethons: Phaethon was a son of the sun-god Helios, who was allowed by his father to guide the sun's chariot for a day. In doing so he was in danger of setting the world on fire, so Zeus killed him with a thunderbolt (Ovid, *Met.* 1. 750 ff.).

28 *Epimenides' record sleep*: the Greek Rip Van Winkle, Epimenides was an early cosmogonist (perhaps sixth century BC) who was said to have slept for fifty-seven years (Diogenes Laertius 1. 109).

Zeus—unless what the Cretans say about you and your grave there is true after all: in the complex mythology of Zeus there was an early Cretan deity who was identified with the Greek Zeus, and Cretan legend told that this 'Zeus' was dead and buried.

Diasia: an important festival of Zeus at Athens, held on 23 Anthesterion.

29 *all those vultures were tearing at his liver*: a reference to the fate of Prometheus.

Anaxagoras: a major philosopher and original thinker, who was charged with impiety at Athens, but escaped from the city with the help of his pupil and friend, the statesman Pericles.

the Anaceum: the temple of Castor and Pollux in Athens, who had the title 'Anakes', 'lords'.

30 *Danae in a bronze or iron chamber*: Danae was shut up in a room by her father, and visited by Zeus through the roof in the form of a shower of gold.

31 *like the dog in the manger . . . the hungry horse to have it*: the well-known Aesopic fable (no. 163, World's Classics edn.), which Lucian quotes again at *Adversus Indoctum* 30.

32 *Tantalus*: one of the famous criminals punished in Tartarus. For some offence against the gods he had to stand thirsty in water up to his chin, but the water receded from him whenever he tried to drink. He also clutched unavailingly at fruit dangling over his head.

Phineus: a blind Thracian king, tormented by the Harpies who carried off or defiled all his food, until they were driven away by the sons of Boreas (Apollonius Rhodius 2. 178 ff.).

carrying water to the Danaids' jar: another famous punishment in the underworld. The Danaids killed their husbands on their wedding night, and were condemned to be forever pouring water into a leaky vessel. The motif became proverbial for any pointless or frustrated activity.

Pluto . . . splendid gifts, as you can tell from his name: the name Pluto is associated with Ploutos, the Greek for 'wealth'.

33 *mill-house*: this figures among the reminders of the ex-slave's past life because slaves were sent to work at the mill.

more handsome than Nireus . . . richer than sixteen Croesuses: Nireus was the handsomest man among the Greeks at Troy next to Achilles. Cecrops was the mythical first king of Athens, and Codrus reputedly another king of Athens some time in the eleventh century BC. Odysseus was a byword for cunning throughout Greek literature. Croesus was the last king of Lydia (*c.* 560–546 BC), and proverbial for his great wealth.

Aristides . . . Hipponicus and Callias: these names are part of the world of early to mid-fifth-century Athenian politics. Hipponicus and his son Callias belonged to one of the wealthiest families in Athens. Aristides was a cousin of Callias but less well off. Plutarch (*Arist.* 25) tells us that Aristides once declined a loan from Callias because he was more proud of his poverty than Callias of his wealth.

34 *pays homage to you, Hermes, for his windfall*: the god Hermes was regularly thought responsible for lucky finds.

Lynceus: see *Charon*, note to p. 16.

'into the deep-yawning sea' and 'down from the lofty crags': these phrases are from Theognis 175–6.

35 *Hyperbolus or Cleon*: Hyperbolus (d. 411 BC) and Cleon (d. 422 BC) were both radical demagogues active in Athenian public life—not the type that Wealth would like to encounter by mistake.

36 *Slayer of Argus*: the usual interpretation of 'Argeiphontes', and a standard epithet of Hermes. He killed Argus, the many-eyed monster Hera set to watch Io when she was turned into a heifer.

37 *Must I take up to Zeus a speech so harsh and so stubborn?*: from Homer, *Iliad* 15. 202: Iris asks Poseidon if he really wants her to take back a defiant reply to a message from Zeus.

38 *Corybants*: priests of the Anatolian mother-goddess Cybele. Timon calls upon them because the frenzied excitement that characterized their rites matches his own mental fervour.

I fear I'll wake up and find nothing but ashes: a proverbial expression which Lucian uses elsewhere, e.g. *Hermotimus* 71.

O gold, to mortals fairest gift: from Euripides' lost play *Danae*, fr. 324 N.

you shine out like blazing fire: adapted from Pindar, *Olympian Odes* 1. 1–2.

Zeus once turned into gold . . . a lover pouring through the roof: see note on Danae on p. 30.

39 *the Altar of Pity*: according to Pausanias (1. 17. 1) there was an Altar of Pity situated in the Agora at Athens, and this has been identified with the Altar of the Twelve Gods on the northern edge of the Agora. See too the account of it in Statius, *Thebais* 12. 464 ff.

40 *I'll summon you before the Areopagus*: the great judicial council of Athens, which met on the Hill of Ares (the meaning of the name), and dealt with charges including, as here, assault and homicide.

41 *Nestor*: king of Pylos, the elder statesman among the Greek leaders at Troy, respected for his age and his (usually long-winded) counsel.

EXPLANATORY NOTES

41 *his turn to distribute the show-money to the Erechtheis tribe*: this refers to the *theorikon*, a state grant at Athens of two obols given to poorer citizens to allow them to attend theatrical shows. Editors point out that Lucian has slipped up in referring here to the Erechtheis tribe, as Timon's deme Collytus belonged to the Aegeis tribe.

The assembly and both the councils: the Council of Areopagus (see note on p. 40.) and the Council of Five Hundred, which prepared measures to be discussed by the Assembly.

42 *it's not clear that you are a free citizen yourself*: an insulting suggestion that one of Timon's parents had been a slave or not an Athenian.

Zeuxis: one of the most famous painters of antiquity. He flourished in the later fifth century BC, working in Athens and southern Italy, and he was noted for the realism of his pictures.

43 *the Nine Springs*: a well or fountain in Athens with nine spouts: its exact location is much disputed. (See Gomme on Thucydides 2. 15. 5.)

44 *two Aeginetan bushels*: 'bushels' is a very rough translation of the Greek *medimnoi*, and the Aeginetan measures (used generally in the Peloponnese) were somewhat larger than the Attic ones. There is of course humorous exaggeration here: Thrasycles' 'pouch' must have been very large indeed.

ICAROMENIPPUS

46 *the Phrygian boy*: Ganymede, the Trojan shepherd-boy who became the cup-bearer of the gods.

Daedalus: see introductory note. The Icarian Sea, to which Icarus gave his name, is part of the southern Aegean, between the Cyclades and Asia Minor.

48 *Another . . . war was the father of the universe*: Heraclitus fr. 53: a metaphor for his theory that the balance of existence in the cosmos is maintained by strife between opposing elements.

49 *others swore by geese and dogs and plane-trees:* Socrates swore by the dog (i.e. the dog-headed Egyptian god Anubis) and the plane-tree (Plato, *Apology* 22a, *Phaedrus* 236e), and one Lampon swore by the goose. Such oaths may have been playful or euphemistic: see Dunbar on Aristophanes, *Birds* 520–1, Dodds on Plato, *Gorgias* 482b5.

the 'high-thundering' men with their 'fine beards': the epithet 'high-thundering' (*hypsibremetes*) is used sardonically, being a stock description of Zeus in Homer. 'Fine-bearded' is also used by Homer to describe lions.

But another thought drew me back: from Homer, *Odyssey* 9. 302: Odysseus ponders how to deal with the Cyclops.

Aesop, who opens up heaven to eagles and beetles, and sometimes even to camels: see Aesop's fables 153 and 510 in the Oxford World's Classics edition (= Perry 3 and 117).

50 *flying from Parnes or Hymettus . . . as far as Taygetus*: these peaks take Menippus and us from the neighbourhood of Athens down through the Megarid, to Corinth, Arcadia, and Laconia.

like Zeus in Homer . . . Mysians: Iliad 13. 4–5.

the Colossus of Rhodes and the lighthouse on Pharos: the Colossus collapsed in an earthquake in 225 BC and lay on the ground for centuries thereafter; so (if it matters) Menippus' journey must be imagined to have taken place before that date. Both the Colossus and the Pharos were counted among the seven wonders of the world.

all that the bountiful earth nurtures: a recurrent phrase in Homer, e.g. *Iliad* 2. 548.

Lynceus: see *Charon*, note to p. 16.

51 *Empedocles . . . looking as if burnt to a cinder and baked in ashes*: a reference to the legend that Empedocles died by throwing himself into the crater of Etna: see below, and cf. *Peregrinus*, note to p. 74.

I am no god: why think me like the immortals?: *Odyssey* 16. 187: Odysseus addresses his son.

by Endymion: an appropriate oath, as Endymion was a beautiful youth loved by the moon, where Empedocles now lives.

52 *I saw Ptolemy . . . broken by a golden cup*: some of the episodes in this list are otherwise unknown—those involving Antigonus, Attalus, Arsaces, and Spatinus. Of the others we can say that Ptolemies did marry their sisters; Lysimachus was a successor of Alexander the Great and ruler of Thrace; Seleucus I was another successor of Alexander and ruler of Babylon: the story alluded to here refers to *c.*292 BC and is widely recorded (elsewhere in Lucian at *The Syrian Goddess* 17–18). Alexander was tyrant of Thessaly in the early to mid-fourth century BC.

Hermodorus . . . brothel: all four of these characters are quite obscure, but the details of the anecdotes are less important than to note that Lucian/Menippus is taking a sideswipe at a range of philosophers and a public figure who behaved disgracefully.

those which Homer portrays on the shield: the shield which Hephaestus makes for Achilles: *Iliad* 18. 478ff.

53 *the Cilicians practising piracy, the Spartans lashing themselves*: the coast of Cilicia was infested with pirates from the second century BC until they were finally suppressed by Pompey in 67 BC. The Spartans regularly flogged their boys as part of a routine training in endurance.

the deaths of so many Argives and Spartans in one day: see *Charon*, 24 and note to p. 25.

54 *Pangaeum*: a mountain in Thrace famous for its gold and silver mines.

Thessalians . . . from ants into men: the original Myrmidon of this race in Thessaly was the son of Eurymedusa and Zeus, who visited her in the form of an ant (Gk. *myrmex*): see A. B. Cook, *Zeus*, (Cambridge, 1914–40) 532 n. 12.

to the palace of Zeus of the aegis, to join all the other immortals: *Iliad* 1.222.

55 *From where there was nothing to see of the labours of cattle and men*: *Odyssey* 10. 98.

56 *What is your name among men, and where are your city and parents*: a greeting that frequently occurs in Homer, e.g. *Odyssey* 1. 170.

Otus and Ephialtes: see *Charon*, 3 and note to p. 14.

56 *Pheidias*: see *Peregrinus*, note to p. 75.

the Diasia: see *Timon*, note to p. 28.

the Olympieion: the temple of Zeus at Athens, begun under the tyrant Pisistratus (d. 527 BC), but abandoned and not completed until the time of Hadrian (reigned AD 117–38).

the men who had robbed his temple at Dodona had been caught: presumably the Aetolians under their general Dorimachus, who in 219 BC ravaged Epirus and destroyed the temple at Dodona (Polybius 4. 67).

And all the streets . . . assemblies: see *Nigrinus*, note to p. 66.

57 *Bendis*: a Thracian goddess whose followers indulged in orgiastic rites. Zeus might also have complained that she was worshipped at the Piraeus.

Anubis: the Egyptian dog-headed god of the dead, sometimes identified with Hermes.

the temple of Artemis: this celebrated temple was regarded as one of the seven wonders of the world.

more frigid than the Laws of Plato or the Syllogisms of Chrysippus: the *Laws* is Plato's longest (and in Zeus' view most tedious) dialogue. Chrysippus (*c.*280–207 BC) was the third head of the Stoa and one of the most formidable of the Stoic thinkers, especially in the field of logic and dialectic. Many fragments and citations of his works survive.

But one thing the Father did grant and another rejected: slightly adapted from *Iliad* 16. 250: Zeus' response to a prayer of Achilles.

like Pyrrho: Pyrrho (*c.*360–*c.*270 BC) was the founder of Greek scepticism.

Hermodorus the Epicurean: another sideswipe: cf. note to p. 52.

58 *Pan and the Corybantes and Attis and Sabazius*: Pan was a god local to Arcadia, half goat in shape. The Corybantes were priests of the Anatolian mother-goddess Cybele, and Attis was her consort. Sabazius was another Anatolian deity, sometimes identified with Dionysus.

eat not bread nor drink of sparkling wine: derived from *Iliad* 5. 341.

Silenus: a creature of the countryside, somewhat like a satyr, usually portrayed as part-horse, and a regular attendant on Dionysus.

Hesiod's Theogony . . . Pindar's Hymns: Hesiod's *Theogony* (somewhere around 700 BC) is largely concerned with the genealogies of the gods. Pindar (518–438 BC) was the greatest lyric poet of Greece, whose *Hymns* survive in fragments and would have contained suitably honorific references to the gods.

The rest of the gods . . . sweet sleep: slightly adapted from *Iliad* 2. 1–2.

59 *a useless burden on the land*: a phrase from *Iliad* 18. 104 (Achilles remorsefully describing himself).

how they lick the dirt off obols: that is, they are so money-grubbing they will pick up the smallest coin from the dirty ground. Or the reference may be to the greasy dirt on coins that have passed from hand to hand.

Having no value in war or in council: almost *Iliad* 2. 202 (Odysseus accusing the fleeing Greeks of cowardice).

Momus: see *Nigrinus*, note to p. 70.

60 *truce from hostilities*: the *hieromenia* ('sacred month') was the period in which the great festivals of Greece took place and hostilities between states were suspended.

So spoke the son of Cronus . . . to confirm it: a Homeric formula for the stated and irresistible will of Zeus: e.g. *Iliad* 1. 528.

the Potters' Quarter: Greek *Kerameikos*, an area in Athens frequented by potters.

the Painted Hall: the *Stoa Poikile*, a public hall in Athens where the early Stoics met and lectured.

NIGRINUS

61 *An owl to Athens*: the proverb derives from the fact that the owl was traditionally associated with Athena and was common in Athens and the surrounding region. It was also a regular motif on coins.

Thucydides' maxim: Thucydides 2. 40. 3 (from Pericles' famous funeral oration).

62 *as they say on the stage, 'thrice-blest'*: in Greek *trisolbios*: a fairly rare word of which we have examples in Sophocles (fr. 837) and Aristophanes (*Ecclesiazusae* 1129).

instead of a slave . . . I am tolerably sane: this seems to be an adaptation of a line from a now lost comedy (Kock, *Com.Adesp.* 1419).

the Sirens . . . and the nightingales and the lotus: these are all references to Homer's *Odyssey*. During his travels Odysseus encountered and evaded the Sirens (whose song would have charmed his sailors to their destruction, *Od.* 12. 166 ff.), and the Lotus-eaters (whose food, the lotus, would have caused them to forget their homeland, *Od.* 9. 83ff.). The nightingale appears in a famous simile in Penelope's talk with the disguised Odysseus (*Od.* 19. 518 ff.).

63 *you are urging on someone who is already keen, as Homer*: *Iliad* 8. 293.

64 *he left his sting behind in all who heard him*: Eupolis (fr. 94. 7 Kock), referring to Pericles. Lucian quotes from the same passage in *Demonax* 10.

Hermes: a suitable god to invoke as he was associated with oratory and orators. The rules for rhetorical introductions (*prooimia*) included informing the audience of the topic of the speech and securing their attention and goodwill. The speaker was also advised to disclaim oratorical ability.

66 *all its streets and all its squares*: phrases from Aratus, *Phaenomena* 2–3 (all streets and squares are full of Zeus). Lucian liked the lines and quotes them again more fully at *Prometheus* 14 and *Icaromenippus* 24.

words of Homer: from *Odyssey* 11. 93–4: Tiresias asks Odysseus why he wants to visit the dead.

67 *Away from the slaughter, the bloodshed and the din*: *Iliad* 11. 164.

You simply have to follow Odysseus' lead: these were Odysseus' tactics in evading the Sirens: see note to p. 62.

greet people they meet through another's voice: this refers to the *nomenclator*, a slave whose duty was to tell his master the names of the people he met.

70 *forcing their way in beside the door*: there is no trace of this phrase in the surviving plays, but the sense is that those who act irrationally in their pleasures are like a man who breaks into a house when he could just step in through a nearby door.

Momus: a figure who personified fault-finding. He plays an important part in Lucian's *Jupiter Tragoedus*, and for the fable alluded to here see another allusion in *True History* 2. 3, and the fuller version in *Hermotimus* 20 and Babrius 59—Momus criticizes the inventions of three deities, including the bull created by Poseidon.

71 *those Phaeacians*: Odysseus held the Phaeacian court spellbound by the story of his wanderings and adventures, and there is a verbal echo in Lucian's text of Homer's lines describing this effect upon them (*Od.* 11. 333–4 = 13. 1–2).

72 *they just scratch the surface*: a phrase from a battle scene in Homer (*Il.* 17. 599).

the Curetes: a semi-divine people who lived in Crete and looked after the infant Zeus, but the reference here is obscure.

Shoot thus and bring perhaps salvation: adapted from *Iliad* 8. 282 (Agamemnon cheers Teucer on in the fighting).

Rhea: the wife of Cronus and mother of Zeus. She was commonly identified with the great Anatolian mother-goddess Cybele, whose frenzied rites among her Phrygian worshippers are here alluded to.

73 *Telephus*: king of Mysia, who was wounded in a fight with Achilles. As the wound would not heal he consulted the Delphic oracle, and was told that the wounder would also heal him. This was eventually achieved by applying rust-scrapings from Achilles' spear to the wound. The story was the subject of Euripides' play *Telephus*, fragments of which survive.

THE DEATH OF PEREGRINUS

74 *Proteus*: a sea-god who could turn himself into all kinds of shapes, including fire: e.g. *Odyssey* 4. 384 ff., where he tries to escape from Menelaus.

Empedocles: the great fifth-century BC philosopher, who was alleged to have thrown himself into the crater of Mount Etna (see section 4).

75 *I was nearly torn to pieces . . . Maenads*: Actaeon was a hunter who saw Artemis bathing, and was therefore turned by her into a stag and killed by his own dogs (Ovid, *Met.* 3. 138 ff.). Pentheus was a king of Thebes who resisted the worship of Dionysus, and in consequence was torn to pieces by the Maenads, the frenzied followers of that god. The story is most famously told in Euripides' *Bacchae*.

Heracles . . . Asclepius and Dionysus, through a thunderbolt: Heracles cremated himself on Mt Oeta in an agony of pain caused by wearing the shirt of Nessus. The story is widely reported, and Lucian makes further sardonic links between Peregrinus and Heracles. Asclepius was killed by Zeus with a thunderbolt for restoring Hippolytus to life. Dionysus appears in this list by association: it was his mother Semele who was blasted by a thunderbolt, and her unborn son by Zeus was rescued to be gestated in Zeus' thigh.

Theagenes: a disciple of Peregrinus, who came from Patrae (section 30), and is known to us entirely from this work.

the man from Sinope, or his teacher Antisthenes: Diogenes of Sinope was probably inspired by Antisthenes (*c.* 445–*c.* 360 BC), the effective founder of Cynicism.

Pheidias: (fifth century BC) was the most celebrated sculptor of Greece, and his statue of Zeus at Olympia was regarded as his masterpiece.

76 *Heraclitus . . . Democritus*: the two philosophers Heraclitus of Ephesus (sixth/ fifth century BC) and Democritus of Abdera (fifth century BC) are regularly paired as the 'weeping' and the 'laughing' philosopher respectively.

Polyclitus: of Argos (late fifth century BC), the most famous sculptor of his day, created a *Doryphorus* (youth carrying a spear) which was regarded as the ideal of harmony and proportion in statuary. We are also told that he wrote a treatise called *Canon* ('Rule'), which discussed the theories of form embodied in this statue (Pliny, *NH* 34, 55). There is a copy of the piece in the Naples museum.

with a radish plugging his anus: this was a conventional punishment for adulterers caught in the act: see Dover on Aristophanes, *Clouds* 1083.

77 *the new Socrates*: it is worth noting that some Christian apologists considered the fate of Socrates as prefiguring the persecution of Jesus and his disciples. (See C. P. Jones, *Culture and Society in Lucian* 122.)

78 *Parium*: in spite of Lucian's scornful tone, Parium was a major port and Roman colony on the southern coast of the Propontis, near to the Hellespont.

wearing a dirty cloak, a pouch at his side and a staff in his hand: cloak, pouch, and staff are routine items in the (usually uncomplimentary) description of itinerant Cynic preachers in the literature of this period.

Diogenes and Crates: Crates (*c.* 365–285 BC) of Thebes was a disciple of Diogenes and one of the most famous of the early Cynics.

Agathoboulos: see *Demonax*, note to p. 153.

an 'indifferent' act: that is, an act neither good nor bad enough to affect a true Cynic. The Greek term *adiaphoron* (if this is the right reading) is a technical one in Stoic ethics, and not apparently in Cynicism, but there is not much difference between Stoics and Cynics in this area, and Peregrinus is just demonstrating the moral indifference of the physical act.

79 *the emperor*: Antoninus Pius.

Musonius, Dio, Epictetus: all three were Stoic philosophers. Musonius was banished by Nero about AD 60; Dio Chrysostom by Domitian about 82; Epictetus also by Domitian in 89.

a man of outstanding culture and renown: this was Herodes Atticus (*c.*101–77), the celebrated sophist, who used his great wealth in generous benefactions, including an aqueduct at Olympia: Philostratus, *Lives of the Sophists*, 2. 551. Philostratus also records Peregrinus' persistent insulting of Herodes (2. 563).

80 *Philoctetes*: one of the Greek leaders at Troy. He assisted Heracles at his self-cremation by lighting the pyre for him on Mt Oeta (Ovid, *Met.* 9. 223 ff.).

Phalaris: a sixth-century BC tyrant of Acragas, who roasted his enemies alive in a bronze bull. He is the subject of one of Lucian's declamations.

set fire to the temple of Artemis of Ephesus: this was done by Herostratus of Ephesus in 356 BC: Strabo 14. 1. 22, Plutarch, *Alexander* 3.

81 *Heracles . . . as the tragic poets tell us*: the agony which made Heracles kill himself was caused by wearing a garment soaked in the poisonous blood of the centaur Nessus, which his wife Deianira had sent to him, thinking it would act as a love-charm. Sophocles' *Trachiniae* and Seneca's *Hercules Oetaeus* deal with the story.

Onesicritus . . . Calanus in the flames: Onesicritus was not only Alexander's steersman but the author of a book about him (see the *OCD* entry for details). Calanus was an Indian Brahmin who was attached to Alexander's army on his eastern campaign. In order to escape the suffering caused by disease he cremated himself on a pyre in Babylon (Plutarch, *Alexander* 69; Arrian, *Anabasis* 7. 3; Aelian, *Varia Historia* 5. 6).

82 *Bacis*: a generic title for a prophet rather than the name of an individual seer: see How and Wells on Herodotus 8. 20. Both these 'oracles' are largely centos of phrases from Homer and Aristophanes' *Knights*. (The OCT apparatus lists the lines concerned.)

Patrae: the birth-place of Theagenes: see note to p. 75.

83 *Nestor noticed the shouting*: from *Iliad* 14. 1: Nestor hears the din of stubborn battle between Greeks and Trojans.

the Hellanodicae . . . in the Plethrium: the Hellanodicae were the judges of the Olympic Games. The Plethrium was an area in the gymnasium at Elis where they matched the competing athletes against each other (Pausanias 6. 23. 2).

a golden tip on a golden bow: Peregrinus goes one better than Pandarus in Homer, who had a golden tip on a bow of horn (*Iliad* 4. 111). He also puns on the Greek word *bios*, which (with different accents) means both 'bow' and 'life'.

85 *a vulture flew up from the midst of the flames*: the vulture here is probably a sardonic substitute (suitable to Peregrinus) for the eagle, which was often associated with the death or transmigration of kings: see D'Arcy Thompson, *A Glossary of Greek Birds* (London and Oxford, 1936), 7.

the Colonnade of the Seven Echoes: this was in the precinct of Zeus at Olympia, and noted for its vocal phenomenon by Pausanias (5. 21. 17) and Pliny the Elder (*NH* 36. 100). The appearance of Peregrinus here after his death somewhat resembles that of Romulus seen after his death, radiant in bright armour, as reported by Plutarch (*Romulus* 28).

86 *Hesiod's tomb*: this refers to a story that Pausanias relates (9. 38. 3) about the people of Orchomenus. When suffering from a plague they consulted the Delphic oracle, and were told that they must bring the bones of Hesiod from Naupactus to Orchomenus, and that a crow would guide them to his tomb—as indeed it did.

Such was the end . . . a man who: these words are a likely echo of part of the final sentence of Plato's *Phaedo*, referring to the death of Socrates.

Troas: probably not 'the Troad' area generally, but the port Alexandria Troas on its coast: see C. P. Jones, *CPh.* 80 (1985), 42.

Alcibiades: the brilliant Athenian statesman and general, who was also a pupil and lover of Socrates.

Aeacus: one of the judges of the dead in the underworld.

88 *the Doctor from Cos*: Hippocrates (fifth century BC), the most celebrated Greek doctor.

89 *Hesiod: Works and Days* 289 ff.

Hesiod: Works and Days 40: Lucian has the same quotation at *The Dream* 3.

like Zeus' golden rope in Homer: *Iliad* 8. 19: the golden rope by which Zeus, to illustrate his omnipotence, says he could if he wished draw up all land and sea to himself.

the Great Mysteries, or the Panathenaea: two of the most famous festivals in Greece. The Eleusinian Mysteries were celebrated in honour of Demeter and Persephone, and the Panathenaea in honour of Athena.

90 *Aornos, which Alexander took by storm in a few days*: a mountain fortress stormed by Alexander the Great in 327–326 BC, during his eastern campaign in the Indus river area: see Arrian, *Anabasis* 4. 28, N. G. L. Hammond, *A History of Greece* (Oxford, 1967), 630.

91 *Heracles . . . became a god*: see *Peregrinus*, note to p. 75.

93 *with a cup as big as Nestor's*: this refers to a famous description in the *Iliad* (11. 632 ff.) of old Nestor's elaborate drinking cup.

94 *Pythian Apollo treat you like Chaerephon*: Chaerephon was a disciple of Socrates, who on consulting the Delphic oracle, was told that Socrates was the wisest of men: Plato, *Apology* 21a.

95 *Margites*: see *Lovers of Lies*, note to p. 163.

96 *Pheidias or Alcamenes or Myron*: all three were celebrated Greek sculptors of the fifth century BC.

97 *the faults Momus found in Hephaestus*: see *Nigrinus*, note to p. 70.

keener sight than Lynceus: see *Charon*, note to p. 16.

98 *But no heed did I pay*: a recurrent Homeric phrase: e.g. *Iliad* 5. 201, *Odyssey* 9. 228.

99 *the poet Hesiod*: see note to p. 89.

100 *going where our feet take us*: a fairly familiar expression in both Latin and Greek authors: e.g. Theocritus 13. 70, Horace, *Odes* 3. 11. 49.

cross the Aegean or Ionian Sea on a mat: we find the expression elsewhere in Euripides fr. 397 N and Aristophanes, *Peace* 699.

Homer's archer . . . cut the cord when he should have hit the dove: the episode occurs during the archery contest at the funeral games for Patroclus: *Iliad* 23. 865 ff.

103 *They do not see my helmet's front*: *Iliad*. 16. 70: Achilles referring to the fact that he is currently out of the fighting.

104 *Hestia*: see *Lovers of Lies*, note to p. 164.

110 *Stay sober and remember to be sceptical*: from Epicharmus (fr. 250 Kaibel), a Sicilian comic writer of the early fifth century BC.

those five years of silence: this refers to the five years of silent study which the students of Pythagoras had to undergo before they were admitted to his presence: Diogenes Laertius 8. 10.

111 *dancing in the dark*: for the proverb see Leutsch–Schneidewin I. 74 (Zenobius).

Tithonus: a lover of Eos, the Dawn. She prayed to Zeus to make him immortal, but forgot to ask that he be ageless too. So he grew older and older and more shrivelled, and in some accounts was at last changed into a grasshopper. For one version see the Homeric *Hymn to Aphrodite*, 218 ff.

113 *nothing that concerns Dionysus*: 'Nothing to do with Dionysus' was apparently the complaint of theatre audiences when playwrights began to write on themes unrelated to the god, and so to the traditional beginnings of Greek tragedy. See Leutsch–Schneidewin I. 137 (Zenobius), and elsewhere in Lucian, *Dionysus* 5.

114 *a youth with both parents alive*: this reflects the practice of Greek cult, in which having both parents alive was a qualification for a boy to take part in some religious rites: see Dunbar on Aristophanes, *Birds* 1737.

116 *the more you empty the fuller it is*: for the proverb see *Trag. Adesp*. 89 N, Leutsch–Schneidewin I. 26 (Zenobius) and 198 (Diogenianus). For the opposite image of the Danaids see *Timon*, note to p. 32.

117 *blaming the blameless, as the poet says*: *Iliad* 13. 775: Paris replies to a bitter accusation from Hector.

the court of the Areopagus: see *Timon*, note to p. 40.

121 *my treasure is but ashes*: see *Timon*, note to p. 38.

fighting over a donkey's shadow: yet another proverbial saying, meaning something not worth fighting about: see Plato, *Phaedrus* 260c, Aristophanes, *Wasps* 191 (with MacDowell's note). A scholiast derives it from a story about a man who hired a donkey, and sat in the donkey's shadow to take a rest. The owner complained that he had hired the donkey and not the donkey's shadow, and took him to law about it.

122 *Hippocentaurs and Chimaeras and Gorgons*: bizarre and incredible creatures from myth. Hippocentaurs ('Horse-centaurs') were half-horse and half-man; the Chimaera was a triple-bodied creature, part-lion, part-snake, and part-goat; the Gorgons were three terrible sister monsters (for details see the *OCD* entry), with whom Medusa was sometimes linked.

Medea fell in love with Jason in a dream: in Apollonius' account of the story Medea's love for Jason is caused by an arrow shot by Eros (3. 281 ff.), and later she has a troubled dream about him (3. 617 ff.). Lucian seems to conflate the two episodes.

124 *Euclides' archonship*: Euclides was archon at Athens in 403–402 BC, when the democracy was re-established and a complete political amnesty agreed between the moderates and the democrats.

126 *how a crocodile carried off a boy ... grow horns*: these are favourite logical conundrums of the Stoics. In the crocodile conundrum the man has to tell the crocodile correctly what the crocodile has decided to do about returning the boy. The one about horns runs as follows: 'If you have not lost something, you have it; but you have not lost horns, therefore you have horns' (Diogenes Laertius 7. 187). Quintilian (1. 10. 5) notes the 'horns' and 'crocodile' fallacies. Lucian has the 'horns' again at *Dialogues of the Dead* 1. 2, and the 'crocodile' at *Sale of Lives* 22; and Seneca also refers to the 'horns' (*Letters* 49. 8).

127 *in that fable Aesop tells*: sea-waves were proverbially uncountable. This fable is in *Aesop's Fables* (Oxford World's Classics edn.), no. 491 (= Perry 429).

128 *drink hellebore, for the opposite reason to Chrysippus*: a favourite jibe of Lucian's against Chrysippus, alleging that he repeatedly had to take hellebore to stave off insanity: see also *A True History* 2. 18, *Sale of Lives* 23.

ALEXANDER

129 *clean up that Augean stable*: a reference to one of the more unpleasant of Heracles' twelve labours.

130 *Arrian*: first half of the second century AD from Bithynia, a public figure and historian, who wrote a history of Alexander the Great and who was responsible for preserving a record of Epictetus' teaching. We know nothing about Tillorobus.

the Cercopes . . . Eurybatus or Phrynondas or Aristodemus or Sostratus: the Cercopes were two mischievous gnomes who pestered Hercules until captured by him. Eurybatus was a proverbial scoundrel, of whom there are different stories: one account says he was one of the Cercopes. Phrynondas, another byword for rascality, lived at Athens during the Peloponnesian War and became a type-name for a rogue. Aristodemus was a more shadowy Athenian, pilloried for his indecency by Aristophanes (fr. 231 Kock). Sostratus must be another pattern of wickedness, but he cannot be clearly identified.

Rutilianus: P. Mummius Sisenna Rutilianus was an important public figure, who had been consul in 146 and later governor of Upper Moesia and of the province of Asia.

131 *Many a drug compounded for good and many for ill*: *Odyssey* 4. 230, describing the supply of drugs Helen had acquired from Egypt.

Apollonius of Tyana: Tyana was in Cappadocia and Apollonius was a Neo-pythagorean who lived in the first century AD and was a very distinguished itinerant philosopher and teacher. Our main source for his life is his biography by Philostratus.

132 *Cocconas*: literally 'pomegranate-seeds', or something similar, but the name probably has an indecent suggestion, e.g. 'testicles'.

Olympias: the mother of Alexander the Great. There was a legend that Zeus was his father, having visited Olympias in the form of a snake.

the war begins here: the opening words of Thucydides 2.

Clarus: a famous oracle and sanctuary of Apollo near Colophon in Ionia.

Branchidae: the priestly clan who looked after another celebrated sanctuary of Apollo at Didyma, which was also itself called Branchidae. Didyma is a few miles from Miletus, so we have a cluster of three well-known shrines of Apollo, Clarus, Didyma, and Miletus, in this corner of Asia Minor.

133 *telling fortunes with a sieve (as they say)*: a reference to *koskinomanteis*, 'sieve-diviners'. We are not told how this method of divination worked, but it was regarded as disreputable: see Artemidorus' treatise on dreams, *Oneirokritika* 2. 69.

Podalirius: a son of Asclepius and one of the doctors in the Greek army at Troy (*Iliad* 11. 833): his home was at Tricca in Thessaly.

EXPLANATORY NOTES

For his name . . . a noble protector: this is an example of an ingenious lexical game played mainly by Greek epigrammatists, and involving 'isopsephs', the interchange of letters and the numbers they represent. Here the numbers 1, 30, 5, 60 stand for αλεξ, the first four letters of Alexander's name. In addition, the Greek form of his name, Alexandros, is concealed in the first four syllables of the last line, *andros alex-*.

134 *the frenzied followers of the Great Mother*: a reference to the frenzied rites associated with the worship of Cybele, the great Mother goddess of Anatolia.

135 *Twice born when other men are born but once*: adapted from *Odyssey* 12. 22.

Coronis, nor even a crow: a pun on Koronis and *korone*, the Greek for 'crow'.

136 *a Democritus*: that is, a man of towering intellect like Democritus, the great fifth-century BC philosopher of atomism. Note the reference to him again in 50.

Metrodorus: a distinguished and favourite pupil of Epicurus.

Amphiaraus: one of the legendary Seven who fought against Thebes.

137 *Bruttium pitch*: the forests of Bruttium in southern Italy produced high-quality pitch which was used in ship-building, and was a major source of revenue to Rome.

138 *Christians*: Christian communities had long been established in Pontus and Bithynia, as we know from the New Testament (1 Peter 1. 1) and Pliny the Younger (letter to Trajan, 10. 96).

139 *Lepidus*: a priest of Amastris, as we learn from an inscription (*CIG* 4149), and an important Epicurean opponent of Alexander: cf. section 43.

Severianus: the Roman governor of Cappadocia, who invaded Armenia in 161 and was utterly defeated by Osroes.

140 *Mallus*: the famous shrine in Cilicia, founded by Amphilochus: see section 19.

142 *Selene . . . to fall for good-looking men in their sleep*: an allusion to the story that the Moon, Selene, fell in love with the beautiful youth Endymion in his sleep. Hence the sardonic term 'Endymion-Alexander' in section 39.

the great plague: brought back from the east by the army of Lucius Verus in 165/6, and it spread from the eastern empire as far as Rome.

143 *Eumolpidae and Ceryces*: these are both titles of officiating priests at the Eleusinian Mysteries: Lucian gibes at Alexander's attempt to imitate the famous rites. On the Eumolpids see *Demonax*, note to p. 158.

145 *Epicurus' Basic Doctrines*: this book, *Kuriai Doxai*, survives and is a collection of maxims which, as Lucian says, cover Epicurus' main doctrines.

146 *squills*: *scilla hyacynthoides*, used in purification rites to avert evil by scourging ritual scapegoats: see Gow or Dover on Theocritus 7. 107.

the Marcomanni and the Quadi: two connected German tribes with whom Marcus Aurelius was at war in 168–74. They had made inroads into Italy as far as Aquileia (mentioned below).

Croesus: king of Lydia (*c.*560–546 BC): he consulted the Delphic oracle about attacking the Persians, and the oracle's defence of its ambiguity is given in Herodotus 1. 91.

148 *Morphen ... phaos*: this and the following oracle appear to be deliberate gibberish, though they contain some Greek words—perhaps a later scribe's partial attempt to translate the 'Scythian'. ('Morphen' is 'shape', 'eis skian' 'into the darkness', 'leipsei phaos' 'you will leave the light of day'.)

149 *Xenophon*: presumably an attendant, but otherwise unknown.

Eupator: king of the Bosporus in the time of Marcus Aurelius.

150 *Timocrates*: see *Demonax*, note to p. 153.

Podalirius: a punning allusion, linking the name with the Greek word for foot or leg, the root of which is *pod-*.

DEMONAX

152 *Sostratus*: a rather shadowy figure, perhaps the same as the man described by Philostratus (*Lives of the Sophists* 1.2). Lucian's treatise on him is lost.

153 *Agathoboulos ... Timocrates of Heraclea*: Demonax had quite a galaxy of teachers. Agathoboulos of Alexandria and Demetrius (who worked mainly in Rome) were famous Cynics; the ex-slave Epictetus (in Rome and then Nicopolis) was one of the most influential Stoics of his time; and Timocrates of Heraclea was another celebrated teacher of mainly Stoic beliefs. Lucian also mentions Agathoboulos in *Peregrinus* 17 and Timocrates in *Alexander* 57.

rush into this with unwashed feet: a proverbial expression meaning 'unprepared'. Lucian has it again in *Pseudologista* 4.

the man of Sinope: Diogenes the Cynic, who came from Sinope on the Black Sea.

154 *Persuasion sat on his lips*: from Eupolis, fr. 94. 5 Kock: cf. *Nigrinus*, note to p. 64.

Anytus and Meletus: two of Socrates' accusers.

the Eleusinian Mysteries: the most famous of the secret cults which were a feature of Greek life, linked with the deities Demeter and Dionysus. Demonax's refusal to be initiated into them might have been in imitation of Diogenes, who similarly refused: Diogenes Laertius 6. 39.

155 *your former victim*: Socrates.

Favorinus: a celebrated sophist from Arelate (Arles) who taught Herodes Atticus. He was a eunuch: hence Demonax's quip.

the sophist from Sidon: he is unknown.

if Pythagoras summons, I shall keep silence: part of the strict discipline of the Pythagoreans was maintaining silence.

156 *Arcesilaus*: because 'Arcesilaus' suggests 'arkos', a Greek word for 'bear'.

Peregrinus Proteus: the Cynic philosopher who is the subject of Lucian's treatise, for which see translation and notes.

you're not doglike: the Cynics were so called because the name in Greek means 'behaving like a dog'.

157 *the great Herodes*: Herodes Atticus of Athens (*c.* 101–177) was the most celebrated and influential sophist of his time. Polydeuces seems to have been a young relative he was particularly attached to.

the Asclepieion: a shrine of Asclepius, the god of healing. The one at Athens dated from 420 BC.

one . . . is milking a he-goat and the other is holding a sieve for him: Proverbial expressions: Diogenianus 7. 95

Agathocles the Peripatetic: this is our only reference to him.

Cethegus: M. Cornelius Cethegus; this episode is probably a few years before his consulship in 170, so Lucian anticipates in calling him 'consular'.

Apollonius: the Stoic of Chalcedon or Chalcis, who was invited to Rome by the emperor Antoninus Pius to be tutor to his adopted son, the future emperor Marcus Aurelius. Demonax links him jokingly with his namesake, Apollonius of Rhodes, whose poem *Argonautica* describes Jason's search for the Golden Fleece: the suggestion is that this Apollonius is after gold too.

158 *Regilla*: the wife of Herodes Atticus, whose mourning for her death was widely noted, like his grief for Polydeuces (note to p. 157).

Eumolpus: a mythical figure associated with Eleusis as one of its rulers and involved in the Mysteries there. He was subsequently said to have been king of Thrace. (See the entry in *OCD*.)

Polybius: possibly the grammarian Polybius of Sardis; in which case he typifies someone who does not practise what he claims to teach.

159 *Admetus*: not otherwise known.

Charon: by this quip Demonax seems to mean he is already marked out for departure to the underworld, i.e. death is in sight. Charon was conventionally represented as the ferryman of the souls of the dead, but the remark here suggests other views which the Etruscans held of Charon as a more monstrous and sinister figure: see Austin on Virgil, *Aeneid* 6. 298 ff.

Stop treating him as your social equal: the Spartans used whipping regularly to train their youth in toughness and endurance.

Danae, but not the daughter of Acrisius: for Danae see *Timon*, note to p. 30. Her father's name Acrisius means 'lawless': hence the pun.

Hyperides: no Cynic Hyperides is know, but the name is chosen as it could mean 'Son of Cudgel' (*hyperos* in Greek).

160 *the Painted Stoa*: the Stoa Poikile, or painted colonnade, built about 460 BC, and so called because it was decorated with pictures by the celebrated painter Polygnotus and other artists. It gave its name to the Stoic philosophy because the early Stoic masters taught there. Cynegirus was a brother of the poet Aeschylus: he lost his hand fighting at Marathon.

Rufinus the Cypriot: he appears only in this passage.

Herminus: a Peripatetic philosopher eminent as a teacher and a writer, but nothing of his work survives.

the Altar of Pity: see *Timon*, note to p. 39.

The idler and the toiler both come to death alike: *Iliad* 9. 320 (Achilles addressing Odysseus).

Thersites: in the *Iliad* Thersites is a common soldier in the Greek army, the only rank-and-filer to be at all characterized. He is an unattractive figure, ugly and foul-mouthed, and he attacks Agamemnon with bitter insults (*Il.* 2. 212 ff.).

161 *Aristippus*: of Cyrene, a close friend of Socrates. Either he or a grandson of the same name founded the 'Cyrenaic' school of philosophy, of which the main tenet was that the pleasures of the senses are man's highest goal.

Now ends . . . your going: these lines are listed as *Carmina Popularia* 19 in Page, *Poetae Melici Graeci* (Oxford, 1962): see the other references given there.

LOVERS OF LIES

163 *Ctesias of Cnidos*: a late fifth-century Greek historian who wrote treatises on Persia and India of which fragments survive. See *A True History* 1.3, where Lucian also alludes to the fabulous nature of his works.

a bull or a swan to gratify a passion: a bull for the sake of Europa and a swan in order to visit Leda.

a bird or a bear: familiar examples are the legends of Procne (nightingale) and Philomela (swallow), and Callisto (bear): Ovid, *Met.* 6.424 ff., 2.405 ff.

Mormo and Lamia: these were bogies or demon-figures whose names were used to frighten children.

Erichthonius: an early Attic hero and king of Athens. He was said to be the son of Hephaestus, whose seed fell to earth from which the boy was subsequently born. The story is reflected in his name Erichthonius, *chthon* meaning 'earth'.

the Thebans' tale . . . a serpent's teeth: a reference to the legend of Cadmus, who killed a dragon and sowed its teeth, from which sprang a harvest of armed men.

a Coroebus or a Margites: proverbial types of the gullible fool. Coroebus is otherwise unknown; Margites is the hero of a lost comic epic attributed to Homer.

Triptolemus: see *The Dream*, note to p. 11.

164 *Boreas*: the north wind, who was said to have carried off his bride Oreithyia, daughter of King Erechtheus of Athens.

In Hestia's name: Hestia was the goddess of the hearth, so calling on her means 'by all you hold sacred at home'.

166 *knocking out one nail with another*: a proverbial expression describing an attempt to deal with a problem which leaves you where you were before. Lucian uses it elsewhere at *Pro Lapsu* 7, and see Aristotle, *Politics* 1314ª5.

Asclepius: the god of healing. His son served as army doctor on the Greek side in the *Iliad* (e.g. 4. 193 ff.).

168 *Hyperborean*: a legendary race who lived in the remote north of the world.

169 *the Syrian from Palestine*: an unknown exorcist. Some have seen a reference here to Jesus, but this is improbable, if only because of the present tenses used. However, this section may well contain some shots at Christianity.

the Forms: a reference to Plato's famous doctrine of the *ideai*, or the perfect archetypal 'forms', of which the objects of our everyday experience are imperfect imitations.

170 *Demetrius*: a sculptor from Alopece in Attica (fifth/fourth century BC), famous for the realism of his portraits.

Myron's: see *The Dream*, note to p. 9.

Polyclitus: see *Peregrinus*, note to p. 76.

Critius and Nesiotes: Greek sculptors (early fifth century BC), who worked together. Their most famous pieces were bronze statues of the Tyrannicides, Harmodius and Aristogiton, which were set up in the Athenian agora in 477.

Pellichus: presumably this is the father of Aristeus, a commander who took part in the Corinthian expedition against Corcyra in 435 BC (Thucydides 1. 29).

171 *Talos*: Tychiades correctly describes Talos, the mythical bronze sentinel who patrolled and guarded the island of Crete: Apollonius Rhodius 4. 1638 ff.

Daedalus' handiworks ... runs away from his pedestal: for Daedalus see introduction to *Icaromenippus*. Here a runaway statue might be credited to Daedalus as he was said to have first created figures which could move their limbs and walk.

173 *Plato and his teaching about souls*: discussions about the soul are found mainly in Plato's dialogues *Phaedo*, *Meno*, and *Phaedrus*.

Tantalus and Tityus and Sisyphus: these three famous sinners and their punishments are a familiar feature of the landscape of Hades.

174 *an Epimenides*: see *Timon*, note to p. 28.

Plato's book on the soul: see note to p. 173. Here the *Phaedo* primarily is referred to, where we find the main discussion on the soul's immortality.

Maltese puppy: a small white dog, which was the most popular pet in the Graeco-Roman world: see *OCD* s.v. 'Pets'.

177 *Democritus of Abdera*: see *Peregrinus*, note to p. 76.

the statue of Memnon ... the rising sun: there were two colossi at Thebes identified as Memnon, a legendary king of Ethiopia, but in fact representing Amenhotep III. At dawn the stones were said to respond musically to the rising sun, and as Memnon was the son of Eos, the Dawn, he was fancifully said to be greeting his mother. (For more details see Courtney on Juvenal 15. 5.)

Pancrates: may be a real character, as there is papyrus evidence of a magician called Pachrates of the previous generation, who greatly impressed the emperor Hadrian: see C. P. Jones, *Culture and Society in Lucian*, 49–50.

179 *Amphilochus in Mallus*: see *Alexander*, note to p. 140.

Patara: an important city in Lycia, where there was a celebrated temple and oracle of Apollo.

HOW TO WRITE HISTORY

181 *Lysimachus*: ruler of the Macedonian kingdom, 285–281 BC.

O Love, you rule o'er gods and men: many fragments of this lost play survive: this one is listed as 136. 1 Nauck.

182 *War is the father of all things*: see *Icaromenippus*, note to p. 48.

the man of Sinope: Diogenes the Cynic (*c.*400–*c.*325 BC).

Philip was reported to be already approaching: Philip II, king of Macedon

(359–336 BC) and father of Alexander the Great, who spent much of his reign building up the power of Macedon by conquests.

Craneion: a wealthy and fashionable suburb of Corinth.

from this billowing spray: Homer, *Odyssey* 12.219, referring to the whirlpool Charybdis.

183 *a possession for ever*: Thucydides thus refers to his own history (1. 22. 4).

184 *Zeus draws up . . . shatter to bits*: see *Hermotimus*, note to p. 89. For Homer's description of agamemnon see *Iliad* 2. 478–9.

185 *Nicostratus*: a celebrated athlete, who was a double victor in wrestling and pancratium at the Olympic Games in AD 37. Quintilian reports meeting him (2. 8. 14); and see also Pausanias 5. 21. 10, Tacitus, *Dialogus* 10. 5.

Argus: a monster with many eyes. When Zeus changed Io into a heifer to hide her from Hera, Argus was set by Hera to watch over the heifer.

Heracles in Lydia: after Heracles killed Iphitus in a fit of madness, an oracle decreed that he could be purified of the crime if he was sold into servitude. Omphale, queen of Lydia, bought him and set him menial women's tasks: see Sophocles, *Trachiniae* 248 ff., Apollodorus 2. 6. 2–3. Lucian refers to the sandal-slapping again at *Dialogues of the Gods* 15.

186 *Aristoboulos*: a technician attached to the army of Alexander the Great, who wrote a now lost history of Alexander. During his Indian expedition (327–325 BC) Alexander's most formidable opponent was the local prince Porus, who so impressed Alexander, that after eventually defeating him Alexander reinstated him in his kingdom.

the engineer . . . on other business as before: this story is reported elsewhere, e.g. Plutarch, *Alexander* 72, who gives the engineer's name as Stasicrates.

187 *Thersites*: see *Demonax*, note to p. 160.

and a far greater man pursuing: slightly adapted from Homer, *Iliad* 22. 158: Achilles pursuing Hector before killing him.

Crepereius Calpurnianus of Pompeiopolis: the reality of this man is disputed: see C. P. Jones, *Culture and Society in Lucian*, appendix A. There is similar uncertainty about the other three named historians, Callimorphus, Antiochianus, and Demetrius.

the sort of plague . . . where it happily stayed: these are echoes of Thucydides' account of the great plague at Athens (2. 17 and 48).

188 *write in Ionic*: he would have thought this appropriate, as the great Greek doctor Hippocrates wrote in the Ionic dialect.

189 *I am going to speak . . . Oxyrhoes*: these are mostly adaptations of phrases from Herodotus, e.g. 2.40. 1, 1. 8. 2, 1. 7. 2.

Vologeses': Vologeses III (see introductory note), who reigned in Parthia from 148 to 192.

190 *Severianus*: see *Alexander*, note to p. 139.

The mountain was in labour: the first words of a Greek proverb: 'The mountain laboured and then brought forth a mouse' (Diogenianus 8. 75). Horace famously gave it Latin form in his *Ars Poetica* 139, where the point is a similar warning against pompous preambles which cannot be matched by the sequel.

Darius and Parysatis had two sons: the opening words of Xenophon's *Anabasis*.

191 *Europus . . . a colony of Edessa*: in fact Europus was situated on the Euphrates.

Thucydides . . . that celebrated war: Thucydides 2. 34 ff.: the celebrated speech by Pericles honouring the Athenian dead.

like Ajax: the death of Ajax was portrayed in a famous scene in Greek Tragedy: Sophocles, *Ajax* 815 ff.

192 *the Zeus of Olympia*: the celebrated statue which was considered to be Pheidias' masterpiece, made about 430 BC.

193 *The ears are more untrustworthy than the eyes*: a quotation from Herodotus 1. 8.

no doubt while taking a stroll from Craneion to Lerna: that is, he imagined it all and never went near Sura.

194 *Nicaea, after the victory*: the Greek word for victory is *nike*.

the Oxydraci: an Indian people living by the river Indus. Muziris was a port on the west coast of India (later Cranganore): Pliny, *NH* 6. 104.

they contrive . . . an ill-timed tongue, as they say: a fragment from an unknown choral poet which had become proverbial: see Page, *Poetae Melici Graeci*, 1020. Lucian has it again at *A Professor of Public Speaking* 18.

Atthis: a reference to a type of history of Attica called *Atthis*, which was popular about 350–250 BC: the names of several 'atthidographers' are known to us.

Momus: see *Nigrinus*, note to p. 70.

195 *create a Titormus from a Conon or a Milo from a Leotrophides*: clearly two pairs of a strong-man and a weakling. Titormus and Conon are hard to trace; but Milo is presumably the famous athlete (late sixth century BC), and Leotrophides was a poet notable for his thin and feeble appearance, and satirized by Aristophanes: see Dunbar on Aristophanes, *Birds* 1405–7.

Antiochus, son of Seleucus: see *Icaromenippus*, note to p. 52.

Theagenes the Thasian or Polydamas of Scotussa: celebrated victors at the Olympic Games in the fifth century BC—Polydamas can be dated to 408.

Philip's eye was put out by Aster of Amphipolis: this incident is noted too in Plutarch, *Moralia* 307 d.

Cleitus was brutally murdered at the banquet: a Macedonian noble who served in Alexander's army, and was killed by Alexander in a drunken brawl, *c*.328/7 BC.

Cleon: one of the most famous of Athenian politicians and demagogues of his time, mainly active in the 420s BC.

196 *Athens . . . the disaster in Sicily*: this refers to an episode in the Peloponnesian War, when Athens launched an expedition to Sicily which turned out a disastrous failure (415–413 BC). Demosthenes and Nicias were both Athenian generals who lost their lives in the expedition. Much of Thucydides' seventh book deals with the affair, with a full account of the incidents Lucian alludes to.

Clotho the Spinner . . . Atropos the Unchanging: 'Spinner' and 'Unchanging' translate the Greek names of these two Fates.

Artaxerxes' doctor: Ctesias of Cnidos, a Greek doctor who served Artaxerxes II of Persia (late fifth century BC), and wrote a history of Persia.

Onesicritus: see *Peregrinus*, note to p. 81.

197 *fearless . . . as the comic poet*: perhaps from Menander: see fr. 717 K (with Körte's note).

Thucydides . . . the present: for these allusions see Thucydides 1. 22.

198 *like Zeus in Homer, . . . the Mysians*: *Iliad* 13. 4–5.

Brasidas leaping forward, or a Demosthenes beating back his attack: Brasidas and Demosthenes were respectively Spartan and Athenian generals, and the clash referred to here was at Pylos in 425 BC (Thuc. 4. 11–14).

200 *so that events will not be forgotten in the passage of time*: Herod. 1. 1.

Tantalus, Ixion, Tityus: famous sinners, whose equally famous punishments were a familiar feature in accounts of the underworld.

Parthenius or Euphorion or Callimachus: these were all Hellenistic writers, whose story-telling technique and interest in narrative detail are contrasted with Homer's more austere style. Parthenius of Nicaea (first century BC) was an influential elegiac poet, who is said to have taught Virgil. Euphorion of Chalcis (third century BC) apparently specialized in mini-epics on mythological themes. Callimachus of Cyrene (*c*.305–*c*.240 BC) was one of the most innovative and influential poets of his time. His best-known poem was *Aetia* ('Causes'), of which fragments survive, and of his other works there are six hymns, which are extant.

201 *Theopompus*: of Chios (fourth century BC) wrote historical works of which we have fragments. The historian Polybius (8. 9–11) is similarly critical of his harsh accusations.

that architect from Cnidos: Sostratus (named below), who around 280 BC built the famous Pharos lighthouse at Alexandria for Ptolemy II. It was regarded as one of the wonders of the world. See also Pliny, *NH* 36. 83.

A TRUE HISTORY I

203 *Ctesias*: see *Lovers of Lies*, note to p. 163.

204 *Iambulus*: author of a now lost description of a journey through Ethiopia to the Island of the Sun, full of fantastic details. He is a totally shadowy figure, but we have excerpts from his work in Diodorus Siculus (2. 55–60).

Alcinous: king of the Phaeacians, at whose court Odysseus gives an extended account of his adventures (*Odyssey* 9–12).

205 *Daphne . . . when Apollo is about to catch her*: see Ovid, *Met.* 1. 452 ff.: she was running away to escape Apollo's attentions, and by divine help was turned into a bay tree (Greek *daphne*).

206 *Endymion*: the moon king's name is that of the beautiful youth Endymion, who was loved by the moon: see Apollodorus 1. 7. 5.

209 *Sarpedon*: son of Zeus and leader of the Lycian force at Troy. He was killed by Patroclus and mourned by his father with a rain of blood: *Iliad*. 16. 459 ff.

210 *belly of the leg*: Lucian's fanciful derivation of the Greek word for calf of the leg, *gastroknemia*, literally 'belly of the leg': i.e. where the leg swells out.

211 *comets, where long-haired men are admired*: English 'comet' derives from Greek *kometes*, 'long-haired', alluding to the 'tail' of the comet.

213 *Cloudcuckoo-city*: the city of the birds in Aristophanes' play (*Birds* 819).

A TRUE HISTORY II

220 *Momus*: see *Nigrinus*, note to p. 70.

Galatea: and Tyro (below) appropriately named, as in Greek *gala* is 'milk' and *tyros* 'cheese'.

221 *Rhadamanthus*: traditionally a ruler and judge in the underworld in many authors. (See the *OCD* entry.)

Ajax, son of Telamon: see *How to write History*, note to p. 191.

hellebore: commonly prescribed as an antidote for madness.

Helen . . . the Amazon and the daughters of Minos: Theseus carried off Helen when she was a child (Plutarch, *Thes.* 31). The Amazon was Antiope or Hippolyte; the daughters of Minos were Ariadne and Phaedra.

Aristides the Just: an Athenian soldier and statesman, and archon in 489/8 BC.

222 *Minoan*: presumably the name is intended to point to the Cretan association through Rhadamanthus.

223 *Eunomus of Locris, Arion of Lesbos, Anacreon, and Stesichorus*: Eunomus was a lyre-player of uncertain date. The others were famous lyric poets of the seventh and sixth centuries BC. Stesichorus was said to have been blinded for writing scurrilous verses about Helen, but recovered his sight when he wrote a recantation (*Palinodia*) of what he had said.

Ajax of Locris: this Ajax was the son of Oileus, and sometimes called the 'Lesser', to distinguish him from the son of Telamon (cf. note to p. 221). He was an unpleasant character, whose most dramatic crime was the rape of Cassandra at the altar of Athena during the sack of Troy: the most familiar account is Virgil, *Aeneid* 2. 403 ff.

both Cyruses . . . Hylas: this is a very mixed bunch. The Cyruses were kings of Persia; Anacharsis was a sixth-century prince of Scythia, who was numbered among the Seven Sages, and in Lucian's dialogue of that name has a discussion with Solon on the subject of athletics; Zamolxis was a Thracian god, or alternatively a man who introduced mystery rites into Thrace (see How and Wells on Herodotus 4. 94); Numa was traditionally the second king of Rome, who was credited with the introduction of laws and religious rites; Lycurgus was allegedly the founder of the Spartan constitution and social system, but traditions differ about his dates; Phocion (fourth century BC) was a distinguished general and statesman, who was much involved in the struggle against Macedon; Tellos was an Athenian mentioned by Solon to Croesus as the happiest man he had ever seen (Herodotus 1. 30: cf. *Charon* 10); Periander was tyrant of Corinth, *c.*625–585 BC; Nestor was the venerable father-figure on the Greek side at Troy, in which Palamedes too served (Palamedes was also credited with the invention of the alphabet). Hyacinthus, Narcissus, and Hylas form a group of beautiful young men who came to a tragic end: Hyacinthus was loved by Apollo and killed by a discus; Narcissus famously fell in love with his own reflection in water, and pined away and died; Hylas was page to

Heracles on the voyage of the Argonauts, in the course of which he went to fetch water from a spring, but was pulled in by the water-nymphs who fell in love with his beauty.

his imaginary city . . . laws he drew up himself: a reference to Plato's most famous dialogue, the *Republic*.

Aristippus and Epicurus: Aristippus of Cyrene (fifth–fourth centuries BC) and Epicurus (341–270 BC) are coupled as having both proclaimed pleasure as the goal of life; but the Cyrenaics preached a fairly blatant form of hedonism, while the Epicureans argued for a pleasure which was much more reasoned and carefully defined.

Aesop the Phrygian: the fabulist (traditionally sixth century BC), though he came not from Phrygia but from Thrace. His own fables do not survive.

Lais: a famous Corinthian courtesan (fifth century BC), among whose lovers was allegedly the philosopher Aristippus: Lucian may be making a mischievous substitution here.

Stoics . . . still climbing the steep hill of virtue: see *Hermotimus passim*.

224 *hellebore*: see *Hermotimus*, note to p. 128.

Homer . . . topic of the keenest interest at home: this was a indeed burning issue, and seven cities claimed the honour of being his birthplace.

hostage . . . changed his name: the Greek for 'hostage' is *homeros*.

the grammarians Zenodotus and Aristarchus: these were two distinguished scholars of the third and second centuries BC respectively, who were heads of the Library at Alexandria, and did important work on the text of Homer. Zenodotus was responsible for the division of the *Iliad* and the *Odyssey* into twenty-four books each.

225 *Thersites*: see *Demonax*, note to p. 160.

the cycles of his soul, His right side was entirely of gold: a variation on the legend that Pythagoras had a golden thigh: see *Sale of Lives* 6. In illustration of his doctrine of metempsychosis Pythagoras claimed to have been the Trojan Euphorbus in a former incarnation (see below).

Empedocles . . . his body thoroughly roasted: see *Peregrinus*, note to p. 74.

Caranus: the text is uncertain and 'Caranus' is a conjecture. Perhaps we should read 'Capros', an Olympic victor in 212 BC (see C. P. Jones, *Culture and Society in Lucian*, 55).

Epeius: a boxer in Homer who won his match at the funeral games for Patroclus (*Iliad* 23. 664 ff.). Areius is unknown, but presumably a real character.

Hesiod won the prize: this reflects an old tradition. There is extant an anonymous text, *The Contest of Homer and Hesiod*, recounting a contest between them, in which Hesiod is declared the victor.

Phalaris of Acragas . . . Pityocamptes: a group famous for their brutality. Phalaris was tyrant of Acragas in the sixth century, who roasted his enemies alive in a bronze bull. Busiris was a mythical Egyptian king, who sacrificed all strangers who came to Egypt. Diomedes was a mythical Thracian who fed strangers to his horses. Heracles' eighth labour was to capture these horses. Sciron was a brigand who operated near Megara, and kicked his victims over a cliff to their death. Pityocamptes means 'pine-bender', and refers to another brigand on the Isthmus of Corinth called Sinis, who tied his victims to two pine trees, which were then released and tore them apart.

226 *Sing to me now . . . shades of the heroes*: a line loosely reminiscent of the opening line of the *Odyssey*.

boiled beans . . . he loathed beans: this recalls the Pyanepsia, an Athenian festival in honour of Apollo at which beans were eaten. Pythagoras ordered his disciples, for obscure reasons, to abstain from eating beans.

227 *Calypso's island*: Calypso was a nymph living on the island of Ogygia, where Odysseus spent seven years with her.

not to stir the fire with a sword: this is a Pythagorean injunction (Diogenes Laertius 8. 17) of uncertain meaning. The others here seem to be Lucianic inventions.

Dear to the blessed gods . . . homeward made his way: these lines adapt recurrent phrases in the *Odyssey* referring to Odysseus' home-coming (e.g. 1. 82).

228 *Timon of Athens*: the notorious misanthrope: see *Timon passim*.

Homer, hasn't given full details: the reference is to Penelope's famous description of the two gates, of horn and of ivory, through which dreams pass (*Od.* 19. 560 ff.).

229 *Antiphon*: a fifth-century sophist and interpreter of dreams, fragments of whose works survive.

the cave, just as Homer described it: in *Odyssey* 5. 55 ff.

231 *And as they thus their woodland voyage pursued*: the poet Antimachus came from Colophon and flourished around 400 BC. This line is listed as fr. 62 Kinkel (= 106 Wyss).

233 *I'll tell you in the following books*: Lucian appropriately signs off with another lie.

DIALOGUES OF THE COURTESANS

1. GLYCERION AND THAIS

235 *a witch who is skilled in Thessalian spells . . . moon*: Thessalian witches were notorious for their skills, and pulling down the moon is often quoted as an example of their power: cf. 4. 1.

2. MYRTION, PAMPHILUS, AND DORIS

the Thesmophoria: an important Greek festival for women in honour of Demeter.

the Admiralty Court: this translates *nautodikai*, a board of officials who presided over trials in cases involving merchants.

4. MELITTA AND BACCHIS

A common use of magic in the ancient world, at least in our literary sources, was in the cause of love, and here a girl invokes magic to bring back her errant lover. The piece strongly recalls Theocritus, *Idyll* 2, and may be modelled on it.

236 *Thessalian women*: cf. 1, note to p. 235.

237 *Piraeus*: the port of Athens.

the Ceramicus: the Potter's Quarter in Athens.

the Dipylon Gate: an impressive double gateway at Athens in the Potter's Quarter: cf. 10. 2.

238 *a magic wheel*: a familiar tool in incantations, this was a spoked disc or wheel with a cord threaded onto it, and increasing or relaxing the tension on the cord caused the wheel to spin. (See Gow on Theocritus 2. 17.)

6. CROBYLE AND CORINNA

239 *Dear Lady Adrasteia*: an alternative name for Nemesis, a goddess who personified retribution and punished excessive good fortune or presumption in mortals. The point of the invocation here is not very clear: possibly she is deprecating the goddess's wrath from her friend's good fortune by saying that she deserves it (see Macleod's Loeb note here). So below she stops herself boasting about her daughter, with a covert apology to Adrasteia (3).

7. MUSARION AND HER MOTHER

240 *the earthly Aphrodite . . . the heavenly Aphrodite of the Gardens*: the 'earthly' and 'heavenly' Aphrodites are distinguished as representing respectively physical love of the body and love of the soul: see Plato, *Symposium* 180e ff. Aphrodite of the Gardens refers to a statue by the celebrated sculptor Alcamenes (second half of the fifth century BC), in some gardens outside the walls of Athens: see Pliny, *NH* 36. 16.

If only my father . . .: the son cannot quite bring himself to say 'would die'.

the two goddesses: Demeter and Persephone.

241 *the Areopagite*: a member of the Areopagus, a very ancient court at Athens.

I find . . . a bit of a pig: the exact meaning of this is unclear, but the general sense must be that she thinks Chaereas physically attractive and the farmer repulsive.

10. CHELIDONION AND DROSIS

242 *the Painted Hall*: see *Icaromenippus*, note to p. 160.

the Academy: a gymnasium in Athens where Plato established his school in the early fourth century BC.

243 *written by a Scythian*: the Scythians were proverbially a harsh and uncouth people, so the meaning is that the letter is rude and discouraging: cf. Aelian, *Epistulae* 14.

244 *help Dromo to run him down*: the translation tries to reproduce a pun in the Greek on the name *Dromon* ('runner') and the verb *syndramein* ('to run'). Cf. 4. 2 for graffiti in the Ceramicus.

14. DORIO AND MYRTALE

I'm shut out and stand weeping before the door: the setting of this dialogue reflects a common situation in Greek and Latin love poetry, especially Latin elegy, that of the *exclusus amator*, the lover shut out on a cold doorstep and complaining bitterly to his mistress within or to a hard-hearted janitor.

245 *donkey playing the lyre to himself*: this proverbial expression, describing a ludicrous effect or situation, is found also in Lucian's *The Mistaken Critic* 7, and elsewhere, and it seems to be the basis of a Greek fable: Phaedrus App. 14 (*Aesop's Fables*, Oxford World's Classics edn., no. 404 = Perry 542).

INDEX OF NAMES

American Literature

Authors in Context

British and Irish Literature

Children's Literature

Classics and Ancient Literature

Colonial Literature

Eastern Literature

European Literature

History

Medieval Literature

Oxford English Drama

Poetry

Philosophy

Politics

Religion

The Oxford Shakespeare

A complete list of Oxford World's Classics, including Authors in Context, Oxford English Drama, and the Oxford Shakespeare, is available in the UK from the Marketing Services Department, Oxford University Press, Great Clarendon Street, Oxford OX2 6DP, or visit the website at www.oup.com/uk/worldsclassics.

In the USA, visit www.oup.com/us/owc for a complete title list.

Oxford World's Classics are available from all good bookshops. In case of difficulty, customers in the UK should contact Oxford University Press Bookshop, 116 High Street, Oxford OX1 4BR.